Mastering Administrative Law

Carolina Academic Press Mastering Series
RUSSELL L. WEAVER, SERIES EDITOR

Mastering Administrative Law
William R. Andersen

Mastering Bankruptcy
George W. Kuney

Mastering Civil Procedure
David Charles Hricik

Mastering Civil Procedure, Volume 1: The Investigative Stage
Peter J. Henning, Andrew Taslitz, Margaret L. Paris, Cynthia E. Jones, Ellen S. Podgor

Mastering Constitutional Law
John C. Knechtle, Christopher Roederer

Mastering Corporate Tax
Reginald Mombrun, Gail Levin Richmond, Felicia Branch

Mastering Corporations and Other Business Entities
Lee Harris

Mastering Criminal Law
Ellen S. Podgor, Peter J. Henning, Neil P. Cohen

Mastering Evidence
Ronald W. Eades

Mastering Elder Law
Ralph C. Brashier

Mastering Family Law
Janet Leach Richards

Mastering Intellectual Property
George W. Kuney, Donna C. Looper

Mastering Legal Analysis and Communication
David T. Ritchie

Mastering Legal Analysis and Drafting
George W. Kuney, Donna C. Looper

**Mastering Negotiable Instruments (UCC Articles 3 and 4)
and Other Payment Systems**
Michael D. Floyd

Mastering Products Liability
Ronald W. Eades

Mastering Professional Responsibility
Grace M. Giesel

Mastering Secured Transactions
Richard H. Nowka

Mastering Statutory Interpretation
Linda D. Jellum

Mastering Tort Law
Russell L. Weaver, Edward C. Martin, Andrew R. Klein,
Paul J. Zwier II, Ronald W. Eades, John H. Bauman

Mastering Administrative Law

William R. Andersen

JUDSON FALKNOR PROFESSOR OF LAW EMERITUS
UNIVERSITY OF WASHINGTON SCHOOL OF LAW

CAROLINA ACADEMIC PRESS
Durham, North Carolina

Library of Congress Cataloging in Publication Data

Andersen, William R.
  Mastering administrative law / William R. Andersen.
      p. cm. -- (Carolina Academic Press mastering series)
  ISBN 978-1-59460-582-6 (alk. paper)
  1. Administrative law--United States. I. Title.
  KF5402. A83 2010
  342.73'06--dc22

                                        2009046261

Carolina Academic Press
700 Kent Street
Durham, NC 27701
Telephone (919) 489-7486
Fax (919) 493-5668
www.cap-press.com

For Mary Ann

Table of Contents

Table of Illustrations

Table of Cases

Series Editor's Foreword

The Carolina Academic Press Mastering Series is designed to provide you with a tool that will enable you to easily and efficiently "master" the substance and content of law school courses. Throughout the series, the focus is on quality writing that makes legal concepts understandable. As a result, the series is designed to be easy to read and is not unduly cluttered with footnotes or cites to secondary sources.

In order to facilitate student mastery of topics, the Mastering Series includes a number of pedagogical features designed to improve learning and retention. At the beginning of each chapter, you will find a "Roadmap" that tells you about the chapter and provides you with a sense of the material that you will cover. A "Checkpoint" at the end of each chapter encourages you to stop and review the key concepts, reiterating what you have learned. Throughout the book, key terms are explained and emphasized. Finally, a "Master Checklist" at the end of each book reinforces what you have learned and helps you identify any areas that need review or further study.

We hope that you will enjoy studying with, and learning from, the Mastering Series.

Russell L. Weaver
Professor of Law & Distinguished University Scholar
University of Louisville, Louis D. Brandeis School of Law

Foreword

Administrative law is something of an exotic in the law school curriculum. That is, the subject is unknown to most students, the field is full of acronyms, alphabet soup initials, and insider jargon. Moreover, most students have had little direct experience with regulatory bodies. All of this can make the subject seem daunting.

But wait! There are two things you need to think about before you get daunted. First, the field is increasingly a vital subject for most lawyers. You can't really function in today's legal world without some introduction to this field, so the time you invest in getting a sense of the subject will not be wasted. And it is an exciting place for a lawyer to be. Administrative law professionals, whether inside government or outside, tend to work at the cutting edge. Administering the same old, same old policies doesn't usually require lawyers. But when the agency or the private client wants to try something new, something different, something innovative, that's when your phone rings.

Answering that phone will introduce you to the variety of roles lawyers play in this field. To agency executives and private clients, lawyers are crucial interpreters of the law, specialists on procedural requirements, drafters, critical arbiters of policy analysis and, of course, advocates in courtrooms and many other places. With this skill set, these professionals are usually at the center of the action, are invited to the meetings that really count. For an elaboration of these professional roles inside government, see McGarrity, *The Role of Government Attorneys in Regulatory Agency Rulemaking*, 61 LAW & CONTEMP. PROBS. 19 (1998).

Second, you should know that administrative law is ultimately a practical subject. When one is dealing with really important matters (think of banking regulation, civil rights, labor/management issues, workplace safety, environmental protection, monetary policy, health care, etc.) there is simply too much at stake to allow endless research or infinite doctrinal refinement. Yes, good regulatory policy must rest on solid research and intelligent principles, but the store must also be kept open. Like the experienced administrative lawyer, you should not be paralyzed by doctrinal complexity. Understand it. But don't let it trap you in a box you can't get out of if more practical resolutions emerge from your thinking. Answers that work are always necessary and usually sufficient.

Finding answers that work may require consideration of multiple perspectives. Effective and workable administrative law doctrines must be consistent with legislative wishes, efficient in the day-to-day work of the executive branch and the independent agencies, sensitive to the attitudes and culture of regulated parties, and ultimately administrable by the courts. These institutions may have different needs and different resources and finding doctrine that works tolerably well for most of them at a given time is one of the real challenges of the field. It is a challenge worthy of the best minds.

So welcome to the field of administrative law. It is sometimes intellectually difficult but always professionally rewarding. It will, without doubt, be a growth experience for you.

Preface

This work is intended for the student or the foreign lawyer in need of a short introduction to the U.S. system of administrative law. Rather than being a contribution to the larger theoretical literature, it attempts to identify central principles in understandable form, and to organize them so that their essential functions are clear. The discussion is accompanied by a number of classroom-tested graphics that should help visualize important doctrinal relationships.

Three essential acknowledgements. I must first note that my students have helped me understand the conceptual difficulties this subject presents the beginner. If this volume is of assistance to future students, it is largely because of what I have been taught by past students.

Second, this book is a survey and necessarily pushes hurriedly through some very deep topics. I owe a heavy debt to the many scholars that have dealt, more adequately than I could have done, with specific aspects of the topic. Several members of that community have also given me the benefit of comments on parts of the manuscript. I would like especially to thank Michael Asimow, Jeff Lubbers, Richard Murphy, and Katherine Watts. I offer the usual caveat exempting them from responsibility for the final product, though their comments resulted in changes which in my view make the book a much better book.

Finally, I have been fortunate in having Kelly Ruhlig as my assistant during the manuscript production process. She contributed greatly—with professional skill, grace, and a sense of humor.

William R. Andersen
Seattle, Washington
November 2009

About the Author

William Andersen is the Judson Falkner Professor of Law at the University of Washington Law School where, over many years, he has taught both Constitutional Law and Administrative Law. Before joining the Washington faculty, Professor Andersen served as Associate General Counsel of the then-Federal Aviation Agency. Since joining the faculty, he has continued to write and speak on administrative law nationally and internationally, has produced a set of CALI computer tutorials on administrative law and was a principal drafter of the Washington State Administrative Procedure Act.

Mastering Administrative Law

Chapter 1

The Role of Administrative Law

Roadmap

- Introduction and History
- The constitutional setting of the regulatory process
- The constitutional problems of accommodating the process
  - authority
  - unfairness
  - unaccountability
- Administrative law defined

A. Introduction

Law is instrumental. Every body of law develops in response to identified problems and is an effort to resolve disputes and give guidance to people confronting those problems. Thus, negligence law allocates the burdens of certain kinds of unintended losses; contract law seeks to facilitate private ordering and exchanges; property law seeks to secure interests in tangible and intangible things and to facilitate transfer of those interests. The doctrines of administrative law are no different; they have purposes, functions, goals.

Understanding the underlying purpose of a set of legal doctrines is not a job solely of interest to the theorist or the philosopher. It is essential to the student. You lay a foundation for deeper understanding of a field if you can get a sense of the reason behind the law—a feel for the problems the doctrine was intended to solve. So in a way, this chapter is the most important chapter in the book. If you work through it carefully you will begin to develop a sense of the underlying rationale of administrative law, a set of perceptions that will pay real dividends in understanding and applying the doctrine and, in the bargain, will provide you with criteria for critique of the system—an obligation of all members of a learned profession.

3

Begin with the thought that we are dealing with government and with the power that government exercises. We are looking at questions about how government instrumentalities get this mysterious stuff called power, how they exercise it, and how it is controlled. Your courses in constitutional law dealt with these issues broadly. Here we look principally at power questions relating to that part of government that is engaged in regulating private conduct.

Whatever may have been the vision of the framers, the subject of regulation today is vast and complex. It touches the daily life of virtually every citizen in seemingly endless ways—from the labels on our foods to the air we breathe; from the crops we grow to the security of our financial and banking system; from the television we watch to the safety of our workplaces. In such connections, the U.S. regulatory process has become a substantial activity with responsibilities for standard setting, enforcement, and direct provision of service in a range of activities that includes agriculture, commerce, education, energy, welfare, labor, transportation, environment, consumer affairs, maritime matters, workplace safety, communications, taxation, and monetary policy, to mention just the obvious.

In each of these areas, a body of *substantive* law will be generated (tax law, labor law, securities law, environmental law, etc.) and the typical U.S. law school will have courses in such substantive areas. The typical law school course in administrative law, by contrast, treats the *procedures* the agencies must follow in carrying out their substantive tasks. In addition, administrative law covers judicial review of agency action—a process raising especially delicate interbranch issues, since the job of the courts is to "police" the other branches, insuring their compliance with the constitution and with any relevant legislative or executive requirements. (We will focus here principally on federal administrative agencies, but somewhat similar arrangements are made for regulatory bodies at the state and local level.)

Regulatory bodies in the U.S. come in a bewildering variety of forms. They may be part of the executive branch or free standing. They may be subject to significant executive branch control or somewhat independent of that control. They may carry names such as commissions, boards, agencies, departments, bureaus, etc. The tasks assigned to them are of many kinds including planning, research, grant administration, and the provision of direct service, etc. But most of administrative law deals with the regulatory function of agencies—actions in which agencies directly impact the private worlds of individuals and businesses. The statutory systems and mechanisms which empower and control these agencies span an impressive range, and the law which regulates procedure in this variety cannot be simply stated. How can we get a handle on this complexity?

We can begin with a mention of the history of the process. It is clear today that the framers had no conception of the size this regulatory function would assume. They wrote before the industrial revolution, before the growth of communications and transportation had welded our nation (and, increasingly, our world) into a single interdependent economic unit. They wrote before the principal players had ceased being farmers and small business owners and had become immense corporate organizations whose size and wealth put them beyond the practical power of individual states to control. The framers wrote, too, before the technical complexities of regulation could have been foreseen and before the magnitude of the process could have been guessed. These factors do more to explain the growth of the regulatory process than any changes in political philosophy. National (and increasingly global) economic interdependence explains why so much of the regulatory process was (and is) lodged at the national level. Technical complexity and the volume of regulatory actions explain why regulation was beyond the ability of the legislative branch as well as beyond the ability of a minimally staffed and ultimately political executive branch. Some process had to be invented which could deal with increasingly technical and complex issues, and deal with them in a careful, professional manner to some degree removed from the play of political forces, yet ultimately accountable to those forces.

The invention process began early. In 1789, the first Congress authorized the president to appoint an administrative officer to estimate import duties. And during the administration of George Washington, executive departments were created (War, State, Treasury, Post Office, Attorney General). Growth was slow, but after the 1860s, the U.S. added cabinet level departments such as Agriculture and Labor. By 1887 the first modern regulatory agency was created—the Interstate Commerce Commission—with important powers to regulate the new railroad industry. Building on that model, agencies were created over the next 30 years to regulate food and drugs (1906), unfair competition (1914), hydroelectric projects (1920), commodity trading (1922), and radio (1927).

With the economic collapse of the Great Depression in the 1930s, industry-specific regulation reached new industries such as securities (1934), wholesale electric power (1935), trucking (1935), airlines (1938), and natural gas (1938). General regulation of labor relations was begun in the Labor Act (1935) though Presidents Roosevelt's broader attempt to regulate prices and business practices was declared unconstitutional by the Supreme Court. Schecter v. U.S., 295 U.S. 495 (1935). After World War II, regulation extended beyond the regulation of business to deal with social and economic problems generally, in such fields as social insurance, public assistance, health care, farm price supports, and housing subsidies.

In the 1960s and 1970s regulation expanded again, now moving into such areas as racial and gender discrimination, consumer fraud, health, safety, and the environment. By the late 1970s the swing of the regulatory pendulum began to slow and, indeed, to move in the other direction. Beginning with the Carter administration and carried forward by later administrations, we began a process of *de*regulation, especially of airlines, trucking, and railroads. Even with the deregulation movement, the size and breadth of the regulatory process is still immense. And we continue to expand the process. No real legislative initiative occurs today that doesn't employ administrative agencies to do the heavy lifting, from the Homeland Security Agency created after 9/11 to the Consumer Financial Protection Agency proposed by President Obama in July 2009 in response to concerns about banking and credit card practices that injure consumers.

Agencies today make rules that for all intents and purposes have the force and effect of legislative enactments—and as any law librarian can attest, ten times as much shelf space is required for published agency rules as is required for all the enactments of Congress. Agencies today adjudicate cases that for all intents and purposes have the force and effect of judicial decisions—and their output is many, many times the number of cases decided by all the federal courts.

The growth of this process has been controversial, and the theoretically minded reader might enjoy some of the academic analyses which have developed, including schools of thought carrying labels like "public choice," "neo-pluralism," "public interest," and "civic republicanism." A recent addition is Steven Croley's "administrative process" theory, which suggests the importance of administrative procedure itself for an effective and legitimate regulatory process. Croley, REGULATION AND PUBLIC INTERESTS (2008).

To keep this essay within limits, we will focus principally on orthodox regulatory agencies. We will not be talking about the governmental organs which take corporate form or whose duties are more operational than regulatory, such as the Public Broadcasting System (PBS) or the Tennessee Valley Authority (TVA). What will be of central concern to us are agencies which regulate private conduct through administrative rulemaking and adjudication. These may be cabinet-level agencies (such as the Labor Department), independent executive branch agencies (such as the Environmental Protection Agency), and so-called independent agencies (typically collegial in form, such as the Federal Communications Commission, the National Labor Relations Board, the Federal Trade Commission, and the Securities and Exchange Commission. The conventional abbreviations for these agencies (EPA, FCC, NLRB, FTC, SEC) give us the storied "alphabet soup" reference to modern government.

Consider the Federal Trade Commission as a typical example. This is an agency with industry-wide authority, not limited to one industry like the FCC or to one aspect of industry such as the NLRB. The FTC is a small agency (barely 1,000 employees), created in 1914 to regulate a variety of matters, including deceptive and unfair commercial advertising, certain kinds of anti-competitive mergers and other business practices that restrict competition. In addition, the Commission carries on a significant economic research effort in support of its law enforcement actions. It works with state and local and international agencies in support of its work, conducts hearings, workshops and conferences for consumers and businesses to develop research and to disseminate information. To give you a sense of the volume of business done by the FTC, in 2003, the Commission received in excess of one million consumer complaints and distributed 22 million pieces of educational literature.

The Commission is headed by a five-person body, all appointed by the president (confirmed by the Senate) for seven-year terms. No more than three commissioners can be from the same political party. Their terms are staggered and are longer than one presidential term so that it will take several years for a new president to fill the Commission with "his" people. As will be noted below, for agencies of this kind the president's power of removal may be sharply circumscribed.

The Commission's formal regulatory work is largely done through rule-making, and rules adopted through the Commission's rulemaking procedures — discussed in Chapter 2 — have the force of law, very like statutes enacted by Congress. The Commission also enforces its rules through adjudication. In a typical Commission formal adjudication, there will be what is essentially a trial — discussed in Chapter 3 — at which the guilt or innocence of the alleged violator is weighed and determined.

The awkward question is, where in our constitutional structure is there provision for a governmental instrumentality exercising powers of this sort?

B. The Constitutional Setting for the Regulatory Process

Our constitution has three functions: it invests the various branches of the national government with power, it separates the branches, and it imposes certain specific limits on the national and state governments. The growth of the regulatory process has raised important issues in all three areas: we will be considering how agencies get their power, whether agency structures violate principles of separation of powers, and when agency conduct violates specific constitutional limits, such as those in the Fourth and Fifth Amendments.

Of special concern to us is the separation of powers notion. The constitution creates the well-known three branches of our government, the legislative, executive and judicial branches. It is clear from the text and from the history of its drafting that the constitution intended to keep the branches separate in important ways. The language empowering the branches supports the idea of separation. Thus, Article 1 vests "all" legislative power in the Congress, Article II vests "the" executive power in the president, and Article III vests "the" judicial power in the judicial branch.

There are places, of course, where the branches share a power, where the powers overlap or where combined action of branches is necessary. For example, the president has a role in the legislative process by the use of the veto; the Senate has a role in the executive's international responsibilities in that the Senate must approve treaties; a court intrudes on the functions of both the other branches when it rules their actions violate the constitution. But at the core of their functioning, the branches are separate and disputes over violation of this principle are often before the courts.

One might think resolving a separation of powers dispute would be relatively easy. One would simply identify the three types of powers, identify the three branches, then ask if a power asserted by actors in one branch was in fact a power that had been vested by the constitution in another branch. If the answer was "yes," we have a violation of separation of powers. Alas, it is more complicated than that. Elizabeth Magill has taught us that both the definition of powers and the identification of branches are very difficult characterizations to make. Looked at intensively, she notes, there are no powers that correspond in any exact way with the words legislative, executive or judicial. And neither are there any governmental branches which correspond exactly with those descriptors.

> The embarrassing secret is that both commitments at the center of separation of powers doctrine are misconceived. The effort to identify and separate governmental powers fails because, in the contested cases, there is no principled way to distinguish between the relevant powers ... Inquiring about inter-branch balance is incoherent because it assumes that branches of government are unitary entities with cohesive interests, but that is not true. The institutions of the national government are made up of individuals and sub-institutions with varying incentives that do not neatly track the institution [i.e., branches] within which they are located. Magill, *Beyond Powers and Branches*, 150 U. PA. L. REV. 603, 604–05 (2001).

Still, the framers had something important in mind and perhaps we can best get a sense of that by focusing on core meanings of the words, recognizing that at the margins there will be considerable inexactness. With that objective, core definitions of the respective powers might look something like this:

- Legislative power is used in the *promulgation of general rules* for the future — rules affecting classes of individuals or events. Article I lodges this power exclusively in the legislative branch.
- Executive power is used *to apply and enforce* the legislative rules — including such functions as administering, investigating, prosecuting, etc. Article II lodges this power in the executive branch.
- Judicial power is used to *resolve individual disputes* arising in the promulgation and implementation of the rules. Such disputes may arise from claims that government action is inconsistent with legislative rules, or from claims that the legislative rules themselves are inconsistent with relevant constitutional or statutory provisions. Article III lodges this power in the judicial branch.

If for present purposes we can settle for these descriptions, we can then ask why the framers thought it so important that the three general repositories of these powers be kept separate from each other. The idea of separating the powers has at least three justifications. The first — surely central to the framers — was the need to avoid concentration of too much power in one place. With the virtually omnipotent British monarch George III in mind, they believed that if power were divided among different branches the potential for oppression and tyranny would be reduced. The branches are constructed such that one can often block action by the other, making control of the whole government by particular interests or individuals much more difficult. This is especially clear when it is recognized that in the ingenious constitutional design, the officials serving in the respective branches are selected by different methods, serve for different terms, and are responsive to different constituencies. It may seem fanciful in this age to worry about monarchial tyranny, but substituting for that 18th Century concern today is the more modern fear that concentrated power facilitates control by those with narrow interests.

A second justification for the separation of powers was simply the obvious fact that specialization brings efficiency. This was not at the forefront of the framers' mind, but it is obvious that we all gain if legislators become skilled at legislating, executives more proficient at executing, and judges more adept at judging.

A third justification for separating powers is of special concern to administrative law. It turns out that if these powers were not separated serious problems of fairness would arise. The three kinds of powers are in some ways inconsistent and combinations could be troublesome. For example, it was ancient history — even in the 18th Century — that those who wrote the laws should not be too deeply involved in their interpretation in individual cases, or that those who investigated and prosecuted alleged law violators should not be judges in those cases. For a discussion of the English antecedents to this view of separated powers, see Pierce, Shapiro and Verkuil, ADMINISTRATIVE LAW AND PROCESS 25–26 (5th ed. 2009).

This concern is raised sharply by the typical administrative agency — such as the FTC described above. All three functions are combined in one agency: the agency writes the rules, prosecutes alleged violators and judges the guilt or innocence of the alleged violator. It would be hard to find a clearer example of combined functions and the problem of unfairness it suggests is palpable.

Yet the administrative process exists. And grows. Has the Court been asleep at the separation of powers switch? The Court has never fully resolved the question. Sometimes it takes a functional view and concludes that necessity requires some combination of functions. You'll recall this functional view expressed in Morrison v. Olson, 487 U.S. 654 (1988). By contrast, the Court sometimes takes a very formal approach, which insists on strict and literal application of the principle of separation. You'll recall that temperament as reflected in cases such as INS v. Chadha, 462 U.S. 919 (1983). As this debate continues, a practical settlement has developed which generally permits the continuation of the administrative process. We will examine this arrangement in more detail in the next section. But note — and this is a crucial insight for those of us who are students of administrative law — a central piece of that settlement is the development of a body of legislative, executive and judicial principles that minimize the problems of combining inconsistent functions. That body of principles is an important part of what we call administrative law. Dealing with these separation of powers shortfalls is one of the functions that administrative law is intended to serve.

C. Dealing with the Separation of Powers Issues in Modern Regulation

Looking at the FTC example above, what would the framers have thought of such an arrangement? There are three ways in which this kind of development would have troubled the framers: its authority, its potential unfairness, and its unaccountability.

1. The Problem of Authority

How can governmental power exist in places where it was not lodged by the constitution? Under the usual notion that the federal government is a government of limited or enumerated powers, no instrumentality of that government can exercise a power unless a grant of the power appears in the constitution. Under the general definitions set out above, the FTC is clearly exercising a legislative power when it makes general rules. Moreover, in its adjudicatory activity the FTC is clearly exercising judicial power. Where did it get those powers?

There have been those who solved that problem by simple denial. Scholars and judges in the past have solemnly stated that administrative agencies exercised only "quasi" legislative or "quasi" judicial power and that linguistic turn was thought sufficient unto the day. Today, most have realized that the problem cannot be solved by word play. When the FTC issues a rule that a particular advertising practice is misleading, businesses are affected in a way that is virtually indistinguishable from the effect of a statutory enactment: a legislative power has been exercised. When the FTC prosecutes a company for engaging in a practice which violates the rule and issues an order requiring the company to cease and desist from using it, the company is affected in a way virtually indistinguishable from enforcement in a court of law: a judicial power has been exercised. If the apparently exclusive constitutional assignment of authority had a purpose and a rationale, as it plainly did, is this obvious divergence from the framers' plan acceptable?

The lack of authority for much of what the regulatory process does is met, in doctrinal terms, by the concept of delegation. The legislative and judicial powers exercised by agencies are said to be authorized because they have been delegated to the regulatory bodies by Congress. But that apparently straightforward proposition is shadowed by something called the nondelegation doctrine — essentially a notion that goes back as far as John Locke and asserts that an agent cannot subdelegate (*delegata potestas non potest delegari*). Nondelegation has no obvious textual basis in the constitution, but is a carryover from the law of agency. The legislature is our agent and the doctrine would forbid that agent from subdelegating the power to somebody else, like an administrative agency. The law of agency, of course, does not forbid the agent from instructing its assistants on operating details, so long as the agent itself remains in control of the basic policy choices. On this basis, Justice Marshall stated that if the important policies had been decided by Congress, subjects of lesser interest could properly be given to others, "to fill up the details." Wayman v. Southard, 23 U.S. 1, 41 (1825). And even earlier, the Court had ruled that Congress could exercise its power contingently, leaving to other instrumentalities the task of determining whether facts existed which called the stated policy into operation. The Brig Aurora, 11 U.S. 382 (1813).

But that leaves the question of how the Court determines when Congress has made the basic policy decision. The best the Court has been able to do is to state that a delegation to an administrative agency will pass constitutional muster if the statute contains an "intelligible principle." J.W. Hampton, Jr., & Co. v.

United States, 276 U.S. 394, 409 (1928). If there is such a criterion in the statute, authority to the administrative agency is lawfully delegated. In the bargain, the intelligible principle will guide agency discretion and will allow a court to determine when the agency is acting within the authority granted. All is well on the authority question. See Figure 1.1

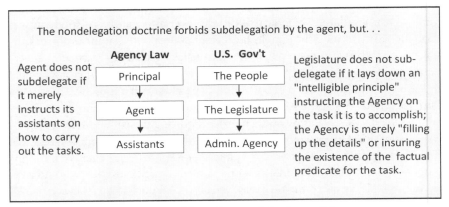

Figure 1.1   Nondelegation and the Law of Agency

This would make perfect sense if one could with a straight face say that the legislature was making basic policies and the agencies were merely "filling up the details." But all today realize this for the fiction it is. The kinds of legislative standards that have been accepted by the Court are of such cosmic breadth as to leave the agency free to exercise basic policy choices over a wide range. When the Court is willing to accept as an "intelligible principle" that the agency is authorized to regulate "in the public interest," no one can doubt that the legislature has turned over major policy-making functions to the agency. What *is* in the public interest, of course, is the real policy issue and agencies get scant guidance from the legislature in statutes of this generality.

The Court's essential disregard of the nondelegation doctrine as an enforceable legal principle has been controversial. Many have felt that the nondelegation should be taken more seriously in aid of forcing the legislature to confront and make basic policy decisions and of assuring accountability to the people (a topic addressed below). Current doctrine, they suggest, insulates Congress from responsibility for policy choice and shifts the venue of policy debate from the halls of the legislature to the corridors of the agency. See, e.g., Industrial Union v. American Petroleum Institute, 448 U.S. 607, 671 (Rehnquist, concurring); Ely, DEMOCRACY AND DISTRUST 131 (1980). The Court, however, has not responded generously to this criticism. Perhaps we have simply come too far to backtrack now. And doctrine aside, if the goal is to identify public sentiment and to allow affected parties meaningful participation in the formulation of policy, it may be that battles over policy at the agency level may be as good as (or even better than) battles in the halls of Congress. Parties' access at the agency level may be easier and cheaper than access at the legislative level. And discussions and negotiations among knowledgeable and experienced experts may be more useful than debates with legislative generalists. Mashaw, *ProDelegation; Why Administrators Should Make Policy Decisions*, 1 J. L. ECON. & ORG. 81, 95 (1985).

Whether and how agency authority is created and transferred can be debated. What cannot be in doubt in the mind of the student or the practitioner is that all agency action must be grounded on some form of statutory authority, that the courts can and do resolve disputes about the adequacy of that authority. Massachusetts v. EPA, 549 U.S. 497 (2007) (EPA *does* have authority to regulate greenhouse gasses); FDA v. Brown & Williamson, 529 U.S. 120 (2000) (FDA does *not* have authority to regulate tobacco). The critical tip for the analyst: the best place to begin thinking about the legality of any agency action is with the exact language of the authorizing statute.

2. The Problem of Unfairness

Among the reasons for the separation of powers noted earlier was the need to assure fairness and the appearance of fairness in the law implementation and enforcement process. If one believes, e.g., that adjudication should be policy-neutral, one might have real concerns if legislative, prosecutorial and judging functions were combined within one body. Suppose the FTC believes a certain type of misleading advertising practice should be prohibited. Acting in its legislative role, the Commission may express this policy in a published rule. Shifting to its role as executive, the Commission may investigate potential violations and decide which violators will be prosecuted. For those violators to be tried, agency personnel serve as prosecuting attorneys. The trial of the alleged violator will be before an FTC Administrative Law Judge (ALJ), whose judgment will be final unless a disappointed party appeals. Parties dissatisfied with the rulings of the ALJ can appeal, but the appeal goes to the Commission itself— the very body that developed, investigated, prosecuted, and judged the case initially. True, any final order of the Commission is subject to judicial review before an independent Article III federal judge, but as we will see in Chapter 6 judicial review is relatively unintensive on questions of policy, on disputed issues of fact within the expertise of the agency, and increasingly on agency legal determinations. If the framers wanted powers to be separated to lend fairness and the appearance of fairness to such governmental action, they would be astonished to see what happens in a typical FTC proceeding today.

Dealing with unfairness concerns has been a principal task of that body of law we call administrative law. You will see as we work through the ensuing chapters, that administrative law is engaged in correcting some of the separation of powers shortfalls that have emerged from the unexpected advent of the regulatory process. For example, when agencies are adjudicating individual cases, we will see procedural requirements about notice, opportunity to be heard, the objectivity of the judge, and the need to base decisions exclusively on the hearing record rather than on untested outside communications.

In informal agency rulemaking, concerns about unfairness are not so obvious since we regard rulemaking as a legislative activity. In the legislature there is no requirement that a legislative decision be based on any discrete "record" compiled in a hearing process—indeed, in the legislative branch there is not even a requirement that there be a hearing. Nor is there any requirement of a neutral decisionmaker. And there will be no limits on outside communications—in a legislative body, it is expected that many people both inside and outside government will be vigorous advocates of their point of view and that advocacy can be both public and private. Assuring fairness in a basically legislative function is more a matter of expanding rather than constricting communications with decisional officials. As we will see, agency rulemaking procedures will usually require much broader participation by those affected than is required in the legislative world.

Even supplemented by statutory and regulatory procedural requirements, of course, the system is hardly perfect, and the lawyer dealing with administrative adjudication and rulemaking will note the imperfections. But most feel the process is generally fair, and continued measurement of the process in light of this criterion is the function of professional critique.

3. The Problem of Unaccountability

The third constitutional question is a problem basic to all representative governments—that of accountability. As is clear from the above description, major policies and their implementation are being developed by unelected officials, none of them removable by the legislature (except by formal impeachment) and many not removable by the president. If a premise of the founders was that officials with such broad-ranging powers should be accountable to the people, it would seem that the growth of these sizable regulatory institutions would frustrate that purpose. It is here that a variety of formal and informal practices have grown up that give those affected significant opportunities to impact the regulatory process. These requirements and practices are not exactly the form of control the framers may have intended, but arguably they offer functionally similar opportunities.

The most obvious control over agencies comes from the legislature. Legislative preferences can be imposed on agencies by the drafting of the original statutes creating the agency and on a continuing basis by statutory amendment and, ultimately, by legislative abolition of the agency—as happened to the venerable Interstate Commerce Commission and the Civil Aeronautics Board. Of course, formal statute writing is not a practical way to fine-tune the thousands of matters agencies deal with in any given year. Efforts to make legislative control more effective with devices such as the legislative veto have not been approved by the Court, INS v. Chadha, 462 U.S. 919 (1983), but Congress has invented devices meeting constitutional requirements which can speed up the process of legislative review of agency rules. See the 1996 Congressional Review Act, 5 U.S.C. § 801 (1996).

Beyond statute writing, the legislature also controls agency budgets, an important avenue of pressure. Budget pressure—even informally threatened budget pressure—can have dramatic effects on agency attitudes. The legislative branch also exercises general oversight of agencies, and through hearings, investigations and reports can have significant effects on agency policies. And, of course, there are many opportunities legislators and legislative staff have to impose informal pressures on the day to day operations of the agencies. None of this is without cost, of course. Some of the techniques have been criticized as vesting disproportionate power in key legislative officials and even key staff members, or opening private avenues of influence to powerful interest groups. These concerns need to be taken seriously, but as anyone who has worked at the policy level in a federal agency will attest, the legislature remains a powerful force to which agencies must give constant and careful attention.

Courts also play an important role in the accountability mission. Courts insist that legislatively authorized procedures be followed. And judicial review of the substance of agency action is another control on agency discretion, tending to keep agency policies accountable to elected legislators. Of course, where the legislative delegation is in vague, amorphous terms, agencies no doubt exercise considerable discretion. But where the legislature has granted power subject to some limits—or where such limits have been developed over time in the course of agency interpretation or practice—reviewing courts can assure that agency rules are consistent with those standards. Still further, courts are authorized to set aside agency action which is arbitrary or is unsupported by evidence in cases where an evidential warrant is required. In all, we will see that an agency's freedom to wander far from its proper substantive and procedural boundaries is substantially limited by judicial action, and all of that adds to the accountability of the process.

Even beyond judicial and legislative control, accountability can be found in controls over the agencies imposed by the executive branch. As you know from your work in constitutional law, the president appoints most high level agency officers, even those in the so-called independent agencies. The power to appoint gives the president a significant initial role in shaping agency policy. Congress shares the appointment power in several respects. The Senate must confirm the presidential appointments of officers. Further, the Appointments Clause gives Congress power to vest the appointment power for "inferior" officers in the president, the courts of law, or in heads of departments. Still further, Congress has some power to establish the qualifications for persons appointed to agencies it creates. Pursuant to that power, Congress has imposed bipartisanship qualifications for membership in most of the independent agencies. There have been very few Supreme Court decisions on the appointment power, but a general picture of the process and the questions it poses can be seen in Figure 1.2.

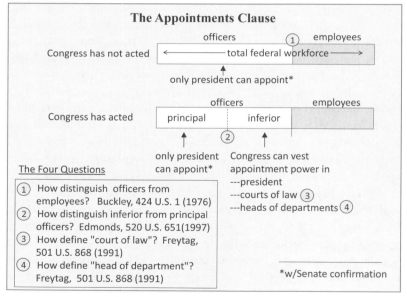

Figure 1.2   The Appointment Power

The president also has the power to remove many high level agency officials which you can be sure adds to the persuasiveness of presidential preferences. The constitution does not provide for removal (except by impeachment) but a removal power seems implicit in the president's obligation to "take care" that the laws are faithfully exercised. In 1926, former president and then Chief Justice Taft ruled (surprise?) that the president's power to remove a postmaster could not be limited by Congress (the congressional act made removal by the president subject to senatorial agreement). Myers v. U.S. 272 U.S. 52 (1926).

Nine years later, the Court considered a case in which the president had sought to remove not an executive official like a postmaster, but a member of a regulatory commission, created under a statute which prohibited dismissal except by an assertion of "cause." President Roosevelt sought to replace an unsympathetic member of the FTC but the Court denied the president that power. Humphrey's Executor v. U.S., 295 U.S. 602 (1935). The Court distinguished *Myers*, treating it as a case involving a "purely executive" official which it contrasted to the work of the FTC which was not executive in nature but was "quasi" legislative (i.e., making reports to Congress) and "quasi" judicial (i.e., agency's adjudicating functions).

No one today is in doubt that the FTC is exercising executive power (i.e., enforcing and implementing acts of Congress), which should make commissioners subject to presidential removal. But *Humphrey's Executor* still stands, and limits the president's power to remove members of a rulemaking and adjudicatory body like the FTC if Congress has specified a fixed term of office. That does not mean, of course, that independent agencies can freely disregard the preferences of the president. Whether or not agency heads are subject to removal, these agencies cannot comfortably function for long if at odds with the White House on important policy matters. Indeed, some of the independent agencies voluntarily comply with executive direction not legally binding on them.

While most high level executive branch officials can be dismissed whenever the president chooses — no Secretary of State will ever have much job security — the presidential removal powers is smaller today than it was in *Humphrey's Executor* days. In Morrison v. Olson, 487 U.S. 654 (1988) the Court adopted a functional approach which would permit Congress to place reasonable restrictions on removal of *any* officers who are not so closely connected with the president that the inability to remove them would seriously impair the president's ability to "take care" that the laws be faithfully executed. That longish sentence means that Congress can protect the tenure of even "purely executive" officers (in *Morrison*, the official was a prosecutor) unless the officer's complete loyalty is central to the presidential function. The future of this functional rather than formal approach to the matter remains to be seen. See Figure 1.3. At this writing (summer 2009), a case has been accepted for argument by the Supreme Court which could produce historic changes in this part of administrative law.

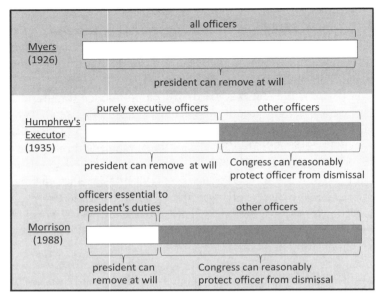

Figure 1.3   The Shrinking Presidential Removal Power

If the case survives preliminary obstacles of exhaustion, ripeness and finality (doctrines discussed below in Chapter 5) — *Morrison* and even *Humphrey's Executor* could be altered by a Court much more interested in a strong presidency than the courts which decided those cases. The case is Free Enter. Fund v. Public Company Accounting Oversight Board, 537 F.3d 667 (D.C. Cir. 2008). For helpful comment on the case see Strauss, Free Enter. Fund v. PCAOB, 672 VAND. L. REV. EN BANC 51; LSN ADMINISTRATIVE LAW Vol. 1 No. 7, 11/02/2009.

Beyond appointment and removal powers, the president also has, and has at times vigorously exercised, a set of general management tools that seek to facilitate agency coordination and budget planning, to bring agency policy views closer to executive preference, as well as to promote better analysis of proposed regulatory measures. You may recall from your work in constitutional law that the debate over the so-called "unitary executive" still rages and has not been illuminated much by Supreme Court opinions. But the president's obligation to "take care" that the laws are enforced surely gives the president implicit management obligations concerning the executive branch. Whether and to what extent the president can direct the exercise of agency discretion remains an unsettled question, and is the subject of considerable speculation and research. A couple of recent empirical investigations are Pressman & Vandenbergh, *Inside the Administrative State: A Critical Look at the Practice of Presidential Control,* 105 Mich. L. Rev. 47 (2006); Croley, *White House Review of Agency Rulemaking: An Empirical Investigation,* 70 U. Chi. L. Rev. 821 (2003).

Most agencies must have their budgets approved by the Office of Management and Budget (OMB)—a part of the office of the White House. Presidents have used this control of budgets to affect agency policy. Legislative proposals of executive branch agencies also need OMB approval. We will return to the question of presidential control of agency rulemaking in Chapter 2. At this writing (summer 2009), the new Obama administration is reviewing the question of executive oversight of the administrative process. There will be changes, but no one expects a radical change in the degree of executive oversight of the administrative agencies.

Finally, there are administrative procedures themselves that contribute to accountability. In the case of agency rulemaking, e.g., we will see that a form of accountability is sought through the public comment process. In this day of electronic information flow, access to the comment system is usually easy and convenient. And the right to comment is in fact exercised; the volume of public comment on a major rule today can be staggering, often in the thousands of comments. Those who believe accountability requires that important policy choices be made by elected legislators might consider that delegating some of those decisions to agencies could in some circumstances be a superior way to fit policies to an accurate and comprehensive sense about public preferences. As we have said, citizen access to the regulatory system is probably easier and cheaper than access to the legislature. Moreover, public inputs to Congress are not always given weight as a function of the validity of their reasoning or the soundness of their factual foundations—many may be more effective because of the political clout of the submitter than by the quality of the submission. By contrast, we will see that under current standards of judicial review, agency decisions must have plausible factual support, must be adequately responsive to public views, and must meet tests for overall rationality—criteria more demanding than would ever be used to judge the outputs of legislatures. Croley, Regulation and Public Interests 135–36 (2008).

In sum, the problem of agency unaccountability does not look quite the same on the ground as it looks at the theoretical level. In practice, agency discretion is cabined at many places by the public, by the industry it regulates, by the courts, by the legislatures and by the president. The avenues of accountability and the linkages of key players do not show the straight lines of the civics books or the official organizational chart. But those experienced with the process usually smile at the wag's observation that the administrative process is a "headless fourth branch." Surrounded as they are by powerful influencing

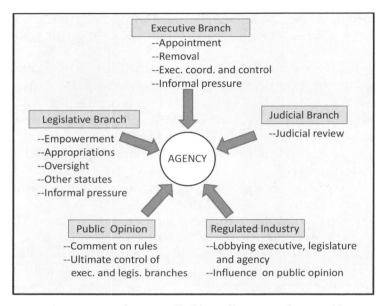

Figure 1.4   The So-Called 'Headless Fourth Branch'

forces, the position of most agencies more resemble that shown in Figure 1.4. (Whether agencies are *too* accountable to inappropriate influences may be the bigger problem, but that is a subject for another book).

D. Conclusion

We have, then, an immense regulatory system with dramatic and comprehensive impact on the daily lives of our citizens which is open to facially plausible charges that it is unauthorized, unfair, and unaccountable. It would be comforting to report that there have been developments in the principles of constitutional law — or amendments of the constitution itself — that would bring these institutions into harmony with the intent of the framers. Unfortunately, no such report can be made. What can be said — and this may be the best one can hope for in a structure needing to satisfy conflicting demands of stability over time and responsiveness to emerging needs — is that a series of accommodating arrangements and practices have developed which seek to lessen the severity of the problems somewhat and seek — by formal doctrine and informal practice — to carry out the underlying purpose, if not the exact structure, the framers intended.

How far and how legitimately these accommodations succeed is a matter of continuing controversy. But central to the settlement is a body of law through which judges are equipped to deal with problems of authority, accountability, and fairness so far as judicial instruments can be sensibly employed for that purpose. That body of law is what we call administrative law. And since this law is applied most obviously by courts, there will be inevitable "rule of law" threads woven into the fabric. Think of the administrative law field as having three distinct but overlapping functions.

> (1) Doctrines of administrative law require agencies to take seriously the various statutory and constitutional procedural requirements imposed on them in aid of values such as authority, accountability, and fairness.
> (2) Doctrines of administrative law insure that when these requirements are enforced by courts, it is done within acceptable standards of judicial competence and legitimacy.
> (3) Doctrines of administrative law insist on important rule of law considerations, such as predictable, principled, and reasoned decisionmaking.

As you work through administrative law doctrine, keep these functions in mind. Insist that every doctrine you examine addresses these functions frontally—that the doctrine supports compliance with statutory and constitutional requirements, that it imposes on courts only tasks that are within their understood portfolios, and that it honors rule of law values. Examining the doctrine through these perspectives will help you understand the doctrines better, apply them more effectively and, finally, will ground your professional critique.

Checkpoints

- The administrative process today is varied, immense, ubiquitous, and touches every aspect of American life.

- The constitutional doctrine of separation of powers seeks to prevent dangerous concentration of power in a single branch and to avoid tyranny and to ensure fairness in decisionmaking.

- Agencies exercise what are effectively legislative and judicial powers in many of their activities; courts have generally permitted this, over nondelegation objections.

- In many agencies, these legislative, executive and judicial functions are combined in a single agency; with some procedures in place to limit dangers, courts have usually permitted such combinations over separation of powers objections.

- The problem of unfairness in combining functions is dealt with by a series of legislative and judicial measures that attempt to keep the hearing process fair and the decisional process objective. Most of administrative law serves these goals.

- The problem of unaccountability is dealt with by significant legislative and executive control over agencies — both formal and informal — and by judicially enforced procedural requirements, insuring that people affected by agency action have meaningful opportunities to participate in the development of those actions.

- The three central functions of administrative law are (1) to facilitate procedural conditions on agency action in aid of such values as authority, fairness and accountability, (2) to insure that this is done within acceptable standards of judicial competence and legitimacy and (3) to insist that certain fundamental rule of law values are honored.

Chapter 2

Rulemaking

A. Why We Use Rulemaking

Let's begin with one of the foundational concepts of administrative law — one you'll need to be very familiar with as we proceed. Leaving complicating details for later, consider that there are two general ways that policy can be developed in the administrative context: (1) through individualized decisions and (2) through general rules.

1. Individualized Decision Making

Policy can be developed as part of the resolution of individual disputes. Thus, in the common law of negligence the policy concerning the level of due care needed to avoid tort liability is worked out on a case-by-case basis. To use a familiar example, in 1928 a court had to spell out due care requirements in the context of an accident at the Long Island Railroad Company's station that injured Helen Palsgraf. Palsgraf v. Long Island R. Co., 248 N.Y. 339, 162 N.E. 99 (1928). Technically, the *Palsgraf* decision was binding only on the named parties, but later courts applied the principles reflected in the opinion, extending

23

and elaborating them in light of the particulars of the cases facing the courts. In this model, policy is thus formulated in the course of deciding a specific case, but the principles developed can have broad impact on "like" cases in the future.

As a student of the common law, you will appreciate the advantages of this way of developing policy. It builds on past experience; it allows policies to be worked out bit by bit as the decision maker feels his or her way in areas that are uncertain; it permits policies to be fitted to the particulars of the case at hand, taking into account special settings or novel situations; and it permits incremental change—the slow, careful evolution of policy to match new needs and circumstances. As we will detail in the next chapter, administrative agencies may be given power to develop and apply policies in a case-by-case manner and these undoubted advantages will be apparent.

But policy development by individualized decisions has some powerful disadvantages as well.

- To begin with, it is famously uncertain. Before Judge Cardozo's opinion in *Palsgraf,* the railroad had little way of knowing when its handling of its equipment would subject it to liability. And even after the decision things were not much clearer; the Cardozo opinion may be a model of elegant judicial rhetoric, but as a detailed inventory of specific steps to be taken to reduce future liability it left vast areas of uncertainty.
- Moreover, there is a certain retroactive quality about individualized policy making. The principle applied by the court in *Palsgraf* was applied to past acts of the railroad, which acts—given the uncertainty of the legal standard—may not have been blameworthy.
- Policy making by individual decisions also can raise the problem of uneven treatment, as possibly irrelevant differences (was Ms. Palsgraf a wealthy socialite or a poor widow?) result in different outcomes in what are essentially similar cases or in which different judges appraise similar facts differently.
- Still further, there are only limited ways in which individualized policy development can address a problem as a whole—to craft a comprehensive approach that might pay major benefits in terms of rule of law values such as rationality, consistency, or predictability.
- Many who may be affected in the future by a principle fashioned in an individual decision will have no opportunity to participate in the formulation of the principle.
- Finally, there is the problem of cost. Litigating a series of individual cases may be a very expensive and time-consuming method for developing policy.

2. The Use of General Rules

The noted inadequacies of policy making through individual decision have produced in most legal systems a second way of determining policy—the use of general rules. A carefully drafted prospective general rule defining the way railroad equipment should be secured might have given the Long Island Railroad advance notice of appropriate conduct and thus might have avoided uncertainty—indeed might have avoided the accident itself. Being prospective, such a rule would not have penalized the railroad for past blameless behavior, would have applied consistently across the whole railroad industry, would have been formulated with the input of other railroads, businesses, passengers and customers, and would surely have saved a great deal of money in litigation and related expenses.

Courts are our model for policy making through individual decisions; when agencies are deciding individual cases we will call that process adjudication. Legislatures are our model of bodies making policy through general rules; when agencies are setting policies through general rules we will call that process rulemaking. Put these two words into you administrative law vocabulary.

| Adjudication | Rulemaking |

You will be working with these two categories of administrative action throughout our discussions. You need to be comfortable with them. The correct classification for any given proceeding may be critical as procedural requirements may turn on the classification.

Usually, it will be clear which category is involved, though the categories are sometimes fuzzy at the margins. When in doubt, begin with the notion that if the action is like what a court does, it is likely to be adjudication; if it resembles legislative action, it is likely to be rulemaking. Then fine tune your initial estimate by consulting relevant statutory and regulatory definitions.

Figure 2.1   Two Fundamental Concepts of Administrative Law

B. Rulemaking and the Rule of Law in a Democracy

In the case of ordinary legislation, legitimacy is assured by direct election of members of Congress who write the laws and by direct election of the President who enforces them. But how do we get legitimacy in a system where rules are written by unelected administrative officials? The basic answer has been touched on in our earlier discussions of how administrative agencies are created and empowered and how their top leadership is selected. Agencies operate under grants of power from the legislature. Statutes creating and empowering agencies are written by elected legislators and signed by an elected President. Further, agencies are managed by top officials who have been appointed by an elected President and confirmed by an elected Senate. Accountability to elected officials is clearest for top officials who serve at the pleasure of the President, but we have seen that even those who have more secure tenure face a range of formal and informal mechanisms through which elected officials seek to conform agency action to political preferences. Indeed, there is often criticism of this political control — agencies sometimes appear to critics to be too accountable — too "political" or too beholden to narrow interests which may have influence in the political arena.

But it is not possible for the most diligent executive and legislative officials and their staffs to attend in detail to all the numerous and highly technical activities of the modern regulatory agency. Administrative law's functional response to this difficulty is a series of procedural requirements that seek to insure that rules are carefully thought out, based on sound factual foundations and that those affected by a proposed rule have some meaningful opportunity to participate in its formulation. The basic structure of what we call "notice and comment rulemaking" is described with appealing simplicity in §553 of the APA. (Excerpts from the APA are set out in the Appendix.)

> (b) General notice of proposed rulemaking shall be published in the Federal Register ... [t]he notice shall include ... the terms or substance of the proposed rule ...
> (c) After notice required by this section, the agency shall give interested persons an opportunity to participate in the rulemaking through submission of written data, views, or arguments ... after consideration of the relevant matter presented, [the agency will issue its rule]. 5 U.S.C. § 553.

The drafters of the APA felt this opportunity for public notice and comment served both to improve the technical quality of rules and to meet legitimacy and accountability concerns. Note that the requirements for public participation go well beyond what the public gets in the legislative process where there are no legal requirements for notice, hearing or even that legislators "consider" views expressed by anyone.

C. The Components of Modern Rulemaking — A Case Study

Federal agencies make thousands of rules each year and for the vast majority of them the procedures in the Administrative Procedure Act work well. There are a few hundred major rules, however—where lots of money and lots of public impact are involved—in which the process has become more complicated and inevitably more cumbersome, slow, and expensive. We will examine the causes of this problem below, but it will be useful now to get a feel for the complexity of one of these proceedings. That will make it easier to grasp what the procedural debates are all about and what hinges on their resolution.

The sketch which follows involves the Environmental Protection Agency (EPA) and its struggle in the past few years to set a standard for smog. (If you'd like more details of this story, see Steven Croley, REGULATION AND PUBLIC INTERESTS, Chap. 9 [2008] or Craig Oren, *Whitman v. American Trucking*, in ADMINISTRATIVE LAW STORIES [Strauss, Ed. 2006]).

The EPA has both the authority and the obligation under the Clean Air Act to identify air pollutants that threaten human health and to write rules prescribing acceptable standards. 42 U.S.C. §7401. Measurement questions vastly complicate these issues, and there is considerable scientific uncertainty about what levels of these pollutants are unsafe. The act requires the agency to review and if necessary revise its standards every five years. Standards for the kind of pollutants that produce what we call smog were established in 1978. In 1982 the agency began its five-year review but no action was forthcoming. Twelve years later, in a lawsuit brought by the American Lung Association, a federal court ordered the agency to review and if necessary to propose a rule to revise these standards as required by the act. American Lung Ass'n v. Browner, 884 F. Supp. 345 (D. Ariz. 1994).

Before a rule is proposed, an extensive process seeks to establish credible scientific foundations for the proposal. During the next several years, multivolume studies and book-length analyses were prepared by EPA staff and by outside advisors—a process in which both industry and environmental groups participated actively. Staff studies finally recommended a rule which would reduce the current standard for smog-producing emissions from 0.12 parts per million (ppm) to 0.08 ppm. (These are major differences. One study showed that the reduction of the standard from 0.09 to 0.08 ppm would have measurable effects on the health of 16,000 children.)

In 1996, the EPA began the public part of the rulemaking process by issuing a notice of proposed rulemaking and inviting public comment. The proposal followed the staff recommendations that emission of smog-producing chemicals be reduced from 0.12 to 0.08 ppm. Along with the proposed rule, the agency made available to the public the many scientific studies it had considered in formulating the proposal. There were thousands of such studies since the agency's last standard revision, most of them showing various levels of adverse health effects of the pollutants concerned. In support of its proposal, the agency estimated that the tighter standards proposed would prevent 15,000 deaths annually, and lead to significant increases in children's health, and between $50 and $120 billion in annual savings in hospital costs, to list just a few of the quantified benefits. Compliance costs were estimated by the agency at between $6 and $9 billion.

If the scientific disputes weren't complicating enough, the governmental relationships added still more complexities. The Clean Air Act was adopted with federalism principles in mind. The EPA does not directly enforce its standards. Instead, the agency's role is to facilitate development of "state implementation plans." There was wide disparity around the country in the degree to which state plans were adequate. And an interesting geographical factor emerged: manufacturing in the midwestern states seemed to be the source of much of this pollution while adverse effects from the pollution fell mainly on northeastern states because of prevailing westerly winds. As you can imagine, this situation had demonstrable consequences in the congressional debates.

Under the provisions of §553 of the APA set out above, the EPA proposals had to run the gauntlet of public comment. In response to the publication of the proposed rule, the EPA received about 55,000 written or oral comments, along with 14,000 phone calls and 4,000 emails (something of a novelty in 1996). In addition to the comment process, the agency voluntarily held public meetings and regional workshops as well as two national telecasts to answer questions. Congress created a panel of distinguished scientists to discuss and evaluate the proposals.

Opposition came from those on whom the immediate costs of compliance would fall: large chemical plants, construction operations, oil refineries, automobile manufacturers, and power plants—a group of powerful and aggressive opponents. In addition, the battle against the proposed rule was supported by the National Association of Manufacturers, the small business community, and the U.S. Conference of Mayors. Millions were spent on lobbying and publicity, challenging the scientific basis of the proposals, the accuracy of the agency's calculation of both benefits (said to be overstated), and costs (said to be understated). Congressional lobbying was especially heavy and some major players in Congress became highly critical of the agency's proposals. A number of legislative hearings were held and the knowledge and credibility of EPA officials were attacked by witnesses as well as by some members of Congress.

The Clinton White House was initially ambivalent about the proposed rule, largely due to congressional opposition, though numerous inter-agency and inter-office meetings were held during this time period, seeking some resolution. Even future presidential politics got involved as Vice President Al Gore—even then a confirmed environmentalist—was criticized by environmentalists for not leading the fight in the White House. Environmental groups sought to enlist the support of Representative Richard Gephart—Gore's rival for the 2000 Democratic presidential nomination—forcing Gore to choose between his environmentalist sympathies and his need for support in the Midwest where the new standards were unpopular. The Vice President finally supported the EPA's proposed rule and brought President Clinton in with him. The rule in its final form was adopted in 1997.

Of course, nothing is ever fully or finally settled in politics. Congressional opponents quickly responded with bills to impose a four-year moratorium. These bills were popular with legislators (some had over 200 sponsors) but none passed, probably because of the vigorous (if late) presidential support of the rule. But congressional opposition to the rule created uncertainty, including questions of funding. By 1998 a bipartisan compromise became law, permitting the agency to implement its rules with some modifications for specially impacted groups (e.g., farmers), some funding for state monitoring efforts, and with some stretching out of the implementation dates.

When the legislative and executive battles had reached this uneasy settlement, the opponents renewed their attacks in the courts. It is in the courts that "administrative law" as such will be explicitly discussed, but don't forget the rest of the iceberg. Most of the judicial opinions you will read in your administrative law study will have been preceded by complex and long-running stories such as this one.

Opponents of the EPA ozone rule were initially successful in the D.C. Circuit Court of Appeals, the court holding that the rules were based on an unacceptable interpretation of the Clean Air Act. American Trucking v. EPA, 175 F.3d 1027 (D.C. Cir. 1999). The Supreme Court reversed this opinion, Whitman v. American Trucking Ass'n, 531 U.S. 457 (2001), and on remand the D.C. Circuit rejected all remaining legal challenges. The administrative law issues debated in these opinions will be treated later in our discussions. They focused on whether Congress can delegate such broad discretionary functions to an administrative agency (it can), whether the correct rulemaking procedure was followed (it was), and whether the final rule was arbitrary or capricious (it was not).

Five years had now passed since the agency's ozone rules were "finally" promulgated. But even the end of this litigation did not lead to immediate implementation of the rules. There was still the problem of determining where in the nation the standards were not being met—plagued by continuing debates of measurement methodology. And when so-called "non-attainment" areas had been identified, there remained the problem of asking states to develop and put in place implementation plans. By 2006, it was estimated that the EPA had identified more than 400 U.S. counties (in which 160 million people lived) that were not yet in compliance with the standards. State plans are in process and it is not expected that the standards will be generally met until 2015. Meanwhile, the science continues to develop and circumstances will change (e.g., with changing patterns of energy consumption). At this writing (summer 2009), litigation about smog standards is still going on. Allegations are flying that the Bush White House interfered with the EPA's efforts and was pushing a more industry-friendly standard. Aspects of one EPA smog rule were struck down by a court in July 2008. North Carolina v. EPA, 531 F.3d 896 (D.C. Cir. 2008). The controversy will continue and it will move at the same glacial speed. Major administrative rulemaking in the United States is not for the short-winded.

A final observation on this story. In thinking about agency rulemaking, we sometimes assume that the accountability mechanisms (executive appointment and coordination, congressional funding and oversight, etc.) is a static process made up of a fixed group of players. But note that in the time period recounted above (1978 to 2008) there were nine EPA administrators who had been appointed by five presidents (three of them Republicans and two of them Democrats) and there had been 15 cycles of elections in the Congress. Rather clearly, the complexities of the regulatory function will take place in a rapidly moving governmental and political environment—another important dynamic to be dealt with.

Whether this process in fact provides the hoped-for foundations of wisdom and legitimacy will always be debated. The sluggish nature of much modern rulemaking is disappointing. There are critics today who believe the rulemaking process has become "ossified" and cumbersome (the classic article is McGarity, *Some Thoughts on "Deossifying" the Rulemaking Process*, 41 DUKE L. J. 1385 (1992) and a typical response is Anthony, *Pro-Ossification*, 31 WAKE FOREST L. REV. 667 (1996)). Further, while the costs of gaining access to the process may be negligible in this day of the Internet, the costs of preparing the kinds of technical and scientific studies needed for many rules today may be huge. The result is that the principal players in modern rule-making will often be dedicated and resourceful interest groups rather than members of the general public. That may create some bias in the system, though dedication and resources can be present in many types of associations, including those representing consumers and environmentalists, civil rights advocates, etc.

Within the agencies, one thing is clear: the cost, delay, and procedural complexity of today's agency rulemaking creates strong pressures for agencies to find what they regard as cheaper and quicker ways to create general policies. They may use interpretive rules or policy statements that, as we'll see, do not require notice and comment. Or they may state a principle in the adjudication of a particular case that — *Palsgraf*-like — may communicate a new policy direction.

In the discussion of rulemaking procedures to follow, we will consider most of the elements shown in this example. In any substantial rulemaking project one will find at least the following steps:

- Initiation of the rulemaking process, through internal initiative or external means
- A phase of study to determine if a rule is necessary and, if so, which available solution seems best — a phase in which various internal and external players will participate
- Intra-executive branch coordination and clearances
- Publication of the proposed rule
- Public comment on the proposal
- Agency consideration of these comments
- Decision on the final rule and, ultimately
- Judicial review of the rule on both procedural and substantive grounds

And all along the way, there are the political threads that are inevitably woven into the fabric.

D. The Legal Framework for Rulemaking

Rulemaking occurs under a complex of statutory and other procedural requirements. We will examine here four major parts of this scheme: the Administrative Procedure Act (APA), which applies to most federal agencies; the agency's own statute; Executive Branch controls over rulemaking; and finally, a scattering of other statutes that touch agency rulemaking in important ways.

1. Preliminary Questions

The first legal question to consider in evaluating the legality of agency rule-making is, of course, the question of authority. Agencies have no inherent power, so every exercise of power by an agency must be supported by a statutory grant. If no statutory authority to make rules can be found, the agency cannot make rules. When rules are challenged on this basis, are courts deferential to agencies? We will discover in Chapter 6 below that courts sometimes defer to agency interpretation of their own statutes. We will see that courts retain the power to decide when and how much to defer. Deference to an agency legal interpretation would seem least supportable when the interpretation goes to the agency's own jurisdiction and authority. FDA v. Brown and Williamson Tobacco Corp., 529 U.S. 120 (2000) (despite the agency's contrary interpretation of its statute, FDA does not have power to regulate tobacco).

Beyond the question of whether an agency *can* make rules is the question of whether there are ever circumstances when an agency *must* make rules. Suppose an agency has general statutory authority to promote air safety, and is authorized to employ both rulemaking and adjudication in carrying out its mandate. Such an agency might write a rule requiring 20/20 eyesight for commercial pilots and in a later adjudication revoke Pilot Green's license if her eyesight was not up to that standard. Alternatively, the agency could forego rulemaking and under its general statutory authority proceed directly to revoke Green's license if the agency could prove her eyesight threatens air safety. Could the latter adjudication be challenged on the grounds that an eyesight standard should first have been embodied in a published rule? In support of such a holding would be the probable facts that a rule would have been fairer (all would have advance notice) and would have been more competently made (wider inputs, more comprehensive solution).

The foundational principle at the federal level is that unless Congress has foreclosed it, the choice about whether to proceed by rulemaking or adjudication "lies primarily in the informed discretion" of the agency. SEC v. Chenery, 332 U.S. 194, 203 (1947). Thus, the federal agency—if authorized to proceed either by rulemaking or by adjudication—is usually free to choose. Concerns have occasionally been expressed that new policies should be announced in advance in rule form before individuals can be disadvantaged for action inconsistent with the policies. NLRB v. Wyman-Gordon, Inc., 394 U.S. 759 (1969). Occasionally, a court will find a due process violation when an agency decides individual cases without "ascertainable standards." Holmes v. N. Y. Housing Authority, 398 F.2d 262 (2d Cir. 1968). But in spite of a clear judicial understanding of the advantages of rulemaking, the federal courts still generally leave the choice to the agency.

At the state level, a few state administrative procedure statutes require (or encourage) rulemaking, e.g., Fla. Stat. Ann. § 120.54(1) (Harrison 1999) (requiring some rulemaking); Wash. Rev. Stat. 34.05.220 (2003) (encouraging some rulemaking). And an occasional state judicial opinion may require rulemaking. Megdal v. Oregon State Bd. of Dental Exam'rs, 605 P.2d 273, 274 (Or. 1980).

2. The Administrative Procedure Act

In 1946 Congress enacted the federal Administrative Procedure Act (APA) and with that measure laid down the basic default pattern for most federal administrative procedure. The Act was the culmination of years of debate over the burgeoning administrative process of the New Deal. Opponents of the New Deal sought to confine and limit the power of agencies. These forces sought to require agencies to follow traditional court-like procedures, and to afford the full protections to individual rights that judicial procedures provided. Supporters of the New Deal sought to liberate agencies from some traditional judicial procedures, regarding those procedures as inflexible, cumbersome, and ultimately as protectors of the status quo. While tempests involving administrative procedure rarely become matters of national debate, in this case Congress in 1940 passed a general administrative procedure act, but it was vetoed by President Roosevelt.

By the end of World War II, the parties had reached an accommodation. The APA as passed in 1946 shows the fingerprints of many contesting interests. Generally, the provisions on adjudication reflect the views of those who wanted agencies to adopt judicial type procedures. Read through Sections 556 and 557 of the Act and see how familiar they sound. On the other hand, the rulemaking functions are almost wholly free of detailed procedures. Section 553 seems to require little except that the agency publish a draft of a proposed rule and listen to public comment on it. The agency can then issue the rule it prefers, explaining its choice in a "concise general statement of basis and purpose."

As we have seen in the case study above, the process has become much more complex today and the procedures employed have been elaborated by a combination of legislative, executive and judicial action. But in 1946, when the APA was passed, rulemaking was seen as a quick, easy, direct way to make general rules with a minimum of formality.

a. Exemptions

Before we look at the rulemaking requirements, a word about rules that are exempted from the APA. Some types of rules are exempted from the §553 process entirely. Section 553(a) exempts rules that involve

(1) a military or foreign affairs function ... or
(2) a matter relating to agency management or personnel or to public property, loans, grants, benefits or contracts.

Subsection (1) exemptions have been interpreted narrowly by the courts.
And some agencies whom the exemptions might excuse from the §553 notice
and comment process (e.g., the Department of Defense) nevertheless have
adopted a policy using notice and comment for many of their rules. The foreign affairs exemption have been used for rules bearing directly on such things
as international agreements and import quotas. See, e.g., Am. Ass'n of Ex-
porters and Importers v. U.S., 751 F.2d 1239 (Fed. Cir. 1985).

Subsection (2)'s exemption of agency management and personnel functions
seeks to permit an agency's internal operational functions to be conducted without the need for public involvement, a generally sensible notion. On the other
hand, the subsection's exemption of rules involving public property, grants,
benefits, and contracts is more troublesome since rules on such matters can
have important impacts on people outside the agency. For this reason, these
exemptions have also been interpreted narrowly by the courts and the weight
of critical commentary clearly supports narrow interpretation. Bonfield, *Public Participation in Federal Rulemaking Relating to Public Property, Loans, Grants,
Benefits and Contracts*, 118 U. OF PA. L. REV. 540 (1970). The Administrative
Conference of the U.S. has recommended that the exemption be eliminated altogether and in the meantime urged agencies to comply with §553 notice and
comment procedures when issuing rules relating to these matters. Administrative Conference Recommendation 69-8, 38 Fed. Reg. 19,782 (1973). A number
of agencies have responded to this urging by the Conference.

Beyond matters exempted from §553 completely, some rules are excluded
from parts of the section. The provisions of the section that require notice and
comment do not apply

(A) to interpretative rules, general statements of policy, or rules of
agency organization, procedure or practice, or
(B) when the agency for good cause finds ... that notice and public
procedure ... are impracticable, unnecessary, or contrary to the public interest.

Subsection (A)'s exemption of interpretative rules and policy statements
will be considered later. Subsection (A) also exempts from notice and comment requirements rules dealing with "agency organization, procedure or practice." This would seem to be a fairly straightforward exemption of internal
housekeeping rules. Rules of procedure, however, may have considerable ef-

fects on outside parties. For a time the courts refused to exempt procedural rules from the notice and comment requirements if the rules had a "substantial impact" on parties outside the agency. Batterton v. Marshall, 648 F.2d 694 (D. C. Cir. 1980) ("The critical question is whether the agency action jeopardizes the rights and interest of parties, for if it does, it must be subject to public comment prior to taking effect." Id. at 708.)

Later courts, however, put more emphasis on an attempt to define what was meant by the term "procedural rules." These opinions tend to identify as procedural those rules—whatever impact they have on the parties—as rules that do not change a basic substantive standard but only the manner in which the standard is used or treated. Hurson v. Glickman, 229 F.3d 277 (D.C. Cir. 2000).

Of course, this is not always an easy distinction to make. Suppose a rule is proposed which would require dog owners to carry with them proof of their dogs' rabies shots. Such a rule might be called "procedural" since it does not alter the underlying substantive standard requiring that all dogs have rabies shots, or that owners must keep records of such shots; it only alters the manner in which the rule will be enforced. But might a court not conclude that a new requirement about what dog owners must carry on their persons was such a dramatic and unpublicized departure from prior practice as to be prejudicial to owners and, as such, better treated as altering the underlying substantive rights of dog owners? Some courts that have exempted questionably procedural rules have added the requirement that agencies must provide adequate notice of such rules and that the procedures used must not operate to the prejudice of the parties. See, e.g., National Whistleblower Center v. NRC, 208 F.3rd 256 (D.C. Cir. 2000).

Turning to subsection (B), the statue exempts from notice and comment requirements any rules where an agency for "good cause" finds that the process is impractical or contrary to the public interest. This is a useful provision that eliminates notice and comment where the time required for such procedures threatens more important values (e.g., airline safety) or where the comment process itself is not useful (the issue is narrow, technical, or not in dispute).

But the exemption is a temptation to short-circuit the public comment process inappropriately and you can expect courts to construe the exemption strictly. Concerns about the good cause exemption have spawned a couple of practices worth noting. One goes by the oxymoronic name, "interim final rules." Here, the agency with a defensible case for a "good cause" exemption puts the rule into effect without notice and comment but voluntarily agrees to receive comment later. If later comment convinces the agency that the rule should be dropped or modified, it will do that, ultimately issuing a truly final rule. In the meantime, the interim rule remains in effect. As Michael Asimow says,

Interim-final rules adopted under the good cause exemption strike a compromise between a perceived need for immediate adoption of a rule and the values of public participation and regulatory analysis. When it adopts an interim-final rule, an agency captures some, but not all, of the benefits of pre-adoption public comment. It also captures some, but not all, of the cost and time savings of adopting a rule without any public participation or regulatory analysis at all. Asimow, *Interim-Final Rules*, 51 ADMIN. L. REV. 703, 710 1999).

Still another way of dealing with the need for prompt rulemaking action is to use a so-called "direct final rule." Here, the agency issues a rule to go into effect in 30 days unless significant adverse comment is received. If such comment appears, the rule is withdrawn and normal notice and comment process begins. The judicial vote is still out on this technique and the commentators are divided. Of course, the use of direct final rules gives the public more opportunity to comment than they would get if the agency successfully used the good cause exemption, and it provides a streamlined process for non-controversial rules. See the discussion in Werhan, PRINCIPLES OF ADMINISTRATIVE LAW 267 (2008).

Finally, remember that even though a particular set of rules is not required to follow §553 procedures, Congress has power to add additional procedures and it sometimes does. We will note examples as the discussion proceeds.

b. The APA Rule Definition

All of the APA's rulemaking requirements apply only to actions that meet the act's definition of rule. Statutes like this are not easy to read and as students we tend to skip over them, looking for the more general comfort of a judicial gloss or paraphrase. But that way is treacherous in administrative law. The exact language of the act must be examined. So you must bite the bullet, dig into the intricacies of a statute and make it your own. Here is the text of §551 of the APA, defining "rule":

"rule" means the whole or a part of an agency statement of general or particular applicability and future effect designed to implement, interpret, or prescribe law or policy or describing the organization, procedure, or practice requirements of an agency and includes the approval or prescription for the future of rates, wages, corporate or financial structures or reorganization thereof, prices, facilities, appliances, services or allowances therefore or of valuations, costs, or accounting, or practices bearing on any of the foregoing;

You can be sure every word in such a definition was the subject of debate in the drafting process and many of the words have been the subject of litigation. Moreover, the definition of rule is especially critical in the APA because it is a reciprocal of the definition of adjudication which we'll examine later.

Figure 2.2 visualizes this definition so you can get a sense of its basic structure.

Several things to note about this definition. First, for all its specificity, the definition has important ambiguities, overlaps and uncertainties, some of which we will explore. Don't be surprised by this; any complex statute will have such problems either by intention (agreement on a more precise formula was not possible) or inadvertence (unforeseen situations have arisen).

Second, the definition goes beyond the normal meaning of a rule (something we think of as "generally" applicable) since it covers actions of "particular" applicability. The drafters apparently thought this necessary because of the inclusion of such things as rate making, which could be proceedings involving only a single regulated party. Read the definition without the "or particular" words to get its general sense, then tuck away these two words until you need them.

Third, there are no subject matter limits here — *all* rules dealing with law, policy, or organization are covered by the definition. The basic drafting strategy here was to use a very inclusive definition of rule, then to provide for nec-

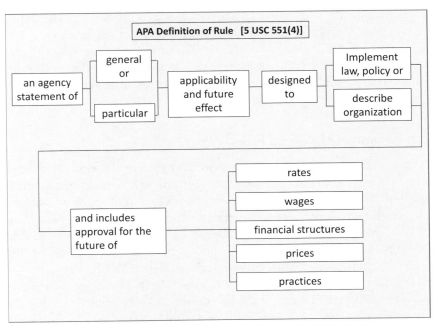

Figure 2.2   Definition of Rule under Section 551(4) of the APA

essary variations through specific exceptions and exclusions, some of which we've already seen.

Fourth, a rule is said to be "of future effect"—a quality that fits with our sense of legislative type action which is usually prospective. But when it comes to distinguishing rulemaking from adjudication (a distinction sometimes required to determine the correct procedure) it should be clear that many adjudications have a kind of future effect as well. The *Palsgraf* case, e.g., certainly had future effect—you're still reading it many years later. Similarly, an adjudication leading to a license revocation or resulting in a cease-and-desist order has obvious future effect. Sometimes it is said that the reference to future effect in the rulemaking definition results from a rule's effort to shape *future* conduct while an adjudication relates principally to *past* conduct of a party. This is a tempting explanation but don't trust it too far—the fact is all rules are in some sense based on past events (we don't pass a rule locking the barn door just on a whim) and all adjudications have some future effects (as in the examples cited above). Perhaps the most we can say is that the main objective of rules is to lay down standards for future conduct—recognizing that past circumstances may have put the issue on the rulemaker's agenda and may play a role in shaping the rule—while the main objective of adjudications is to assert something about the legality of past events—recognizing that future arrangements may be needed to make remedies effective and that the adjudication's justifying principles may have future impacts in similar cases.

Finally, stay flexible: the APA's rule definition is broad enough to cover a lot of things that won't look like rules. An agency statement designed to implement policy could come in the form of a memo, an email, a bulletin or even a luncheon speech.

c. Formal and Informal Rules

Once you have concluded that the instrument you are looking at (or that is being contemplated) is a rule, there are three procedural tracks that might be required. See Figure 2.3. Section 553(c) provides two of these: an *informal* track (essentially the notice and comment process we will examine below) and a *formal* track (requiring use of the more formalized provisions of §556 and §557). Incidentally, the words "formal" and "informal" do not appear in the APA, but have become conventional usage in judicial opinion and commentary. And note that the words formal and informal do not always carry their usual meaning—the elaborate EPA case study we examined earlier followed §553 notice and comment process and is, despite its complexity and length, "informal" rulemaking. The third track—the so-called *hybrid* track—is used where other

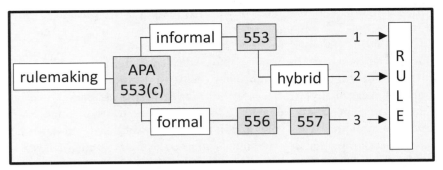

Figure 2.3   Three Types of Rulemaking Procedures

statutes or rules add procedural requirements to what would otherwise be required by §553's informal rulemaking process.

How do you tell which track an agency must follow in any particular rulemaking? Figure 2.3 tells us that the decision as to which track to follow is governed initially by § 553(c). The last sentence of that subsection provides

> **When rules are required by statute to be made on the record after opportunity for an agency hearing, sections 556 and 557 of this title apply instead of this subsection.**

If Congress were always clear about this question when it authorized an agency to make rules our lives would all be much simpler. Unfortunately, Congress is often unclear. Suppose Congress authorizes an agency to promulgate rules "after hearing." Does this trigger the formal provisions of §§556–557? The answer today is, "no." As we will detail in the next chapter, §§556–57 require such formal processes as cross-examintion, discovery and a decision on a closed, exclusive record. Rulemaking works best when it is handled like legislative action. As a result, formal procedures are not favored in rulemaking. In U.S. v. Florida East Coast Railway, 410 U.S. 224 (1973), the Supreme Court made it as clear as anything gets in administrative law that the mere word "hearing" in a congressional grant of rulemaking power does not necessarily trigger the formal provisions of §§556–57. The ICC in this case had required evidence and argument to be submitted in written form only, had thus denied personal presentations and cross-examintion, procedures that usually are required in formal hearings under §§556–57. The Court conceded that the rulemaking involved had fiscal impacts on the regulated railroads — very like rate orders as to which due process historically required fuller hearing. Yet it found that in this case the word "hearing" in the ICC Act did not require the ICC to hear testimony, to permit cross-examination or to hear oral argument, either under the ICC Act itself or by triggering §§556–57 of the APA.

Does this mean that formal procedures are never used in rulemaking? Not exactly. There are some advantages to formal rulemaking (fuller deliberation, full participation by parties, more objectivity in decision making, etc.) so Congress occasionally prescribes it. But *Florida East Coast Railway* teaches that before an agency can be required to use those procedures, Congress will have to be very precise in expressing its wishes. Any drafter worth his or her salary will express that congressional intent by using the actual triggering words of the APA — they will write that the rules are to be made "on the record after opportunity for an agency hearing." In the absence of such explicitness, you can usually assume all rulemaking will be either informal or hybrid.

d. "Nonlegislative Rules" (Herein of Interpretive Rules, Policy Statements, etc.)

In a subject as diverse as administrative agency rulemaking, you can expect there to be many ways in which agencies can express general policies. Section 553 rulemaking is one method. But suppose an agency wishes to advise regulated parties about a policy that

- the agency wishes to implement quickly without the delay and expense of the notice and comment process, or
- doesn't seem of broad enough impact to justify full scale notice and comment proceedings, or
- is still in the formative stage and needs more experimentation and flexibility than a final notice and comment rule would provide, or
- is a policy that the agency is not anxious to publicize widely.

Can the agency express the policy in a statement issued without notice and comment? In a press release? In a bulletin? In an email statement? In a notice posted on its web page?

You might begin by noticing that the APA rule definition is broad enough to cover all these forms of expression — i.e., they are all agency statements of future effect designed to implement policy. But a category of rules that are not typical notice and comment rules raises several difficult legal questions.

(1) is compliance with §553's notice and comment process required for their validity?
(2) if they are valid without §553 notice and comment, what is their effect?
   (a) are they binding on the agency ?

(b) are they binding on outside parties?
(c) can they be changed without any sort of process?
(d) what weight will courts give them on judicial review?

We will focus on the first question here, the others later. In deciding whether §553 procedures must be used in formulating these kinds of rules it is useful to think of rules in two broad categories which we might label *legislative* and *nonlegislative* rules. Legislative rules are so named because of their legal effect—they are very like statutes. Violation of legislative rules can earn your client license revocations, fines, and in some cases even criminal penalties. They are "law" in almost every sense of the word. Sometimes these rules are called "substantive" rules. For these kinds of rules, the first question above (must §553 be followed?) is answered, "yes." This is classic rulemaking, following §553 notice and comment process and resulting in binding legislative rules.

Nonlegislative rules are more difficult to describe. As suggested above, they come in many shapes, sizes and forms. When an agency wishes to notify its own staff about preferred enforcement tactics, when it wants to inform outside parties about agency views as to the meaning of its statute, when it wants the public to know about the policies it wishes to follow—in all such cases, the agency may communicate its views in interpretive statements, policy papers, bulletins, memos, manuals, letters, press releases, and even speeches. Some courts and writers have come to describe these expressions under the generic title, "guidance materials." As you might expect, these kinds of agency expressions are much more numerous than legislative rules. They can also be extremely valuable—both to affected outsiders seeking to anticipate agency action and to agencies themselves seeking appropriate and consistent work by agency staff.

In §553(b), the APA uses the phrases "interpretative rules" and "general statements of policy" which seem to cover some of these expressions. The section explicitly exempts such statements from the notice and comment requirements, though still requiring their publication.

So we can begin with this:

- legislative rules must comply with all of §553 and
- some nonlegislative rules (interpretive rules and policy statements) are exempt from the notice and comment process of §553 but remain subject to the APA's publication requirements, §552(a)(1)(D), (to be discussed in Chapter 7), and
- other nonlegislative rules (bulletins, manuals, staff instructions, press releases) are exempt from the notice and comment process, and from publication requirements, but some may be subject to public inspection and copying requirements if they affect members of the public. §552(a)(2).

Now the hard question: how does one determine whether one is looking at a legislative rule or a nonlegislative rule?

The courts have struggled mightily with the distinction and a number of theories have been advanced. Starting from our preliminary definition of legislative rule above, some courts have said that if the agency's issuance has "the force of law" it is a legislative rule rather than a nonlegislative rule and, accordingly, §553 notice and comment are required. Initially, that is an attractive notion, but as we will discover in our discussion of the *Chevron* doctrine in Chapter 6C, "force of law" is a term beset with its own definitional problems.

Some courts have looked carefully at the language of the issuance and the conduct of the agency with respect to it to see if the agency purported or intended it to encapsulate a final and an authoritative policy choice — a conclusion that would lead to its characterization as a legislative rule. The court might examine the title of the instrument or the prose surrounding it to look for such signs as peremptory language of command (words like "shall" imply that the instrument was intended to have regulatory force), or by the absence of any willingness to consider variations (which implies that the agency has settled on a final policy regarding the matter). If such a court believes the issuance reflects a finally decided policy choice, compliance with which was expected, the court will likely regard the rule as legislative rule. It will be invalid if not promulgated through §553 notice and comment.

While this is not an easy test to apply — or to predict — it does have a certain functional justification. That is, it is precisely when the agency is making a definitive and final policy choice that the values of §553 notice and comment are most useful. Of course, the theory can facilitate evasion of the §553 process by allowing agencies so disposed to include in their rule elaborate verbal disclaimers of finality and bindingness.

A third approach has been suggested by a thoughtful scholar who suggests that one should focus on the *process* the agency followed in expressing its policy: if the agency used §553 notice and comment procedures, the resulting rule is a legislative rule; if not, it is nonlegislative rule. Funk, *When Is A "Rule" A "Regulation"? Marking A Clear Line Between Nonlegislative and Legislative Rules*, 54 ADMIN. L. REV. 659 (2002). This view has the benefits of clarity and simplicity and these are rare and treasured values in administrative law. But the cost of collecting these benefits may be significant if a rule classified as nonlegislative under this test — and thus lacking *legal* force — nevertheless has *practical* impact on the parties.

For example, suppose a federal health agency is authorized by statute to ensure "good restaurant sanitation practices" in private restaurants operating in federal facilities. The agency issues a bulletin that in the future it will regard a restaurant as in violation of this provision of the statute if the restaurant does not have a comprehensive contract with an accredited pest exterminator. Under the theory being examined, this bulletin — not having gone through the notice and comment process — will not be a legislative rule, will not have the force of law. That is, to enforce it, the agency will have to prove not just that the restaurant has no exterminator contract but that the restaurant does not meet the statutory standard of having "good sanitation practices." So far so good: the rule was not promulgated through notice and comment and should not have legal force.

But the bulletin — even with no legal effect — may have substantial practical effect. Even if the restaurant owner believed the restaurant fully met the statutory standard, it would surely be cheaper for the restaurant to comply with the bulletin (by contracting with a pest exterminator) than to face the economic and public relations consequences of defending a public health enforcement action. When a nonlegislative rule has this kind of practical impact, shouldn't those affected have the opportunity to comment on it before it is adopted? And are you comfortable with allowing the agency itself to decide — in choosing a label for its rule — when §553 procedures will and will not be required?

Still another view is that one should look at how the agency *uses* the rule. If the agency calls the rule nonlegislative but seeks to enforce it merely by citing it, the agency is seeking to give the rule the same kind of legal effect as a legislative rule would have. A court might be persuaded by this conduct to classify the rule as a legislative rule and strike it down if §553 notice and comment procedures were not followed.

Finally, there is a group of cases holding that if the rule itself contains a substantive standard it is a legislative rule; if the instrument is merely clarifying a substantive standard in its authorizing statute the rule is interpretive. That theory requires some very difficult distinctions. Consider Figure 2.4.

In Case 1, it could be said that the standard is in the rule itself and the rule must thereby be considered legislative. In Case 2, by contrast, the standard is in the statute and the rule merely interprets the statute, leading to a conclusion that the rule is only interpretive. One can draw such a picture, but it is not really very convincing. What, after all, is the "standard"? Why couldn't the standard in Case 1 be "citizen protection" and the rule merely an interpretation about what that protection requires in this setting? Perhaps all that can be said about this theory is that when the rule seems to particularize a very broad statute (as in Case 1) there is a stronger sense that a basic policy choice is being made, leaning the court toward a view that §553 notice and comment procedures would be useful; the classification of the instrument as a legislative rule will accomplish this goal.

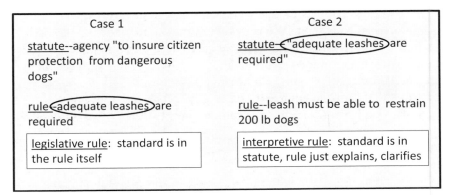

Figure 2.4 **Distinguishing Legislative from Interpretive Rules**

How do we make sense of this variety of ways of distinguishing legislative and nonlegislative rules? Here are a couple of clues. First, take a deep breath and remember that the courts are dealing here with a tension between important values, and law developed in that setting will seldom be easy to state or apply; expect some judicial opacity and some difficulty in predicting judicial outcomes.

Second, see if you can identify the functional values in conflict here. On the one hand we don't want to lose the considerable benefits of nonlegislative rules—including advising the public (and agency staff) of agency enforcement preferences—and agencies might use them less if courts too often required full §553 notice and comment. On the other hand, the core APA idea that parties should be allowed to participate in the formulation of important policies that affect them could be threatened if agencies too often used nonlegislative rules to avoid the notice and comment process.

If you are representing a private client, you need to look concretely and in detail at the problem being considered and attempt to determine precisely where and how both values might be maximized or how prejudice to those values might be minimized. In law study we tend to make you think inside the judicial review box (what would a judge say?). But you shouldn't be shy about thinking outside that box. For example, discussion and negotiation with agency staff might be useful (never over-relying on agency advice, of course, because of the usually true maxim that "estoppel does not run against the king"). Contacts with legislators might, in appropriate cases, be a useful tactic. If you are representing an agency and need to exert a regulatory force but circumstances don't permit full §553 notice and comment, consider some variations on the APA's options discussed above (good cause exemption, interim final rules, etc.), for issuing legislative rules without public comment.

There have been executive branch attempts to correct potential misuse of nonlegislative rules. See, e.g., E.O. 13,422, (Jan. 23, 2007) which provided for presidential review of some agency nonlegislative rules or "guidance documents" as they are called. (This executive order was revoked by E.O. 13,497 [Jan. 30, 2009]). And there have been proposals to address these problems by requiring some opportunity for public comment before nonlegislative rules can be issued. Mantel, *Procedural Safeguards for Agency Guidance*, 61 ADMIN. L. REV. 343 (2009).

e. Starting the Process — The Rulemaking Petition under APA § 553(e)

How is the rulemaking process started? There are as many ways of beginning the rulemaking process as there are for beginning a legislative proposal. The process may be wholly internal to the agency as when staff studies or inspector reports identify a problem that can be addressed by a general rule. It may be initiated by pressure from the legislature — formally by a statutory command or informally through a congressional expression of dissatisfaction with existing agency policy or conduct. Or it could be pressure from the executive branch in the form of a "prompt letter" from the Office of Management and Budget (OMB), from informal discussions with executive branch officials, or as part of the president's regulatory planning process itself. It could be a response to recommendations from other government agencies, advisory committees, or states. The new policy suggestion may arise in communications with regulatory beneficiary groups. Sometimes, rulemaking may be required as part of a judicial settlement. See Rossi, *Bargaining in the Shadow of Administrative Procedure*, 51 DUKE L. J. 1015 (2001).

Rulemaking can also be a response to a citizen petition for rulemaking. Section 553(e) entitles a citizen to petition the agency to issue, amend or repeal a rule. Section 555(e) requires prompt explanation if the petition is denied. In addition, there may be provisions in an agency's rules, in other statutes, or in OMB requirements that affect the manner or timing of an agency's response to petitions, such as a requirement that the agency ask for public comment before denying petitions or a requirement that explanations for denials be published.

What can an agency do in response to such a petition? Since filing a petition is a matter of right, Massachusetts v. EPA, 549 U.S. 797 (2007), the agency is not free to ignore it. That leaves three other possibilities. The agency can (1) deny the petition, (2) grant it and begin a rulemaking proceeding and (3) delay ruling on it, perhaps setting it aside for further study.

If the agency denies a petition for rulemaking, there has been "final agency action" within the meaning of §704 of the APA and the decision is judicially reviewable. We will return to this in Chapters 5 and 6, but appreciate that the courts

are likely to be very deferential to agencies where the denial reflects agency judgment about where and when the agency will expend its scarce rulemaking resources. If there are congressional requirements for rulemaking, of course, the scope
of review of a denial may be more intense, as in *Massachusetts. v. EPA*, supra.

The hardest question for the courts is presented when the agency adopts
the third option — it does not grant or deny the petition, but simply delays
any action on it. Section 555(b) of the APA requires response in a reasonable
time and §706(1) provides for judicial relief for unreasonable delay. But there
are serious practical problems with enforcing such requirements. A classic example is International Union v. Chao, 361 F.3d 249 (3rd. Cir. 2004) where the
union filed a petition for rulemaking with OSHA, asking for a rule to protect
workers from certain kinds of machining fluids. Ten year later, no official response to the petition having come from the agency, the union filed a suit
claiming unreasonable delay. The agency responded by a letter officially denying the petition, explaining that in its view the fluids were not especially dangerous and that in any event the agency had limited resources that were being
used to deal with what it considered more serious risks. The court accepted
OSHA's argument, not wanting either to interfere with the agency's technical
decision on the merits or its judgments about priorities and resource allocations. The court said holding for the union "would have us intrude into the quin-
tessential discretion of the Secretary of Labor to allocate OSHA's resources and
set its priorities. . . . This is a step we are not prepared to take." The court could
only throw the union one bone, lecturing the agency, "we trust that we will
not again see delays such as were seen here." 361 F.3d at 256. There is an occasional victory for a plaintiff in an unreasonable delay case, but it is rare.
Luneburg, *Petitioning Federal Agencies for Rulemaking*, 1988 Wisc. L. Rev. 1
(1988).

f. Publication of the Proposed Rule; What Notice Is Required

When we first consider the idea of a proposed rule, we tend to think of this
as the beginning of the rulemaking process. But as we have seen in our case study,
most proposed rules are issued only after a long process of research, study, legal
and political analysis, including discussions with stakeholder groups, executive
branch officials and legislators. When those discussions and clearances are concluded, the proposed rule is ready for public comment. Public comment has
many purposes, including assuring legitimacy, rationality and public acceptance.
Further it may inform the agency about potential enforcement problems. Comment on proposed rules is, of course, only one part of the full public participation process. For major rules, the process may include investigations, conferences,

consultation, advisory committees, oral and written communication to agencies, and hearings of varying levels of formality. When the APA was written, the drafters set simple notice and comment as the minimum, leaving the parties, the agencies and the legislature to elaborate the process where that was felt useful.

Legally, the proposal must be published in the Federal Register, although today most people use the Internet to learn of and comment on proposed rules. The requirements of §553 are straightforward:

> (b) General notice of proposed rulemaking shall be published in the Federal Register ... The notice shall include—
> (1) a statement of the time, place, and nature of public rulemaking proceedings;
> (2) reference to the legal authority under which the rule is proposed; and
> (3) either the terms or substance of the proposed rule or a description of the subjects and issues involved.

Many agencies today go beyond Federal Register and Internet publication and provide information about proposed rules in press releases, trade publications, loose leaf services, trade association publications, etc.

As to what must be contained in the notice, the text of §553 above states the bare minimum. Most agencies today include a final draft of the proposed rule, as well as statements indicating compliance with the various assessments required by statutes and executive orders. The extent to which the notice of proposed rulemaking should include or identify agency studies and reports considered in formulating the proposal depends on the function of the notice and comment process. The drafters of the APA probably believed the public comment process was intended to inform the *agency* about how the rule would impact regulated parties. Today, largely by reason of the judicial pressure we will examine in Chapter 6, the notice requirements seem more to function as a way of informing (a) the *public* about the factual bases of the agency's views in order that those bases can be understood and, if need be, challenged, and (b) the reviewing *courts* which must rule on those challenges. Here is a more contemporary judicial attitude.

> In order to allow for useful criticism, it is especially important for the agency to identify and make available technical studies and data that it has employed in reaching the decisions to propose particular rules. To allow an agency to play hunt the peanut with technical information, hiding or disguising the information that it employs, is to condone a practice in which the agency treats what should be a genuine interchange as mere bureaucratic sport. An agency commits serious pro-

cedural error when it fails to reveal portions of the technical basis for a proposed rule in time to allow for meaningful commentary. Conn. Light & Power Co. v. NRC, 673 F.2d 525, 530–31 (D.C. Cir. 1982).

With this shift in the purpose of the comment process, the simple rulemaking model described in §553 of the APA no longer mirrors current practice.

Perhaps the quickest way for you to get a sense of the current practice is to take a break from your reading, turn on your computer, and take a look at www.regulations.gov. Put in a search word (e.g., "smog"), then narrow the search by picking an agency, then narrow further by picking "proposed rules." Now take a look at some of the proposals and some of the public comment on them. (Incidentally, you are free to comment yourself on those rules—easy to do, just type in your comment or attach a previously written document.)

Pick a proposed rule of interest to you and examine the text of the notice. At first glance, you will probably see a myriad of technical details, mysterious acronyms, a long development history behind every proposal (which may include legislative action and judicial interventions) and the elaborate documentation the agency will almost always include or reference in its notice, in response to judicial attitudes such as that noted above. This material contains the scientific, economic and other studies on which the agency relied in deciding on the proposed rule. Don't be intimidated by the elaborate profusion of this arcane material. In practice, experienced players in this field (soon could be you!) will usually have been involved in the development of the proposed rule and will be familiar with these details long before the notice of proposed rulemaking is published.

What kind of comment is possible? Section 553(c) entitles commenters to submit comments in writing; oral presentations may be available at the option of the agency. As will be seen below, some agency statutes, agency rules and agency practices may provide more opportunities for oral presentation. Much comment today, of course, arrives in electronic form. For a summary of the prospects and problems of electronic rulemaking see Coglianese, *E-Rulemaking: Information Technology and the Regulatory Process,* 56 ADMIN. L. REV. 353 (2004).

Who can comment on proposed agency rules? Section 553 says "interested persons" can comment which may suggest some limits, but the underlying theory of notice and comment rulemaking requires that the phrase be very broadly interpreted—essentially, anyone can comment.

Who does comment on proposed agency rules? While the idea of public comment has a populist ring to it, the opportunities for lone individuals alone to have major impact—the Ralph Nader model—are rare. If you spent a little time on www.regulations.gov, you will quickly see that dealing effectively with contemporary rulemaking requires financial resources, technical expertise and the ability to mobilize others. As a result, most comment received today comes from organized interest groups. While the system does not technically discriminate against the individual commenter, the need for resources does some inevitable filtering of potential commentators. But as was true in our case study above, agencies will hear from a diverse body of such groups. And we will see in Chapter 6 that — unlike legislation — the final legality of a rule will turn more on the quality of the agency's reasoning and the soundness of the rule's factual support than on the number of commenters, their political influence, or the resources which they may command.

What do members of the public comment about? Comments address such matters as the cost of compliance, the time for compliance, the quality of information on which the proposed rule is based, the proposal's clarity, and the agency's authority to issue the rule.

The published notice is inadequate if it does not give fair notice of the rule as finally promulgated. So the agency cannot propose rule *A* and, after the comment period, promulgate rule *B*. But the matter is more complicated than it seems. Everyone understands that the final rule cannot be limited to the exact form of the rule proposed, else the public comment process is pointless. Similarly, all understand that if every difference between the proposal and the final rule requires reopening the comment period, the process could be endless.

At the practical level, courts have sought to assure that the final rule is close enough to the rule as proposed as to make the opportunity to comment meaningful. The blackletter doctrine for this judicial accommodation is called the "logical outgrowth" rule: if the final rule can be characterized as a "logical outgrowth" of the rule as proposed, notice was adequate. Chocolate Manufacturers Ass'n v Block, 755 F.2d 1089 (4th Cir. 1985). But like most blackletter rules, this one is not of much practical help to the lawyer shaping an argument. The final rule will in some sense always be a "logical outgrowth" of the proposed rule — final rules do not, after all, come from outer space. A more usable statement is that the final rule should have been *foreseeable* from examining the rule proposed. That is, what matters is not the logical connection of the proposed and final rule, but whether the proposed rule put all parties on notice about the issues that were "on the table" as the agency worked its way toward a final decision. As the D.C. Circuit put it, "Notice was inadequate when the interested parties could not reasonably have anticipated the final rulemaking from the draft." National Mining Assoc v. MSHA, 116 F.3d 520, 531 (D.C. Cir. 1997). What the agency must avoid is what the D.C. Circuit colorfully called a "surprise switcheroo" in the final rule. Envt'l Integrity Project v. EPA, 425 F.3d 992, 997 (D.C. Cir. 2005).

Some courts have found adequate notice when an issue that appeared in the final rule was drawn from public comments on the proposed rule. United Steelworkers v. Schuykill Metal, 828 F.2d 314 (5th Cir. 1987). Sometimes agency action itself can serve notice as to what issues are or are not "on the table." In *Chocolate Mfrs.*, supra, the court thought the agency's long standing practice — sharply changed by the final rule — had misled the parties. One can doubt whether an industry as large as those involved here would have been wholly innocent of agency plans, but the court was convinced. Lawyers should never let their clients be surprised by agency action when information is relatively easy to get.

The agency is, of course, always free to begin a second cycle of notice if comments received on the first proposal show the need for substantial modification. And if there are clear alternative solutions to the problem, the agency might publish them with its proposed rule, inviting comment on them. No surprise there. For more discussion of useful agency strategies, see Lubbers, A GUIDE TO AGENCY RULEMAKING, Chap. 3 (4th ed. 2006).

g. Agency Consideration of Public Comment — Drafting the Final Rule

(1) The Puzzle of the Administrative "Record"

Section 553 tells us that after the comment period it is the agency's job to "consider" all public comment and decide on the shape of the final rule. The great puzzle has been to decide what it means to "consider" this mass of material. Recall the difference between the judicial and the legislative models. In a judicial proceeding the material received in the hearing (transcript of testimony, documents, etc.) would be called the "record" and the court would be bound by what is in that record. That is, a court cannot consider matters not in the record and cannot "find" facts unless there is competent evidence of those facts in the record.

On the other hand, legislative hearings may produce an enormous volume of material (testimony, documents, reports, etc.) but it is not a "record" in the judicial sense — it does not bind the legislature in its final decision. The legislature is free to consider anything else it chooses and it can pass a law even though all the views expressed in its hearings were opposed.

Which model do we follow in considering an administrative rulemaking proceeding? As Figure 2.5 illustrates, the agency in rulemaking seems more like a legislative body and the notion of the record is quite different from the judicial record. As it "considers" comments on the proposed rule, to what extent is the agency restricted to the material the process has generated? The idea that there is a rulemaking "record" first emerged in the APA's legislative history, which makes it clear that "the agency must keep a record of and analyze and consider all relevant matter presented prior to the issuance of rules." H.R. REP. No 1980, 79th Cong., 2d Sess. 259 (1946).

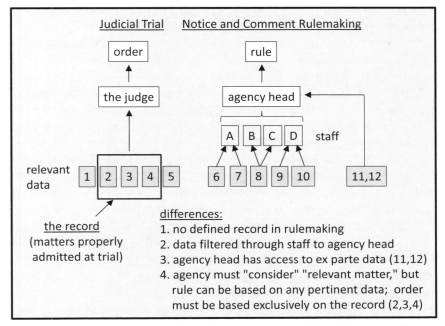

Figure 2.5   Comparing Judicial and Agency Rulemaking Records

Modern courts have struggled with defining the set of materials the agency must consider and the reviewing courts must examine in assessing the legality of a rule. In 1971, the Supreme Court was considering an informal agency adjudication (since it was informal there was no "record" in the conventional sense); the Court remanded to the district court to examine the agency's action in light of "the full administrative record that was before the secretary at the time he made his decision." Citizens to Preserve Overton Park v. Volpe, 401 U.S. 402, 420 (1971). Building on that perhaps unwise choice of words—no one really knew what a "full administrative record" was—lower courts have slowly developed a sense that there exists in the words of one influential court, "a body of material—documents, comments, transcripts, and statements" against which "it is the obligation of [the] court to test the actions of the agency for arbitrariness...." Home Box Office Inc. v. FCC, 567 F.2d 9 (D.C. Cir. 1977). Perhaps from force of habit, judges tended to label that "body of material" a rulemaking "record" though more careful labeling sometimes calls it a rulemaking "docket" or a rulemaking "file."

However named, while it is not an exclusive record in the judicial sense, the statute requires that the material must be considered. We will see in Chapter 6 that reviewing courts have increasingly required evidence of serious consideration.

Several important questions have arisen about rulemaking records, two of them of interest to us here. First, what must be included in the record? There is no fully agreed answer, since the ideas of a definitive record and an essentially legislative process do not fit comfortably together. And there are many aspects of agency expertise, experience and insight that—however vital they may be in the final decision about a rule—simply cannot be encapsulated in identifiable documents or reports. Perhaps the best general guide is the recommendation of the Administrative Conference of the United States which suggested that the rulemaking record (which it helpfully called a rulemaking "file") include all rulemaking notices, copies of all written factual material "substantially relied upon or seriously considered" by the agency, and all written comments submitted. ACUS Recommendation 93–4, 58 Fed. Reg. 4670 (1994).

Second, when a rule is challenged and is reviewed in a judicial proceeding, is the agency confined in its defense to material developed during the notice and comment process? May new studies and arguments be used on judicial review—material that was not in the agency's contemplation when it decided on the rule? Various answers have been given by the courts, and Congress has provided a number of special statutes bearing on the question. The safest practice for a rulemaking agency is to compile a record that is full enough to support any arguments that may be needed on review since courts have clearly signaled that they do not favor "post hoc rationalizations"—i.e., factual information and arguments appearing only after a rule has been challenged. Courts tend to be suspicious of such material because of doubts about its objectivity or because of a sense that material of this importance should have been available to the public for comment and adversarial testing. Cf. Citizens to Preserve Overton Park v. Volpe, 401 U.S. 402, 419 (1971).

When important information is developed after the comment period is over, a court might order reopening the comment period, though the potential for endless reopenings might limit this remedy to cases where the material is especially critical. Chamber of Commerce v. SEC, 443 F.3d 890 (D.C. Cir. 2006).

(2) The Agency as Decisionmaker

When an agency is deciding on its final rule, agency decisionmakers are quite different from judges in a judicial proceeding. Two special differences are relevant here. First, in the U.S. judicial system the judge functions as an individual and makes a personal decision. The agency, on the other hand, produces a group product, drawing on expert staff, analysts and policy-makers. The agency head who signs the final rule will not be as familiar with the details of the matter as a judge will be—much of what the agency head considers will be drawn from summaries and analyses of lower level staff. There is simply no other way for an agency head to handle the number and complexity of matters under his or her purview. This is regarded by most observers as one of the comparative strengths of the administrative process. The rulemaking decision is said to be "institutional" rather than personal and derives from that circumstance much of its technical sureness and policy depth.

Second, it will be clear from the foregoing description that while the judge is presumably neutral regarding the outcome of a case, the agency and its staff are committed to a legislatively declared policy. Don't expect neutrality from the SEC on questions of fraud in investment practices, disinterest from the EPA on questions of clean water, or indifference from the FTC on questions of misleading advertising. One hopes for objectivity in making first level factual determinations (who did what, when, etc.). But as the matter moves up toward ultimate decision, it will increasingly depend on inferences, implications, guesses about future consequences, choices among competing policies and, ultimately, political preferences. This has been frustrating to the courtroom-oriented lawyers, but seems an inevitable consequence of using administrative bodies to carry out these tasks. We will return to this tension in Chapter 6. For now, just understand that agency rulemakers—unlike many judges—will tend to have an attitude.

(3) Ex Parte Communications

During the agency's consideration of public comment and in the course of making its decision about the final rule, how should we treat ex parte communications to the agency decisionmakers? (By ex parte communications we mean communications addressed to the decisionmaker outside the presence of the other parties.) Again, the judicial and legislative models are suggestive but not dispositive. Ex parte communications are strictly forbidden in judicial proceedings but they are every day, bread and butter components of the legislative process. How should they be treated in administrative rulemaking?

Where do ex parte communications come from? They may come from any private person (such as those impacted by the proposed rule). In addition, such comments might come from public sources such as the executive branch, from legislators, from people within the agency, or from other agencies. Considering these diverse sources—and the various motives that may have produced them—are these communications beneficial or, on balance, harmful?

The agency may find them quite useful. As Judge Patricia Wald has stated,

> Informal [ex parte] contacts may enable the agency to win needed
> support for its program, reduce future enforcement requirements by
> helping those regulated to anticipate and shape their plans for the fu-
> ture, and spur the provision of information which the agency needs.
> Sierra Club v. Costle, 657 F.2d 298, 401 (D.C. Cir. 1981).

But there are obvious dangers as well. If you believe strongly that the policy-for-
mulation process should be transparent, that the public should know and be able
to comment on all transmissions to the agency, and that on judicial review a court
trying to assess the rationality of the rule should also know about important substantive communications to the agency—if these considerations reflect your
views, you will have concerns about ex parte communications in rulemaking.

What are the legal standards? As we will see in Chapter 3, the APA contains important restrictions on ex parte communications, but those provisions appear in
sections of the act dealing with formal proceedings (§§554, 556–57). For informal, notice and comment rulemaking, there is simply nothing in the APA which
forbids ex parte communications. However, the sense of impropriety that law
trained people have about ex parte communications has resulted in a few limits.
There have been occasional due process limits applied to ex parte communications
in informal proceedings where those proceedings involved "conflicting private
claims to a valuable privilege." Sangamon Valley v. U.S., 269 F.2d 221 (D.C. Cir.
1959), and a narrow holding of that sort still seems alive in the D.C. Circuit. ACT
v . FCC, 564 F.2d. 458 (D.C. Cir 1977). For a discussion, see Beermann, *Repro-
cessing Vermont Yankee*, 75 Geo. Wash. L. Rev. 856 (2007) and the following responses by Pierce (Id. at 902). Beyond that, few courts have been willing to go,
and the Court's lecture on lower court humility in Vermont Yankee Nuclear Power
Corp. v. NRDC, 435 U.S. 519 (1978) suggests that there will be little judicial pressure to restrict ex parte communications in informal rulemaking in the future.

But the risks and appearances of uncontrolled ex parte communications have
not been lost on either the legislative or the executive branches. Today, some
statutes, some executive orders, and most agency procedural rules will contain
provisions limiting such communications or requiring their full disclosure. See
Lubbers, A Guide to Federal Agency Rulemaking 341–55 (4th ed. 2006).
The lawyer tempted to contact agency rulemaking officials outside of public
proceedings should not, therefore, look merely to the APA for guidance.

(4) The "Concise, General Statement"

When final rules have been decided upon, §553 requires that the agency prepare and publish a "concise general statement of their basis and purpose." The

legislative history of the APA makes clear that these adjectives were to be taken literally—that the statement accompanying the final rule was to be both concise and general. Today, however, under pressure from reviewing courts setting aside rules the courts considered inadequately explained, agencies in preemptive self defense have converted this concise statement into a lengthy and detailed document—called a preamble—reviewing the evidence, the scientific foundation of the rule, the alternatives considered, and the weight given to public comments.

There has been much criticism of this development since it enormously complicates and delays the rulemaking process which the framers of the APA intended to be short and simple. It is one of the chief sources of the "ossification" we mentioned earlier. But neither Congress (which in its hybrid rulemaking procedures has added "ossifications" of its own) nor the Supreme Court has curbed the courts of appeal in this movement. We will examine these issues more fully in the Chapter 6 on judicial review.

Finally, as the rule is published, there may be other clearance and reporting obligations under executive orders or statutes. For example, the 1996 Congressional Review Act, 5 U.S.C. §§801–08 requires that major rules be laid before Congress for 60 days during which time Congress can pass a joint resolution rejecting the rule. Joint resolutions must be signed by the president or passed over his veto. While an earlier attempt at permitting a legislative veto of agency rules was rejected by the Supreme Court, INS v. Chadha, 462 U.S. 919 (1983), the Congressional Review Act was carefully drafted to comply with the bicameralism and presentment requirements of the constitution. It has not been widely used.

3. Beyond the APA

As we have noted, required APA procedures are minimums. Additional procedural requirements can come from other places. Lawyers working in the field need to be familiar with them all. Some examples follow.

a. Congress

Congress has enacted a number of general statutes that seek to further specific goals or to protect certain interests in the field of regulatory action. Just to mention a few, the Regulatory Flexibility Act (5 U.S.C. §601) requires rulemaking agencies to consider the impacts of significant rules on small business enterprises. The Paperwork Reduction Act (44 U.S.C. §3501) seeks in part to minimize the paperwork burden of regulatory activities. The Unfunded Mandates Act (2 U.S.C. Chs. 17A, 25) seeks to protect subnational governments (including Indian tribes) from onerous burdens without providing adequate resources to carry them out. More broadly, the National Environmental Policy Act (42 U.S.C. §4321) requires assessment of the environmental impact of significant agency rules. All of these acts require agency assessment of a proposed rule's impact—a study and reporting process that can be costly and time consuming, surely beyond anything contemplated by the drafters of the APA rulemaking provisions.

A number of agencies' own statutes require more formality in rulemaking than §553 requires—the category of so-called "hybrid" rulemaking—neither informal nor formal but somewhere in between. As we have seen, for example, the APA does not require any opportunity for oral presentations. But legislative type hearings are mandated by such statutes as the Occupational Safety and Health Act (OSHA), 29 U.S.C. §655, the Consumer Product Safety Act, 15 U.S.C.§§2056, 2058, and the Clean Water Act, 42 U.S.C. §7606(d). Even more elaborate procedures, including cross-examintion are contained in statutes such as the Magnuson Moss Warranty—FTC Improvement Act, 15 U.S.C. §57a, and the Securities Act Amendments, 15 U.S.C. §78f(e).

In 1990, Congress added to the APA sections 561–70 which authorize agencies to accomplish some aspects of the rulemaking process by negotiation. Negotiated rulemaking (reg-neg as it unfortunately has come to be called) involves convening a group of major stakeholders—those parties principally affected by the contemplated rule—and seeing if a consensus about the new rule can be developed. A draft thus worked out is published as a proposed rule and the usual public comment process ensues. Negotiated rulemaking is thought by its supporters to produce technically better rules, rules which more clearly identify the diverse concerns of those affected by the rule, and rules that will lead to simpler enforcement and less judicial review. The concept has, however, generated controversy. Critics worry that some affected interests will not be invited to the party; others are concerned that the system transfers too much power to the private sector. The debate is reviewed in Lubbers, A GUIDE TO FEDERAL RULEMAKING 214–17 (4th ed. 2006).

b. Executive Controls over Rulemaking

As touched upon in Chapter 1, recent presidents have been active in seeking controls on agency rulemaking. Starting with President Reagan in the 1980s, presidents have used the executive order and the power of the president as "manager" of executive branch agencies to impose a complex and far reaching set of additional requirements on rulemaking agencies. The current foundational document (at this writing) is E.O. 12,866. The Order is based on the original Reagan Executive Order (E.O. 12,291) as modified by Presidents Clinton, George

H.W. Bush and George W. Bush. Among its stated principles, the order requires executive branch agencies to conduct a cost/benefit analysis of all "economically significant" rules (e.g., those with more than an annual $100 million effect on the economy), to adopt the least intrusive regulatory alternative available, to regulate only in clear cases of private market failure, to emphasize incentive strategies (such as user fees) as alternatives to command and control regulation, to base its decisions on the best obtainable scientific data, to regulate by specifying general objectives not particular behavior, to utilize state and local governments where possible, and to express its regulations in simple, clear language.

E.O. 12,866 is administered through the Office of Information and Regulatory Affairs (OIRA), a component of the president's Office of Management and Budget (OMB). In addition to the foregoing efforts to improve the quality and political acceptability of agency rules, the Order also seeks to coordinate the vast executive rulemaking enterprise. The Order requires all agencies (including the so-called independent agencies) to prepare a regulatory agenda of all rules under development. These agendas are circulated by OIRA to other agencies for review, and an effort is made to eliminate conflict, duplication or rules that are not consistent with the president's regulatory objectives. Executive agencies are further required to periodically review all existing rules to assure they are still needed. See Congressional Research Service (Copeland), *Federal Rulemaking: The Role of the Office of Information and Regulatory Affairs*, June 9, 2009.

This vast expansion of presidential control over the agency rulemaking process has been controversial. As a matter of policy, there are many who doubt the propriety of the system's underlying emphasis on cost/benefit analysis. A good picture of the complexity of this analysis can be seen in OMB Circular A-4, a statement of good practices originating in the Clinton administration. Its current form can be seen at http://www.whitehouse.gov/omb/circulars/a004/a-4.pdf. Critics have said that having to show that benefits exceed costs in a setting where benefits cannot convincingly be quantified (human health, safety, human life, etc.) inevitably loads the dice against protecting those values. Moreover, the use of political officials (the president, OMB, OIRA) to review the scientific conclusions of the agencies is thought by some to undercut the value of agency expertise and to produce less than objective science. Finally, some have expressed separation of powers concerns since under this system executive branch officials interfere with or dramatically affect the outcome of legislatively delegated agency powers. Supporters of presidential control of agency rulemaking cite the need for coordination—which only the president can accomplish—and accountability—which supporters believe can best be provided by an elected president.

The tension here is palpable and as usual in the world of administrative law, the language of the constitution does not signal a clear answer. The result is a series of uneasy settlements beset by increasing procedural elaboration and shifting as new presidents arrive at the White House. At this writing (summer 2009), President Obama has requested and received comment on proposals to revise the executive role in agency rulemaking, revisions which seek to make the process more effective in working with massive cross-cutting regulatory problems, such as global warming, as well as responding to concerns about ossification. You can expect some changes in the process but not a dramatic reduction in executive control. Some good reviews of the debate are Bressman and Vandenbergh, *Inside the Administrative State: A Critical Look at the Practice of Presidential Control*, 105 MICH. L. REV. 47 (2006); Heidi Kitrosser, *The Accountable Executive*, 93 MINN. L. REV. 1741 (2009).

c. The Agencies

Agencies' own regulations provide much more detail than the barebones provisions of §553. And agencies are constantly fine-tuning the rulemaking process. Recent action by some Obama administration agencies, e.g., is exploring fuller use of technology, including using blogs and other social media to generate public input before proposed rules are drafted. Among the claimed advantages: people commenting on issues could also comment on other comments, enriching the dialog. See: http://www.federaltimes.com/index.php?S =4137205.

d. The Courts

This subject is so broadly important we have treated it at some length in Chapters 5 and 6 which discuss judicial review generally. Here, we mention only the role of courts in imposing procedural requirements on the rulemaking process. Courts cannot use constitutional provisions to police rulemaking procedure as the constitution imposes virtually no limits on legislative type procedures. Bi-Metallic Invest. Co. v. State Board, 239 U.S. 441 (1915). For that reason, the courts will have a limited role here. In the celebrated decision in Vermont Yankee v. NRDC, 435 U.S. 519 (1978) the Court sharply criticized the courts of appeal for seeming to add procedural requirements beyond those laid down by Congress.

But the courts are not wholly without the ability to have some impact on rulemaking procedure. In the *Vermont Yankee* opinion itself, the Court left room for courts to add some procedures in rulemaking cases involving "adjudicatory questions," an invitation that has not been wholly ignored by the courts of appeal. United Airlines v. CAB, 766 F.2d 1107 (7th Cir. 1985). More broadly, we will see in Chapter 6 that reviewing courts remain authorized to review the substance of agency decisions for arbitrariness. That broad power leaves the courts with some indirect control over agency procedure. *Vermont Yankee* only limits reviewing courts from specifically requiring particular procedures; it does not prevent them from reversing agency decisions that might have passed muster had better procedures been followed. Agencies will probably be able to connect these dots and adjust their procedures in ways intimated by the courts.

Checkpoints

- The fundamental distinction between rulemaking and adjudication — there is no more important distinction in administrative law.

- By making it possible for those affected by agency rules to be meaningful participants in the shaping of those rules, rulemaking procedures advance both sound decisionmaking and accountable government.

- Agencies with power both to make rules and to adjudicate cases usually can decide which process to use in adopting new policies; seldom is rulemaking required.

- Section 553 of the APA contains the basic rulemaking process. Exempted from all of §553 are rules concerning certain military and foreign affairs functions and certain internal management activities. Exempted from the notice and comment requirements of §553 (but remaining subject to its publication requirements) are interpretive rules, policy statements and rules of procedure, along with matters where the agency for good cause believes notice and comment would not serve the public interest.

- There are three types of rulemaking procedure: formal, informal and hybrid; most rulemaking is informal under §553 of the APA, but Congress is increasingly adding procedures to produce something between formal and informal rulemaking, called hybrid rulemaking.

- Informal rulemaking can be initiated by the agency itself, by outside public bodies and by petitions from citizens. Citizens petition as of right and their petitions cannot be ignored by agencies. If the petitions are denied, the denial must be explained and the explanation is subject to judicial review.

- Although not required by the strict language of §553, publication of the notice of proposed rulemaking today requires that agencies notify the public of studies, reports, research and other material used by the agency in its formulation of the proposal in order that public comment can be informed.

- As decisionmakers, agency officials deciding on a final rule are regarded more as legislators than as judges and can (so far as the APA is concerned) freely engage in ex parte communications.

- Other sources of rulemaking procedures include executive branch requirements, legislation beyond the APA targeting special areas, and an agency's own procedural rules.

Chapter 3

Adjudication

A. The Nature of Adjudication

As we come to adjudication — the second great model on which the APA is built — we come to a technique that is at once more familiar and in some ways more complex than the rulemaking model we have looked at. Adjudication is more familiar to us as it more closely resembles what courts do. Indeed, many of its details will be "old hat" to law students who have seen the technical apparatus of adjudication in other law school courses — not to mention the endless stream of courtroom trials which TV and movies provide us.

But though some of its details may be familiar, adjudication is quite a complex set of practices. From the functional point of view taken in these discussions, it is worth considering some of its unique features. The classic American discussion of adjudication is Fuller, *The Forms and Limits of Adjudication*, 92 HARV. L. REV. 353 (1978). Professor Fuller teaches that what is distinctive about adjudication is the manner of participation the parties are guaranteed. He contrasts adjudication with other forms of social ordering such as elections (where we participate by voting) and contracts (where we participate by negotiating). In adjudication, parties participate by presenting proofs and reasoned argument in an effort to resolve a dispute according to pre-existing principle. From that perspective, an ideal adjudication system would guarantee the parties:

- An agreed set of principles that will function as the substantive criteria for resolution of the dispute. These principles may be specific as in a statute, or may be very general as in common law doctrines. They are agreed in the sense that all parties accept that they are the correct principles and that they will be controlling. Beyond serving as criteria for the ultimate outcome, the principles will shape the discussion, will identify the issues, and will define what is relevant in the way of proof and argument.

- A meaningful opportunity to present proof and argument in support of each side of the dispute. Independent presentation by advocates on either side of the dispute — as distinguished from having the decision-maker assemble facts and arguments — guards against what Fuller calls "the natural human tendency to judge too swiftly in terms of the familiar that which is not yet fully known." Fuller, *The Forms and Limits of Adjudication*, 92 HARV. L. REV. 353, 383 (1978).

- That the deciding official is obligated to listen to and consider the argument and proof presented. The decider in an election (the voter) may sleep through a political speech intended to influence his vote and we'd not be concerned. But the judge in an adjudicative proceeding is not permitted that sort of inattention.

- That the deciding official will resolve the dispute exclusively on the basis of the principles stated and the proof and argument presented by the parties. This gives real meaning to the opportunity to participate, and it minimizes the risk that the decision will be affected by facts outside the record or considerations beyond the agreed principles.

- That the final decision will be accompanied by a statement of reasons. A required statement of reasons disciplines the decisional process itself — judges have been known to say that a particular decision initially seemed correct but "won't write." A statement of reasons has three additional benefits: it exposes the decision's rationale to professional critique, it communicates to the parties that their participation has been meaningful and, in a precedential system, it may provide guidance for future decisions.

You will readily see that this process is not at all like the legislative-type functions we considered in our discussion of rulemaking in the last chapter. In the legislative process, there is:

- No ex ante set of governing principles — legislative outcomes are based on policy preferences of legislators and the people they represent, which may change radically from one session to another.

- No guarantee of an opportunity to present proof and argument. Legislative hearings may be conducted but they are wholly at the discretion of legislators and are intended more to inform legislators than to allow advocates to speak.

- No legal obligation on the part of a legislator to consider or weigh any views of the parties that may be expressed. Legislators can wholly disregard any presentations made and are free to collect and make dispositive use of information from any source they choose with or without notice or any opportunity to respond.
- No need for an explanation of the legislative outcome, beyond what the decider chooses to say and no restriction on what bases can be used to support the conclusion if the decider chooses to say anything.

Of course, administrative adjudication will be somewhat different from adjudication in the judicial setting. Consider three major differences. First, there is the obvious problem of volume. Federal agency adjudication takes place millions of times each year, as compared to the thousands of cases heard by our courts. The pressure from this volume will sometimes require simpler and quicker procedures than are typical in courtrooms.

Second, there are many different types of adjudications, and those differences may call for quite different ways of structuring the proof and argument process. For example, consider the procedural design implications of these different types of adjudications:

- The agency is trying to stop what it regards as unlawful conduct by a party.
- The agency action will result in conferring or denying a benefit to a party.
- The agency action will permit conduct that could not be engaged in without permission.

All these types of adjudications will present different design problems—differences concerning whether the parties are adversarial, whether the disputed issues focus more on policies and future estimates rather than historical facts about individuals, and whether the consequences of the decision affect people and situations far removed from the immediate participants. These sorts of variations will require us to be nuanced in our procedural designs. See Koch, ADMINISTRATIVE LAW AND PRACTICE § 5.10 (2d ed. 1997).

Third, the person making the final decision in agency adjudication is seldom going to be the neutral generalist judge we expect to see presiding in a courtroom. In some manner, our adjudicatory design must guarantee the parties meaningful hearings and objective decisions while at the same time bringing the agency's technical expertise and political mission into the equation.

Despite these differences, administrative and judicial adjudications have similar goals. An obvious first goal is factual accuracy. Adjudicatory procedures that are too hurried, that rely on inference and impression rather than on more reliable foundations, or that reduce or eliminate adversarial testing might not give us the required level of accuracy. Most of the procedures we will discuss below dealing with such matters as evidence, burdens of proof, cross-examintion, internal appeals, and the qualifications of the judge have fact finding accuracy as a principal objective.

But factual accuracy can be expensive and we live in a world of resource constraints — especially in the high volume settings frequently encountered in administrative adjudications. So cost and efficiency must not be forgotten in our design criteria, even where doing so may reduce accuracy. For example, eliminating or reducing cross-examintion in an adjudication will surely lower costs, but might impede the goal of factual accuracy. Similarly, giving parties the opportunity to appear with counsel may add costs, but its absence may reduce accuracy. The design task here is to consider nuance and subtlety in an effort to maximize accuracy at minimum cost. Can cross-examintion be limited to situations where the issues in dispute make cross-examintion especially useful? Can the participation of counsel be limited to narrowing and sharpening the issues? The effort to seek accuracy at low cost will be seen in many of the procedures discussed below.

Accuracy and low cost do not exhaust our list of design criteria. In our culture, the procedure also must be acceptable to those affected. Perceived fairness may seem something beyond technical legal requirements, but it is a principle deeply embedded in our legal culture. Hamlet's complaint about the "insolence of office" is a palpable concern. People expect officials to deal with parties fairly and openly, to give them meaningful opportunities to participate and to provide rational explanations of the action taken. Procedural requirements for keeping official action true to these principles are important. For a thoughtful discussion of some of these criteria, see Cramton, *A Comment on Trial-Type Hearings in Nuclear Power Plant Siting*, 58 VA. L. REV. 585, 592–93 (1972).

All of these issues will be touched in the discussion below. You are encouraged to measure the degree to which the procedures available are meeting these goals.

B. The Sources of Procedural Requirements in Adjudication

When searching for procedural requirements in agency adjudications, where does a lawyer look? As usual, we'll need to examine a number of sources, including the APA, the agency's own statute, other relevant statutes, the agency's regulations and, of course, any minimums required by the due process clause. Figure 3.1 shows one preliminary way to think about some of these parts and their relationships. The chart tracks the four principal sources of procedural requirements.

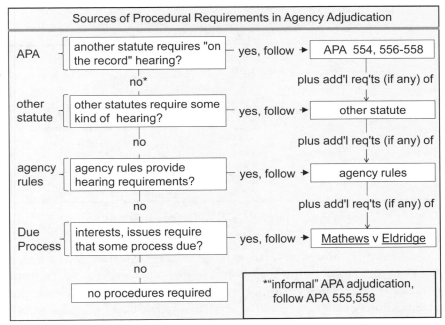

Figure 3.1   The Sources of Procedural Requirements in Adjudication

This chapter will discuss the first three of these sources, focusing principally on the APA. Chapter 4 will treat requirements imposed by the due process clause.

C. The APA's Treatment of Adjudication

Before the formal adjudication procedures of the APA apply to an adjudication, two preliminary tests must be met. First, the proceeding has to come within the APA's definition of adjudication and second, another statute (such as the statute authorizing the agency to adjudicate) must demand the use of formal process. Looking at the first, the APA's definition of adjudication is easy, if a little surprising. After defining adjudication as a process for formulating an order, the APA defines order simply as:

> "The whole or a part of a final disposition ... of an agency in a matter other than rulemaking but including licensing." 5 USC § 551(6).

As Figure 3.2 shows, the definition is residual; it covers every final agency action except rulemaking.

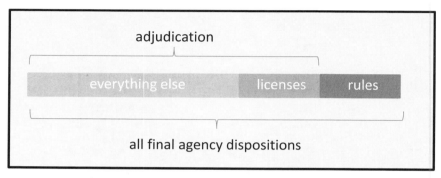

Figure 3.2   The APA Definition of Adjudication

Pretty clearly, this definition is too broad to be taken literally. Many agency functions that cannot be included in the category of rulemaking can hardly be considered adjudication in any normal use of that word. For example, agency investigations, planning, research, legislative activities, advising the public about regulatory matters, etc. are actions that surely cannot be considered adjudication and, just as surely should not be required to follow the trial-like procedures the APA provides for formal adjudications. In Chapter 2 we distinguished rulemaking from adjudication by noting that adjudication usually was an agency decision turning on specific facts about the private individuals involved. That remains a good starting place for identifying an agency adjudication.

Notice that the adjudication definition includes licensing. Licensing is thus a special kind of adjudication and usually involves a citizen asking for permission to engage in a certain kind of conduct. "License" is broadly defined to include "an agency permit, certificate, approval, registration, charter, membership, statutory exemption or other form of permission." 5 U.S.C. § 551(8). The act goes on to define "licensing" to include about anything the drafters could think of that an agency might do with a license, including the "grant, renewal, denial, revocation, suspension, annulment, withdrawal, limitation, amendment, modification, or conditioning of a license." 5 U.S.C. § 551(9).

As we proceed through the sections of the APA dealing with formal adjudication procedure, it will turn out that one kind of licensing—so-called initial licensing—will be treated differently in several particulars from other adjudicative (and other licensing) matters. We will see, e.g., that § 554's separation of functions rules and its ex parte communication prohibitions do not apply to initial licensing. And § 556's requirement of cross-examintion is less severe in cases of initial licensing. Finally, § 557's requirements about who may issue an initial decision in an adjudication is considerably more flexible in the case of initial licensing.

The reasons for these relaxations appear to be several. Unlike a license revocation case, the *parties* in an initial licensing case may not appear as adversaries, lessening the need for the kinds of protection that adversary proceedings require. Beyond that, the *issues* in an initial licensing case may bear more resemblance to rulemaking issues than typical adjudicatory issues. For example, when an applicant seeks an initial license to operate a nuclear reactor, the real question may not be the applicant's technical skill, his financial responsibility, the quality of his equipment, or his history of complying with regulations. These are classic adjudicatory issues—historical facts personal to the applicant for which formal adjudicatory procedures might be appropriate. But if the real question in the licensing proceeding is whether society needs another nuclear reactor, the case may present the kind of general policy analysis and the kind of predictions about the future that mark the typical rulemaking process. By exempting initial licensing from some of the formalities of adjudication, the drafters were attempting to be sure the agency would not be bound too tightly to trial-like procedures in considering these broader issues. See Attorney General's Manual on the Administrative Procedure Act 50-53 (1947).

D. Hearing Requirements of the APA

Let's assume now that we have a clear case of an adjudication and we want to know what procedures the APA requires. The APA formal adjudication requirements, though highly general (and usually fleshed out with detailed agency procedural rules), are quite stringent, are surely above the due process minimums we'll examine in Chapter 4. Rather than describing APA adjudication procedures in general prose, the discussion which follows quotes the relevant text of the APA and adds comments to clarify meaning, mentions important practices that have developed under the provision, and signals important judicial decisions that have interpreted the sections. This immersion in the actual text of the statute will give you a chance to become familiar with the syntax and structure of the act. This framework, in turn, will facilitate your understanding of the details we will discuss. If you seek mastery of administrative law, there is no better beginning point than learning your way around the APA, and no better way of doing that than just confronting its text; paraphrasing may work for casual readers; it doesn't work for masters.

Let us begin by looking in general at the way the APA is structured. We have examined part of the structure in our consideration of rulemaking in Chapter 2. (See Figure 2.3 in that chapter.) Figure 3.3 displays the full chart showing both the rulemaking and adjudication provisions. You will note that there are only four APA procedural tracks: formal and informal rulemaking and formal and informal adjudication. (Hybrid rulemaking comes from other statutes.)

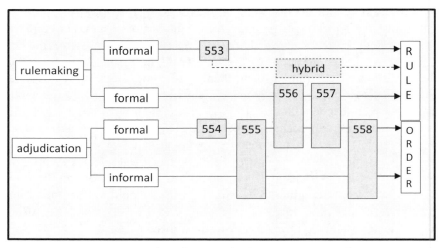

**Figure 3.3   Rulemaking and Adjudicative Procedures
in the Administrative Procedure Act**

For the formal adjudications that will concern us mostly in this chapter, five sections of the APA (§§ 554–558) must be consulted. You might find it helpful to begin by reading these five sections in their complete form in the Appendix. Then return here to look at each separately and consider some commentary on them.

APA § 554

Adjudications

(a) This section applies, according to the provisions thereof, in every case of adjudication required by statute to be determined on the record after opportunity for an agency hearing . . .

Comment: Part of the unusual breadth of the APA's definition of adjudication is cured by § 554(a)'s requirement that the formal adjudicative procedures of the APA apply only to a special class of adjudications — those required by *another* statute to be determined "on the record after opportunity for an agency hearing." Given this phrase, it is probably accurate to say that the APA itself *never* requires formal adjudicative procedure. The requirement must be found in another statute. When such a requirement is found, the APA spells out the sorts of procedure that will be required.

We have discussed the meaning of the phrase "on the record" in Chapter 2's consideration of rulemaking. There we concluded that the phrase essentially refers to the kind of hearing in which the decision following the hearing must find its support in proofs and argument presented in the hearing itself. Stated otherwise, in an "on the record" hearing the record is the exclusive basis for the final decision — both in the sense that the order must be supported by evidence produced in the hearing and in the sense that the decisionmaker is not allowed to consider evidence and argument that was not presented (and tested) in the hearing. In general, "on the record" is similar to the kind of judicial proceeding with which we are all familiar.

If Congress were always careful in drafting agency statutes, there would be no uncertainty about this issue. All Congress has to do — if it wants an agency to follow the formal adjudication procedures spelled out in the APA — is to follow the formula of § 554(a) and say that the determination the agency is being authorized to make must be made "on the record after opportunity for an agency hearing." Unfortunately, Congress is not always careful. Sometimes, it just authorizes an agency adjudication (e.g., a license revocation) with no mention of hearings at all. Sometimes it just requires a "hearing" and one is not sure if Congress intended the hearing to be "on the record" or is rather a public meeting type of hearing, or merely an opportunity for interested persons to submit written comments as in rulemaking.

Where Congress is not clear, the courts are left to figure this out and they have not been of one mind. We saw in our rulemaking discussion that the courts have come to the view that if the proceeding is a rulemaking proceeding, the word "hearing" standing alone probably will *not* trigger the "on the record" language of § 553(c). By a parity of reasoning, some courts have followed the Attorney General's early advice and held that if the proceeding being authorized is an adjudication—especially one involving disputed facts—a statutory reference to a "hearing" probably *was* intended to refer to an "on the record" hearing. Seacoast Anti-Pollution League v. Costle, 572 F.2d 872 (1st Cir. 1978). See also, Attorney General's Manual on the Administrative Procedure Act 43 (1947).

Other courts—perhaps not anxious to impose unnecessary formalities on the agency—have held otherwise, virtually requiring Congress to use the magic words "on the record" before they will insist on use of the full APA formal hearing process. See, e.g., City of West Chicago v. NRDC, 701 F.2d 632 (7th Cir. 1983). And today, under the sway of the famous *Chevron* doctrine (*Chevron* is discussed in Chapter 6), some courts have deferred to an agency's interpretation that its statute did *not* intend to require formal hearing procedures. Dominion Energy Brayton Point v. Johnson, 443 F.3d 12 (1st Cir. 2006) (effectively overruling the First Circuit opinion in *Seacoast*, supra). For a recent discussion of cases on the so-called § 554(a) trigger, see Jordan, *Chevron and Hearing Rights: an Unintended Combination*, 61 Admin. L. Rev. 249 (2009) (criticizing use of *Chevron* analysis in interpreting § 554(a)).

The uncertainty about how the formal adjudication provisions of the APA are triggered is significant. There are thousands of adjudications conducted annually by federal agencies that are (a) supposed to turn on evidence submitted by the parties but (b) do not trigger APA formal hearing procedures because they are authorized by statutes in which the magic words "on the record" or their equivalent do not appear. We will discuss the problem below in Part E, "Informal Adjudication," and raise the question whether the APA as currently written stops short of providing needed procedural protection for this important class of adjudications.

(a).... [Section 554 applies] except to the extent that there is involved—

(1) a matter subject to a subsequent trial of the law and the facts de novo in a court;

(2) the selection or tenure of an employee, except an administrative law judge appointed under section 3105 of this title;

(3) proceedings in which decisions rest solely on inspections, tests, or elections;

(4) the conduct of military or foreign affairs functions;

(5) cases in which an agency is acting as an agent for a court; or

(6) the certification of worker representatives.

Comment: Each of these exclusions describe proceedings that the APA drafters felt would be better handled by procedures other than the kind of trial-like procedures the APA provides for covered adjudications. You can see the logic in most of these. Tenure of public employees, for example, may be better covered by special civil service procedures. An adjudication involving the strength of an airplane wing (or, for that matter, your qualifications to practice law) may be better handled by tests than by the method of trial. Two things to remember about these exclusions: first, they will be narrowly interpreted and second, they do not rule out the possibility that other statutes or agency regulations will impose procedural requirements.

(b) Persons entitled to notice of an agency hearing shall be timely informed of—
   (1) the time, place, and nature of the hearing;
   (2) the legal authority and jurisdiction under which the hearing is to be held; and
   (3) the matters of fact and law asserted.

When private persons are the moving parties, other parties to the proceeding shall give prompt notice of issues controverted in fact or law; and in other instances agencies may by rule require responsive pleading. In fixing the time and place for hearings, due regard shall be had for the convenience and necessity of the parties or their representatives.

Comment: Under subsection (b) notice must be timely and must be complete regarding the details listed. In addition, adequate notice is a requirement of due process. The basic concept is that notice (its content, its timing, its transmission, etc.) must be adequate to apprise parties of agency action that will affect their interests. While the requirement is practical and the agency need not disclose everything it knows about the matter, notice should include enough information about the theory of its case, the issues to be decided and the information supporting the proceeding to allow a party to begin its preparation. Where agency rules provide for pleading, it is "notice" pleading and seeks the same practical objective—notice that is sufficient to allow a fair response. Administrative pleadings are liberally construed and easily amended. 2 Koch Administrative Law and Practice § 5.32-33 (2nd ed. 1997).

> (c) The agency shall give all interested parties opportunity for —
>
> (1) the submission and consideration of facts, arguments, offers of settlement, or proposals of adjustment when time, the nature of the proceeding, and the public interest permit; and

Comment: These are pretty standard opportunities for parties to conduct their cases, but note that it is all subject to time and public interest constraints. The agency has considerable discretion here. Don't be surprised if an agency exercises this discretion to limit participation, and do be ready to assert your client's rights if they could be prejudiced by shortcuts.

> (2) to the extent that the parties are unable so to determine a controversy by consent, hearing and decision on notice and in accordance with sections 556 and 557 of this title.

Comment: This is the language which triggers the hearing and decision provisions of §§ 556 and 557 which we will examine in detail below.

> (d) The employee who presides at the reception of evidence pursuant to section 556 of this title shall make the recommended decision or initial decision required by section 557 of this title, unless he becomes unavailable to the agency.

Comment: A principal design feature of the APA adjudication process is that the person who hears the witnesses and sees the evidence will usually make the first decision in the case. Some variations will appear in § 557, below, but in the typical case, the person who presides over the hearing will also be the person to render the first decision (called initial, tentative, recommended, etc.). This means that real chips are on the table at the agency hearing. You are not trying a case before a shorthand reporter whose job is merely to collect the evidence and argument and forward them to higher officials for decision. You are trying the case before a person with full decisional responsibility whose decision—barring internal review—will become the agency decision.

As we will see below, unless the agency's statute provides otherwise—or unless the agency members themselves wish to preside (which is rare)—the presiding official must be a so-called Administrative Law Judge (ALJ). The agency is not generally free to appoint another staff member to preside at hearings. This is a very important part of the design process. We will also see below that the ALJ—though technically an employee of the agency—will have considerable independence from agency views through structural devices we'll examine below.

> (d).... Except to the extent required for the disposition of ex parte matters as authorized by law, such an employee may not—
>
> (1) consult a person or party on a fact in issue, unless on notice and opportunity for all parties to participate; or
> (2) be responsible to or subject to the supervision or direction of an employee or agent engaged in the performance of investigative or prosecuting functions for an agency.
>
> An employee or agent engaged in the performance of investigative or prosecuting functions for an agency in a case may not, in that or a factually related case, participate or advise in the decision, recommended decision, or agency review pursuant to section 557 of this title, except as witness or counsel in public proceedings.

Comment: This is a very complicated piece of drafting and the drafters were not always successful in making their meaning clear. The language set out above deals with two different but related matters.

1. Section 554(d)(1) is part of the APA's restrictions on *ex parte communications*; more limits will appear in § 554(d)(2) and in § 557(d).

2. Section 554(d)(2), along with the language that follows in the flush paragraph, is also part of the APA's *separation of functions* provisions.

(1) *Ex Parte Communications.* Looking first at the ex parte communications limit in § 554(d)(1), note that it limits the ALJ's ability to discuss facts in the case with "any person or party," except in the presence of all other parties. This is obviously intended to insure that the decision is truly made "on the record" and that any factual considerations asserted by a party are subjected to adversarial testing. Because § 557(d) will prohibit ex parte communications with persons *outside* the agency, this provision is generally treated as having its principal application to communications *inside* the agency. The section seems to forbid the ALJ from having private discussions with any members of

the agency staff. But wouldn't that reading make unnecessary the language of § 554(d)(2) which prohibits a special class of agency employees (prosecutors and investigators) from participating or advising in the decision? Or is the *consultation* prohibited in § 554(d)(1) different from the *participation* banned in § 554(d)(2)? Obviously, some drafting clarity would have been helpful.

Begin with the notion that these can be serious limits on agency action. One of the things we hope to get from adjudication by administrative agency is the full use of agency expertise. But that expertise is resident in agency staff, not in ALJs. Wouldn't we get more expert decisions if the ALJ, say, after the hearing, could consult with experts in the agency staff about the meaning or significance of material in the hearing record? And wouldn't it be fairer to the parties if this kind of consultation had the consequence of making the ALJ's initial decision a more accurate reflection of the full rationale of the decision, so the parties would be on notice of the issues that had to be addressed on appeal?

Largely for reasons such as this, the Attorney General's Manual on the APA would soften the § 554(d)(1) prohibition somewhat by interpreting it to mean that while the language prohibited the ALJ from engaging in an ex parte discussion of facts in issue with any person during the *hearing* phase of the proceeding, during the later *decisional* phase, the ALJ could "obtain advice from or consult with agency personnel ... [such as]the agency heads, supervisors of the [ALJ] and persons assigned to assist the [ALJ] in analyzing the record."ATTORNEY GENERAL'S MANUAL ON THE APA 55 (1947).

Neither the Supreme Court nor lower courts have resolved the matter. Butz v. Economou, 438 U.S. 478, 513–14 (1978) is sometimes cited as a Supreme Court ruling on the matter, but the Court's statements are clearly dicta. And while lower courts now and then remind us of the difference between ex parte issues in courts and in adjudicating agencies—suggesting that we shouldn't read the ex parte prohibitions in agency cases as strictly as they are read in judicial cases— the question before us has not been settled. White v. Indiana Parole Bd., 266 F.3d 759, 766 (7th Cir. 2001)

As a result you can find differing views on the propriety of ALJ consultation. Thus, one respected scholar can say that "internal [ALJ] contacts with other than prosecutors are not expressly prohibited [by the APA]," Koch, ADMINISTRATIVE LAW AND PRACTICE § 6.12[1] (1997), while another can say that "because section 554(d)(1) extends to consultations with 'any person,' an ALJ may not have such discussions with other agency personnel, regardless of their duties or lack of involvement in the case." Werhan, PRINCIPLES OF ADMINISTRATIVE LAW § 5.1(b) (2008).

If it is felt that such ALJ consultation would improve the quality of the decision—or would provide clearer notice to the parties about the issues on appeal—yet it is not feasible to reopen the hearing or to produce the expert for cross-examintion, perhaps § 554(d)(1)'s "facts in issue" phrase could be read narrowly. If the prohibition extends only to ALJ consultation on specific and disputed issues of adjudicative fact, the ALJ could still consult with non prosecutors and investigators on issues of law or policy. Consultation would even be possible on factual questions if they were not disputed issues of adjudicative fact. For example, while an ALJ could not consult with anyone on whether the alleged violator committed the act charged, the ALJ could consult with non prosecutors on questions such as whether there was an increasing trend in this kind of violation (a question of fact) that might warrant increasing the usual sanctions (a question of policy). Finally, never forget that most agencies have rules which contain further limits on ex parte communications. We will return to ex parte contacts below in our discussion of § 557(d) which focuses on ex parte communications from those outside the agency.

(2) *Separation of Functions.* Beyond its implications for ex parte communications, § 554(d)(2) is part of the APA's treatment of separation of functions issues. As we have seen in Chapter 1, at the top of our government, the constitution separates what are regarded as inconsistent functions (such as judging, legislating and prosecuting) by placing those powers in different branches. But the administrative agency combines all three functions within one governmental unit. The Court has told us that the constitution does not always prohibit this combination of functions; indeed, there is a presumption that it does not. Withrow v. Larkin, 421 U.S. 35 (1975). But as we have repeatedly said, it is precisely this sort of separation of powers shortfall that administrative law (and the APA) were created to help correct. To provide some assurance of objective decisionmaking, § 554(d)(2) first insures that ALJs are not supervised or directed by those in the agency who perform investigative or prosecutorial functions—employees who might be expected to have a mind set inconsistent with objective decisionmaking.

Then, more broadly, the flush paragraph goes on to prohibit prosecutors or investigators from participating or advising in the decision of the case and in the internal review of the case except as witnesses or counsel in the public hearing itself. Notice that this limit applies to the case at hand and to any "factually related" cases, that is, to different cases arising out of the same set of facts. Pretty clearly, the APA attempts to seal off prosecutors and investigators, except as open participants in the hearing itself.

We will see further statutory provisions to protect the independence of the ALJ in later sections.

> This subsection does not apply —
>
> (A) in determining applications for initial licenses;
> (B) to proceedings involving the validity or application of rates, facilities, or practices of public utilities or carriers; or
> (C) to the agency or a member or members of the body comprising the agency.

Comment: This is an important provision, rendering all of the § 554(d) limits (on decisional authority, separation of functions and ex parte communications) inapplicable in the three situations listed. We will see that later § 557(d) which prohibits ex parte contacts from people outside the agency, is *not* subject to these exceptions.

The initial licensing exemption (A) relates to our earlier discussion of that particular kind of adjudication. We noted that such proceedings might turn more on general, policy views (do we need more nuclear reactors?) than on contested issues of adjudicative fact (is this applicant for a reactor license qualified?), in which case perhaps the separation of functions and ex parte limits should be relaxed. But where an initial licensing case does turn on the qualifications of the applicant, combining prosecuting and judging functions and permitting ex parte communications with staff could be troublesome. Be sure to check the agency rules to see whether these limits are reimposed in some initial licensing cases. And, of course, in a case where there has been a clear and prejudicial ex parte communication in an initial licensing case that turns on disputed adjudicative facts, the due process clause might offer some relief. See the discussion in Chambers v. Department of Interior, 515 F.3d 1362 (Fed. Cir. 2008).

The exclusion of public utility rates and practices (B) was thought necessary because questions about past reasonableness of rates were often consolidated with the making of future rates. Since, as we've seen, the APA definitions put ratemaking into the rulemaking category, §554(d)'s quintessentially adjudicative protections were thought less necessary.

Finally, the exclusion of the agency or "members of the body comprising the agency" (C) is necessary because of the organizational structure of the administrative agency. Be careful to note that the exclusion is not of agency staff generally, but only the agency head (e.g., the Administrator in an agency with a single head) or "members of the body comprising the agency" (e.g., the 5 commissioners of the FTC or the 7 board members of the NLRB). The section continues to apply to all other members of the agency staff, whatever their title. When you look at the agency as an organization, it is clear that the agency head *is* the prosecutor and the investigator—that is, those functions are being performed in his name and by his authority. To apply the provisions of §554(d) to the head of the agency would make agency prosecutions impossible; hence, the exclusion of the head of the agency is necessary.

The result of the exclusion of agency heads also means that §554(d)'s restrictions on internal ex parte communication are relaxed, permitting the agency head somewhat fuller access to relevant agency staff in making the final decision. That may be a benefit in aid of enriching the decision with agency staff expertise, but could come at an obvious fairness cost. Judicial review remains the last corrective to any inappropriate addition of untested argument or evidence which this relaxation may permit. And remember that the Attorney General Manual expresses the view that agency heads are still prohibited from having ex parte contact with investigators or prosecutors. ATTORNEY GENERAL'S MANUAL ON THE APA 56–57 (1947).

> (e) The agency, with like effect as in the case of other orders, and in its sound discretion, may issue a declaratory order to terminate a controversy or remove uncertainty.

Comment: The declaratory order fulfills a similar function in administrative law as it does in regular litigation—to "develop predictability in the law by authorizing binding determinations 'which dispose of legal controversies without the necessity of any party's acting at his peril upon his own view.'" ATTORNEY GENERAL'S MANUAL ON THE APA 59 (1947). Declaratory orders are discretionary with the agency, but when issued are usually judicially reviewable. When compared to the less formal techniques for giving advice that we looked at in Chapter 2 (interpretive rules, policy statements, etc.) they seem likely to qualify for so–called *Chevron* deference — a set of mysteries we'll examine in Chapter 6.

APA § 555 Ancillary Matters

(a) This section applies, according to the provisions thereof, except as otherwise provided by this subchapter.

Comment: This section of the APA applies to both formal and informal adjudications.

(b) A person compelled to appear in person before an agency or representative thereof is entitled to be accompanied, represented, and advised by counsel or, if permitted by the agency, by other qualified representative.

Comment: Except for hearings required by due process — where a *Mathews v. Eldridge* calculation might in some cases require a different result, see Chapter 4 — witnesses have no general constitutional right to counsel in administrative proceedings. In re Groban, 352 U.S. 330 (1957). Thus, any entitlement to the assistance of counsel will come from statute or from the agency's own rules. The above language of the APA grants a right to counsel to persons compelled to appear — as, for example, witnesses who appear in response to an agency subpoena . Voluntary witnesses receive no protection from this provision.

Look carefully at what is granted: the right to be "accompanied, represented and advised" by counsel. These words have somewhat different meanings from agency to agency and from one type of proceeding to another. Your safest bet is to examine the agency's own procedural rules to see exactly what kinds of assistance will be permitted. You would find, for example, that the Federal Deposit Insurance Commission rules provide that "[a]ny person compelled or requested to provide testimony as a witness" is entitled to be represented in agency investigatory proceedings by counsel, who may: "(1) Advise the witness before, during, and after such testimony; (2) Briefly question the witness at the conclusion of such testimony for clarification purposes; and (3) Make summary notes during such testimony solely for the use and benefit of the witness." 12 CFR § 308.148. While this rule goes beyond § 555 in entitling *voluntary* witnesses to representation, the attorney's role is quite limited. Nothing is said about the attorney's opportunity to object to questions, to make and argue objections for the record, or to cross examine other witnesses. In the administrative agency context, these roles are usually not thought to be included in the word "represented." FCC v. Schreiber, 329 F.2d 517, 526 (9th Cir. 1964). See the discussion in Moritz, *The Lawyer Doth Protest Too Much*, 72 U. Cinn. L. Rev. 1353, 1384–87 (2004).

A thoughtful recommendation of the Administrative Conference of the U.S. has been persuasive to some agencies that have broadened the role of counsel representing witnesses. See Selected Reports of the Administrative Conference of the U.S., Sen. Doc. 24, 88th Cong. 1st Sess. at 223 (1963). For example, the FTC practice rules permit the witness to consult with counsel on each question, permit counsel to object on the record to some issues, including making brief statements in support of the objection, and permit counsel, on completion of the examination, to request that the witness be allowed to clarify any answers given. The attorney will be kept on a relatively tight leash. The presiding official retains discretion to regulate the course of the hearing and is specifically authorized to sanction attorneys for any behavior that is "dilatory, obstructionist or contumacious." 16 CFR § 2.9.

(b) ... A party is entitled to appear in person or by or with counsel or other duly qualified representative in an agency proceeding.

Comment: Beyond the rights of representation of *witnesses*, this provision deals with representation of *parties* to the proceeding. The provision has two parts. First, those who are parties have the right to a personal appearance in an "agency proceeding" (defined in § 551 to include rulemaking, adjudication, licensing). Because of the opening clause of § 555(a), this entitlement does not extend to situations where other provisions of the APA rule out personal appearances. Thus, it does not entitle someone interested in an informal rulemaking to a personal appearance if the agency has exercised its discretion under § 553(c) to limit participation to written comment. And even in a formal adjudication, as we will see, there may be places where the submission of one's case in written form is authorized by the APA (see, e.g., § 556(d)) and in such cases this section does not entitle a party to present evidence orally.

Second, the language entitles parties to appear "by or with" counsel. Presumably, "by" includes an opportunity for counsel to speak on behalf of the party and, subject to other discretion conferred on the agency in § 556 below, to examine witnesses, make objections, etc.

> (b).... So far as the orderly conduct of public business permits, an interested person may appear before an agency or its responsible employees for the presentation, adjustment, or determination of an issue, request, or controversy in a proceeding, whether interlocutory, summary, or otherwise, or in connection with an agency function.

Comment: Taken at face value, this is a remarkable section of the APA. It extends the right of personal appearance beyond the parties to a case. It gives any interested citizen the right to appear before the agency, and to appear before "responsible employees" to discuss any issue involved in a "proceeding" (rulemaking, adjudication, licensing) or any other "agency function." It is true that the citizen's right may not impair the "orderly conduct of public business," and that the language does not impose on agencies the duty to provide notice to citizens of matters that may affect them or to invite their participation. But even with these limits, the provision celebrates the principle of participation generally and specifically supports citizen requests for hearings, meetings, conferences or informal discussions.

> (c).... With due regard for the convenience and necessity of the parties or their representatives and within a reasonable time, each agency shall proceed to conclude a matter presented to it.

Comment: As we have seen, delay in completing agency action is often a problem, and courts have only a limited ability to deal with it despite § 706(1)'s grant of authority to courts to compel action unreasonably delayed. Perhaps the general injunction here — that matters should be concluded within a reasonable time — is the most that can be done to encourage good management by agencies and to support courts in cases of truly unacceptable delay. The many cases on unreasonable delay suggest that courts will tolerate even multiple-year delays, but only if reasons can be advanced by the agency that plausibly relate to the special nature of the problem, or to the agency's resources and priorities.

> b).... This subsection does not grant or deny a person who is not a lawyer the right to appear for or represent others before an agency or in an agency proceeding.

Comment: This provision retains agency discretion over whether non-lawyers can be authorized to practice before an agency. Generally, any attorney in good standing can represent parties before federal agencies and without specific statutory authority those agencies cannot impose additional restrictions on attorneys' rights to appear. 5 USC § 500. However, a few agencies (e.g., the Patent and Trademark Office) have statutory authority to do so.

(c) Process, requirement of a report, inspection, or other investigative act or demand may not be issued, made, or enforced except as authorized by law. A person compelled to submit data or evidence is entitled to retain or, on payment of lawfully prescribed costs, procure a copy or transcript thereof, except that in a nonpublic investigatory proceeding the witness may for good cause be limited to inspection of the official transcript of his testimony.

Comment: This permits compelled witnesses to obtain copies of transcripts of their testimony or copies of material submitted in response to an agency subpoena. Note, these rights are not given to voluntary witnesses and the right given is only to receive copies of what the witness provided, not material provided by other witnesses or parties. In confidential investigations, e.g., inquiries that may lead to later prosecution, the agency may limit the availability of copies on a showing of good cause.

(d) Agency subpoenas authorized by law shall be issued to a party on request and, when required by rules of procedure, on a statement or showing of general relevance and reasonable scope of the evidence sought. On contest, the court shall sustain the subpoena or similar process or demand to the extent that it is found to be in accordance with law. In a proceeding for enforcement, the court shall issue an order requiring the appearance of the witness or the production of the evidence or data within a reasonable time under penalty of punishment for contempt in case of contumacious failure to comply.

Comment: Note this for now. We will discuss it in Chapter 7.

(e) Prompt notice shall be given of the denial in whole or in part of a written application, petition, or other request of an interested person made in connection with any agency proceeding. Except in affirming a prior denial or when the denial is self-explanatory, the notice shall be accompanied by a brief statement of the grounds for denial.

Comment: This section requires that agency denials of citizen requests in connection with "agency proceedings" (rulemaking, adjudication, licensing) be prompt and that the denials be accompanied by a brief statement of reasons. The language reflects a key principle of the rule of law—that some explanation of harmful action is owing to those affected. The section doesn't require a full dress opinion and it could even be delivered orally in some cases. Courts have been relatively generous with agencies, but the essentials of an explanation must be made available.

APA § 556

Hearings; presiding employees; powers and duties; burden of proof; evidence; record as basis of decision
(a) This section applies, according to the provisions thereof, to hearings required by section 553 or 554 of this title to be conducted in accordance with this section.

Comment: Sections 556 and 557, to be examined now, lay out procedures for what we have been calling formal proceedings—whether rulemaking or adjudication. Thus when another statute requires rules to be made "on the record," § 553(c) directs you to these two sections. And when a statute requires an adjudication to be "on the record," § 554(c)(2) directs you to these two sections.

(b) There shall preside at the taking of evidence—

(1) the agency;
(2) one or more members of the body which comprises the agency; or
(3) one or more administrative law judges appointed under section 3105 of this title.

This subchapter does not supersede the conduct of specified classes of proceedings, in whole or in part, by or before boards or other employees specially provided for by or designated under statute.

Comment: Subsection (b) is one of the most important provisions in the entire APA. It deals with one of the critical design features of the act. In the decade before the APA, fierce criticism was directed at the burgeoning administrative process. A central tenet of that criticism was that formal decisions were being decided not by independent life-

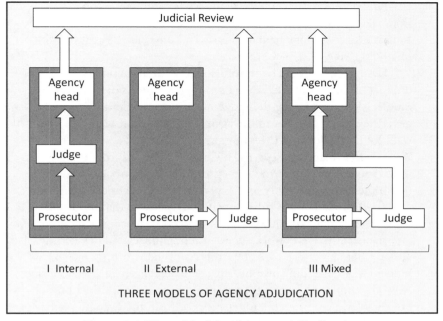

Figure 3.4 Three Models of Agency Adjudication

tenured judges as in the federal court system, but by agency employees. Even if one granted that these employees were "experts," they were
not objective and they were not independent but were seen by many
(especially the bar) as mission-oriented servants of the political appointees at the head of the agency.

You can quickly see the design problem facing the drafters of the APA.
They had on the one hand to insure that agency decisions took advantage of agency expertise. On the other hand, formal proceedings
in which the interests of individuals could be severely affected should
entitle the individual to objectivity in decision making. The design
problem was how to reach both goals. Figure 3.4 shows three possible approaches to this design problem.

The *Internal* model will insure that agency political and technical
expertise is employed fully in all phases of the case, since all actors are
agency employees. But, of course, objectivity may suffer. The citizen
whose license is revoked under this process may feel like a character in
a Kafka novel—all phases of the process seem lined up against him.

The *External* model addresses the Kafka problem. With the decisionmaker outside the agency, some objectivity in making the decision can be expected. This benefit, however, comes at the cost of minimizing the role of agency expertise.

The *Mixed* model is a compromise and a variation on it is what the drafters of the APA finally settled on. It seeks some objectivity in initial decisions by placing the judge not quite outside the agency but nevertheless insulated from the agency in important respects, which we'll look at below. At the same time, this model seeks to capture some degree of agency expertise by bringing appeals from the judge's initial ruling back within the agency for final decision. Of course, how this tradeoff of objectivity and expertise actually works depends on how free the agency is to substitute its judgment for that of the judge. We'll discuss that explicitly below.

For such a system to work, a new group of judges had to be created. Today, there are close to 2,000 officials called Administrative Law Judges (ALJs) presiding over hearings in federal agencies. Technically, ALJs are employed by the agency over whose hearings they preside, but they have considerable independence from the agency. We have seen in § 554(d) that they cannot be subject to the direction and control of agency investigators or prosecutors. More broadly, agencies are not free to select their own ALJs — they must be selected from a roster of qualified applicants provided by the Office of Personnel Management (OPM), and their pay and tenure are determined by the OPM system rather than by agency choice or recommendations. The agencies do have some controls over ALJs and in the litigation over these controls you can see sharply the tension created among the conflicting goals: management efficiency and loyalty to agency policy preferences on the one hand and decisional independence on the other. See, e.g., Nash v. Bowen, 869 F.2d 675 (2nd Cir. 1989). Information about the selection, powers, evaluation, compensation and tenure of ALJs is reviewed in ABA, A GUIDE TO FEDERAL AGENCY ADJUDICATION, Chap. 10 (Asimow Ed. 2003).

Of course, if agencies were permitted to appoint others to judge formal adjudications — employees not protected from agency pressure — the design would not function as intended. Hence, § 556(b) tells the agency that they must assign ALJs to preside at formal hearings unless the agency heads themselves are going to preside (which would be rare).

Remember that § 556 applies only to formal proceedings. The thousands of adjudications annually that are not required to be "on the record"—and thus are not required to follow APA §§ 556–557—are presided over by non-ALJs who lack the status and independence of the ALJs. See Conference on Fair and Independent Courts: A Conference on the State of the Judiciary, Appendix I: Tiers of Federal Judges, 95 Geo. L. J. 1009, 1021–22 (2007). The serious procedural shortfalls that may occur in such cases are discussed below in Part E, "Informal Adjudication."

(b)…. The functions of presiding employees and of employees participating in decisions in accordance with section 557 of this title shall be conducted in an impartial manner. A presiding or participating employee may at any time disqualify himself. On the filing in good faith of a timely and sufficient affidavit of personal bias or other disqualification of a presiding or participating employee, the agency shall determine the matter as a part of the record and decision in the case.

Comment: The process for asserting the disqualification of an ALJ or other agency decisionmaker is very like what you would find in a federal court—a party files an affidavit asserting personal bias of the ALJ and the matter is decided by the agency, the decision becoming part of the record for judicial review.

If the process is familiar, however, the grounds for disqualifying bias in the administrative law world are different from what you might expect in a courtroom. As we have seen, administrative agencies are not likely to be neutral in the sense that a courtroom judge is supposed to be neutral. The agency has a substantive mission assigned to it by Congress and its whole reason for being is to carry out that mission. How do we draw the line between acceptable agency fidelity to its mission and the party's right to a fair hearing?

The broadest form of the question about agency objectivity is structural; whether any acceptable level of objectivity can be expected from an agency which combines investigating, prosecuting, fact-finding, and judging within one governmental unit. As we noted in Chapter 1, avoiding the potential injustice from combining the functions of this kind was one of the concerns of the framers and one of the justifications for dividing government powers into separate branches. Might the constitution, then, forbid combining inconsistent functions within one administrative agency?

The answer seems to be, "no." As the court stated in Withrow v. Larkin, 421 U.S. 35 (1975), "the combination of investigative and adjudicative functions does not, without more, constitute a due process violation." 421 U.S. at 58. There is a general presumption of honesty and integrity of public officials that supports the Court's conclusion, along with an obvious practical need to permit agencies to function effectively.

If combination of inconsistent functions will not support a claim of disqualifying bias, what will? You can begin with the notion that if the decisionmaker's bias is personal to a party, it may be disqualifying. Similarly, if it can be shown that the decisionmaker has some pecuniary or other personal interest in the outcome of the case, the bias may be disqualifying.

The harder cases arise where the agency decisionmaker evidences a strong predisposition on the issues in the case. Here we need to look further at the nature of the issues concerned. If it is a prejudgment of a deciding official about adjudicative facts at issue in the case, the bias may be disqualifying. If Captain Green's commercial pilot's license is being revoked because of her allegedly poor eyesight, a decisionmaker who had made up his or her mind about the quality of Green's eyesight would presumably be disqualified.

If, on the other hand, the prejudgment is about more general facts (is 20/20 the appropriate standard for commercial pilot licensing?) it would not necessarily be disqualifying. This would be especially true if the judgment were the "official" view of the agency, extracted over time from agency experience. To the pilot with 20/30 eyesight, of course, this prejudgment would be fatal to his case, but this kind of factual development is precisely what we expect agencies to do.

Moreover, the prejudgment may not be disqualifying if it is about policies ("we need to crack down on eyesight problems this year") or law ("our statute may not seem this clear to others but our reading of it is that we must be especially tough on the visual qualification of pilots"). In FTC V. Cement Institute, 333 U. S. 683 (1948) the Court pointed out that it is one of the duties of the administrative agency to study and inform itself about relevant policies and carrying out that function should not prevent the agency from applying those policies.

If a disqualifying bias can be shown, what is the remedy? In the judicial world, when bias is successfully asserted against a judge the remedy is simply to substitute another judge. Presumably a biased ALJ could similarly be replaced. But how do you handle the disqualifying bias of the head of the agency (the administrator of a single-headed agency or the board or commission members in a collegial body)? There simply is no substitute for such people. If disqualifying bias means license revocation action against Pilot Green must be dropped, the result leaves Green at the controls of a jetliner despite concern over her eyesight, hardly a victory for the public interest. In such a case, the ancient (15th Century!) "rule of necessity" may be applied — the agency will be permitted to make the decision despite the bias. One suspects there will be especially intensive judicial review of such a decision if the matter later reaches court. For a discussion of the rule in both its judicial and administrative forms, see McKevitt, *The Rule of Necessity: Is Judicial Non-Disqualification Really Necessary?*, 24 Hofstra L. Rev. 817 (1996).

(c) Subject to published rules of the agency and within its powers, employees presiding at hearings may —

(1) administer oaths and affirmations;

(2) issue subpoenas authorized by law;

(3) rule on offers of proof and receive relevant evidence;

(4) take depositions or have depositions taken when the ends of justice would be   served;

(5) regulate the course of the hearing;

(6) hold conferences for the settlement or simplification of the issues by consent of the parties or by the use of alternative means of dispute resolution as provided in subchapter IV of this chapter;

(7) inform the parties as to the availability of one or more alternative means of dispute resolution, and encourage use of such methods;

(8) require the attendance at any conference held pursuant to paragraph (6) of at least one representative of each party who has authority to negotiate concerning resolution of issues in controversy;

(9) dispose of procedural requests or similar matters;

(10) make or recommend decisions in accordance with section 557 of this title; and

(11) take other action authorized by agency rule consistent with this subchapter.

Comment: This list of 11 powers of the ALJ is similar to the list of powers we would expect to be given to a trial judge. There are a couple of differences to note. First, as noted above, the ALJ is an employee of the agency and as such subject to agency management controls in aid of productivity, training, integrity, and conduct.

Another difference between an ALJ and a federal trial judge is that the ALJ has an affirmative obligation to develop a full record. Especially when individuals are not represented by counsel (as would be typical, e.g., in a social security disability case), it is essential that the ALJ act affirmatively to assure that the record contains all the relevant facts. It would not be unusual in such a case for the ALJ to do some questioning of the parties or the witnesses. See Block, Lubbers and Verkuil, *Developing a Full and Fair Evidentiary Record in a Nonadversary Setting [disability adjudications]*, 25 CARDOZO L. REV. 1 (2003). Indeed, failure of the ALJ to fulfill this obligation to a private party may rise to the level of a due process violation. Gjeci v. Gonzales, 451 F.3d 416 (7th Cir. 2006).

Item (2) concerning subpoenas does not itself grant authority to issue subpoenas. That authority must be found elsewhere as we'll see below in Chapter 7.

Items (6) (7) and (8) reflect the congressional preference for dispute resolution through flexible and informal measures such as mini-trials (simulations), mediation, arbitration and other simplified procedures. By amendment to the APA in 1990, Congress specifically authorized and encouraged the use of alternative dispute resolution techniques. 5 USC §§ 571–583.

Item (10) is an important part of the overall APA design; it reflects the usual practice where the head of the agency does not preside and the ALJ makes the first decision in the case. That process will be discussed below in connection with § 557.

(d) Except as otherwise provided by statute, the proponent of a rule or order has the burden of proof.

Comment: This language puts the burden of proof on the party proposing something. Hence, in an enforcement proceeding, the agency would have the burden of proof. When a private party seeks a license, on the other hand, the burden of proof is on the private party.

What is the burden of proof? You may recall from your courses in evidence that the term "burden of proof" can refer either to the obligation of producing evidence on a matter (sometimes called the "burden of coming forward"), or the phrase can refer to the burden of establishing the truth of the evidence (sometimes called the "burden of persuasion"). The Attorney General's Manual found "some indication" that the drafters meant by the phrase only the burden of coming forward. The Attorney General's Manual on the Administrative Procedure Act 75 (1947). The Court, however, seems to have adopted the view that the phrase includes the burden of persuasion. Director v. Greenwich Collieries, 512 U.S. 267 (1994).

The dispute may not be important in most administrative cases. In the typical case — where the agency, say, authors a complaint — the agency will have both burdens. And as a practical matter, the agency may carry both burdens even in a license application case. While the license applicant is a "proponent" and as such should carry the burden of proof, an agency denial of the license without adequate proof would be subject to reversal under prevailing standards of judicial review (which we'll examine in Chapter 6).

(d).... Any oral or documentary evidence may be received, but the agency as a matter of policy shall provide for the exclusion of irrelevant, immaterial, or unduly repetitious evidence.

Comment: While it is everywhere accepted that administrative adjudication — even at its most formal — can be free from many of the restrictive evidentiary rules that prevail in jury trials, it remains true that a knowledge of evidence is important to the adjudicatory process in administrative agencies. All the above quoted language establishes is that agencies have much discretion about the admission of evidence — it is seldom reversible error for an ALJ to receive evidence that would be incompetent in a jury trial setting. As issues vary, as agencies vary and as presiding officials vary, one can expect different expressions of that discretion — some of it far from the jury trial restrictions, some of it much closer.

Agency rules for the conduct of formal proceedings will typically include rules relating to evidence and those rules need to be carefully noted by practitioners. A 20-year-old report by the Administrative Conference of the U.S. surveyed the almost 300 agency evidence rules, finding that some were as broad as the APA provisions cited above and some were considerably more restrictive. Reporter Professor Richard Pierce also surveyed presiding officials and found they much preferred the more restrictive Federal Rules of Evidence to the wide discretion of the APA. Pierce, *Use of Federal Rules of Evidence in Federal Agency Adjudications*, 39 Admin. L. Rev. 1 (1987).

The statutory language quoted above clearly implies that hearsay evidence can be admitted, and its admission is not uncommon. The absence of a jury and the presence of an experienced fact finder (the ALJ) make concerns about hearsay less troubling in the administrative context. But the rule against hearsay can aid in accurate fact finding by insisting that a declarant be present in the hearing room for cross-examintion. Where it matters—i.e., where some increase in accuracy might be obtained by applying the hearsay rule—and where it is feasible, litigators before agency hearings still can object to hearsay evidence. Remember, in this connection, that there is no absolute right to cross-examintion—or to unlimited cross-examintion—provided by the APA.

(d).... A sanction may not be imposed or rule or order issued except on consideration of the whole record or those parts thereof cited by a party and supported by and in accordance with the reliable, probative, and substantial evidence.

Comment: This provision goes not to the admissibility of evidence but rather to the weight of the evidence admitted. As we will see in the discussion of judicial review below (Chapter 6), a final order must be supported by "substantial evidence." The legislative history of the APA suggests that the additional words "reliable, probative" were not intended to alter the basic test stated in § 706. ATTORNEY GENERAL'S MANUAL ON THE ADMINISTRATIVE PROCEDURE ACT 76 (1947).

So the question with regard to hearsay evidence becomes whether hearsay evidence alone can be "substantial" within the meaning of the APA judicial review provisions. The old rule was that it cannot. The Court in Consolidated Edison v. NLRB, 305 U.S. 197 (1938) held that there must be at least a residuum of "competent" (i.e., non hearsay) evidence in the record to support an order. This so-called residuum rule was in effect overruled by Richardson v. Perales, 402 U.S. 389 (1971) where the Court—without mentioning *Consolidated Edison*—upheld an order based exclusively on uncorroborated hearsay. With a sense of the practical burdens some agencies would face if hearsay could not be relied upon, the Court noted that there is good and bad hearsay, and listed a number of indicators that the hearsay in this case was good hearsay—it was reliable since it was mostly made up of written reports of standard and routine medical examinations that were consistent and were made by trained professionals. An order based on this kind of hearsay would not violate the fundamental fairness required by due process—especially for an agency that had to process half a million such claims annually. Absent factors of this kind, a different result might be expected.

(d) ... The agency may, to the extent consistent with the interests of justice and the policy of the underlying statutes administered by the agency, consider a violation of section 557(d) of this title sufficient grounds for a decision adverse to a party who has knowingly committed such violation or knowingly caused such violation to occur.

Comment: Section 557(d) to be discussed below prohibits persons from outside the agency from making ex parte communications in agency formal proceedings. The section quoted above provides a sanction for use in such cases—essentially it gives the agency authority to rule against a party on the merits of the case where the party made (or caused) a prohibited communication.

Note the very careful introductory conditions stated—ruling against the party must be consistent with the public interest and with the policy of the underlying agency statute. Suppose A and B are competitors for a single television license and A is highly qualified but B is just barely qualified. If A makes an illegal ex parte communication, it would not be in the public interest to disqualify A and grant the license to B. Remedies in ex parte communication cases are difficult; sometimes disclosure and an opportunity to respond are the only practical remedies available.

(d).... A party is entitled to present his case or defense by oral or documentary evidence, to submit rebuttal evidence, and to conduct such cross-examination as may be required for a full and true disclosure of the facts. In rule making or determining claims for money or benefits or applications for initial licenses an agency may, when a party will not be prejudiced thereby, adopt procedures for the submission of all or part of the evidence in written form.

Comment: The first sentence of this quote is self explanatory—parties to formal proceedings are entitled to present their cases personally, to present rebuttal evidence and to conduct cross-examintion if necessary. Note especially the limit on cross-examintion; it is not an absolute right, and the courts have held that the party seeking cross-examintion has the burden of showing that it is required for a "full and true disclosure of the facts." Citizens Awareness Network v. U.S., 391 F.3d 338 (1st Cir. 2004).

The second sentence of the section lists three kinds of cases in which the protections are somewhat less. (1) In rulemaking (and this would refer to formal rulemaking as § 556 doesn't apply to any informal proceedings) the right to personal appearance may be limited. As we have seen, when the relevant evidence in the case is mostly economic or statistical — likely in some rulemaking proceedings — agencies should be able to receive it in written form rather than having it read into the record by a witness. Evidence submitted only in documentary form, of course, cannot be tested by cross-examintion. The drafters did not think cross-examintion was of particular value in resolving disputes over most rulemaking issues. If you can make a persuasive case for limited cross-examintion for some issues, an ALJ might permit it to some degree.

(2) Sensibly, in determining claims for money or benefits, the drafters thought agencies should be allowed to require that papers filed in support of such claims contain the relevant factual material. ATTORNEY GENERAL'S MANUAL ON THE ADMINISTRATIVE PROCEDURE ACT 78 (1947).

(3) In cases of initial licensing, as in rulemaking, if the relevant evidence in support of an application is largely economic, technical or statistical, written presentations may be sufficient. To refer to our example earlier, cross-examintion might be required if the taxi licensing issue is whether this applicant is qualified, but not if the real question to be decided is whether the community needs more taxis.

In all three cases, the reduced opportunity for oral presentations is conditioned on the absence of a showing that this will be prejudicial to the party.

(e) The transcript of testimony and exhibits, together with all papers and requests filed in the proceeding, constitutes the exclusive record for decision in accordance with section 557 of this title and, on payment of lawfully prescribed costs, shall be made available to the parties.

Comment: This "exclusive record" provision is close to the heart of what we mean when we speak of an "on the record" hearing. One side of the exclusive record coin assures us that all evidence in support of the decision was presented (and tested) in open hearing with opportunity for all to participate. The other side of the coin affirms that the decision cannot be affected by testimony, exhibits or other papers that were not presented in the hearing.

We can expect this classic form of the exclusive record requirement to be present in a conventional judicial proceeding. (Look at Figure 2.5 in Chapter 2 to refresh your recollection of the judicial model.) In a criminal trial, e.g., a finding that defendant was in Omaha on June 13 will require testimony or documentary evidence in the record in support of that finding. Moving this principle from the judicial to administrative setting, however, raises some difficult questions. We have said that the strength of agency adjudication is that it brings agency expertise into the decisional process. Expertise may be reflected in studies and reports that can be introduced into the hearing record. But beyond that, the agency may also have accumulated judgment, insight, situational sense and "feel" from their extended experience. This may be the most important kind of expertise the agency has. If this kind of expertise cannot be encapsulated into discrete documents or if it resides in the minds of those for whom testifying at the hearing is not feasible, must the expertise be ignored on pain of violating the exclusive record requirement?

Suppose a company advertises that its "charm school" will virtually guarantee graduates positions as airline flight attendants. The FTC believes the ads are misleading and seeks to enjoin them. A formal adjudication follows and in the hearing the agency is unable to get anyone to testify that they were naive enough to believe the ads. On the contrary, the company produces many witnesses who testify that they did not believe the ads, treated them as mere commercial "puffing." On such a record, can the FTC conclude that the ads were misleading?

If the exclusive record concept is applied too tightly, the FTC will fail, as there is no direct record support for its conclusion that the ads were misleading—indeed evidence in the record would seem to show the opposite. But shouldn't the agency be allowed to evaluate the evidence in the record in light of its prior experience? The FTC might have developed the view over the years that companies do not spend money on advertising unless it has been shown to persuade some buyers. Or the agency may have concluded from past hearings in consumer cases that while it is relatively easy to find witnesses willing to show their sophistication by claiming not to have believed ads, it is difficult to find witnesses willing to show their naiveté by admitting to having been duped. If this background information could be used to evaluate the evidence in the record, should it be ignored by the agency under a strict exclusive record requirement? We will consider judicial review of agency fact finding in Chapter 6. For now, consider the exclusive record requirement as generally permitting the use of agency experience in evaluating evidence in the record so long as the agency is careful to explain how its experience bears on its factual findings. The critical question is whether the agency is using expertise to *evaluate* evidence or using it as a *substitute* for evidence. The Model State Administrative Procedure Act addresses the matter directly: "The presiding officer's experience, technical competence, and specialized knowledge may be utilized in the evaluation of evidence." Uniform Law Commissioners, MODEL STATE ADMINISTRATIVE PROCEDURE ACT § 4-215(d) (1981); for a similar provision, see Revised Code of Washington, 34.05.461(5)(2008). If the agency does not adequately explain its treatment of the evidence, of course, it may not be so successful. See Cinderella Career and Finishing School v. FTC, 425 F.2d 138 (D.C. Cir. 1970).

When an agency decision rests on official notice of a material fact not appearing in the evidence in the record, a party is entitled, on timely request, to an opportunity to show the contrary.

Comment: The exclusive record requirement is a mainstay of the formal adjudication. But at times it would be wasteful to require an agency to enter in the record through testimony and documents material facts that do not seem to be disputable. In the judicial setting, the federal Rules of Evidence permit a court to take judicial notice of facts that are "generally known" or which can be readily determined from reliable sources. Fed.R.Evid. 201(b). In the administrative world there are, in addition, facts that may not be "generally known" but which are well known to the agency by reason of its prior experience, study and decision. The quoted language permits an agency to take "official notice" of such facts, eliminating the need for evidence of such facts to be developed at the hearing.

What kinds of facts can an agency notice? The range of facts is much broader than what can be judicially noticed. The courts have generally accepted the statement of the Attorney General's Manual that official notice can extend to "all matters as to which the agency by reason of its functions is presumed to be expert, such as technical or

scientific facts within its specialized expertise." ATTORNEY GENERAL'S
MANUAL ON THE ADMINISTRATIVE PROCEDURE ACT 80 (1947). For
example, an agency can take official notice of the harmful effects of nude
dancing, City of Erie v. Pap's AM, 529 U.S. 277 (2000), a change in
the rate on 10-year Treasury bonds, Union Electric Co. v. FERC, 890
F.2d 1193 (D.C. Cir. 1989), and whether the lack of binocular vision
does significantly diminish a disability claimant's opportunity for certain types of work. Sykes v. Apfel, 228 F.3d 259 (3rd Cir. 2000).

But along with this liberality in allowing the agency to take official
notice of facts within their specialized expertise comes the qualification
noted in the language quoted above. Unlike judicial notice, official notice requires that a party be notified that a fact is going to be noticed
and must be given an opportunity to show that the fact is untrue.

For notice of what we have called legislative facts (i.e., facts about
general matters, not about the party) a written opportunity to rebut
may be sufficient. When official notice is taken of adjudicative facts
(specifically about the party) the matter is more complex. If the facts
are central to the controversy, they may not be noticeable at all—their
development in the record by the traditional methods may be a requirement of due process. Dayco v. FTC, 362 F.2d 180 (6th Cir. 1966).
If they are capable of being noticed, the opportunity for rebuttal should
include oral presentations and even cross-examintion in an appropriate case. See the discussion in 2 Koch, ADMINISTRATIVE LAW AND
PRACTICE 209 (2d ed. 1997).

APA § 557

Initial Decisions; conclusiveness; review by agency; submissions by parties; contents of decisions; record
a) This section applies, according to the provisions thereof, when a
hearing is required to be conducted in accordance with section 556 of
this title.

Comment: You will recall that a hearing is to be conducted under this
section when, in the language of §§ 553 and 554, it is to be "on the
record." In this Chapter we are working with adjudications, so you
can begin by noting that § 557 applies only to *formal* adjudications.
Adjudications not required by another statute to be on the record—
so-called *informal* adjudications—will be noted briefly at the end of
the Chapter.

(b) When the agency did not preside at the reception of the evidence, the presiding employee or, in cases not subject to section 554(d) of this title, an employee qualified to preside at hearings pursuant to section 556 of this title, shall initially decide the case unless the agency requires, either in specific cases or by general rule, the entire record to be certified to it for decision. When the presiding employee makes an initial decision, that decision then becomes the decision of the agency without further proceedings unless there is an appeal to, or review on motion of, the agency within time provided by rule. On appeal from or review of the initial decision, the agency has all the powers which it would have in making the initial decision except as it may limit the issues on notice or by rule. When the agency makes the decision without having presided at the reception of the evidence, the presiding employee or an employee qualified to preside at hearings pursuant to section 556 of this title shall first recommend a decision, except that in rule making or determining applications for initial licenses—

(1) instead thereof the agency may issue a tentative decision or one of its responsible employees may recommend a decision; or
(2) this procedure may be omitted in a case in which the agency finds on the record that due and timely execution of its functions imperatively and unavoidably so requires.

Comment: The drafters' basic problem here is to bridge the gap between the person who presided at the hearing and the top agency officials who finally decide the case. Well before the APA was adopted, the Supreme Court had held that the administrative official who finally decides a case must in some sense have "heard" it. Morgan v. U.S., 298 U.S. 468, 480 (1936). This didn't mean, of course, that the head of the agency had personally to sit through the full hearing. A subordinate could preside at the hearing and the final agency decision could be based on summaries and analyses of other subordinates. But the deciding official had to "consider and appraise the evidence" on which the final agency order rested. 298 U.S. at 481–82. These provisions of the APA spell out that process.

In the most typical scenario, the ALJ will both preside and make the initial decision. If the agency prefers to have an ALJ preside at the hearing but to reserve to itself power to make the initial decision, it may do so, in which case the ALJ will make a "recommended" decision.

As we have noted earlier, in any case in which the ALJ presides and makes some form of preliminary decision, the ALJ is an officer with decisional responsibility much like a trial judge. He or she will have to make qualitative judgments, to compare and evaluate the proofs and arguments submitted by the parties, to integrate them into a single decision which includes a judgment about which way the proof and argument preponderates. The responsibility of the ALJ is made clear by the language quoted above that the ALJ's initial decision "becomes the decision of the agency" if there is no appeal. ALJ authority and responsibility will be palpable in the hearing room.

Though neither the due process clause nor the APA requires it, Guentchev v. INS, 77 F.3d 1036 (7th Cir. 1996), agency rules will usually provide for an appeal of an initial decision. The appeal may be by a party or, if the agency lost before the ALJ, by agency staff itself. The appeal will go to the head of the agency or to some internal appellate body acting for the agency head. These arrangements will vary from agency to agency, so consulting agency rules will be important.

How free is the reviewing body to overturn the ALJ decision? This is a variation of the "scope of review" discussion we will have in Chapter 6 when we look at the power of a court to set aside the final decision of the agency. It is also similar to the scope of review issue you have when an appellate court reviews a trial judge or, for that matter, when a trial court evaluates a jury verdict. Look at some of the comparisons in Figure 3.5.

In reviewing a jury verdict—at (4) in the chart—a trial judge must defer substantially to the jury on questions of fact but not on questions of law. When a trial judge's order is on review in an appellate court— at (3) in the chart—some deference will be shown the trial judge's fact findings—though not as much deference as is shown jury verdicts— and virtually no deference is shown the trial judge's rulings on law.

We'll spend most of Chapter 6 looking at judicial review of the agency's final action—at (1) in the chart. Our focus now is on the agency's review of its ALJ—at (2) in the chart. Section 557(b) as quoted above says that "On appeal from or review of the initial decision, the agency has all the powers which it would have in making the initial decision …". That would suggest very little deference need be shown to the decision of the ALJ. The agency would thus be free to make its own decision largely independent from the ALJ's initial decision. In the language of the Attorney General's Manual, "the agency is in no way bound by the decision of [the ALJ]; it retains complete freedom of

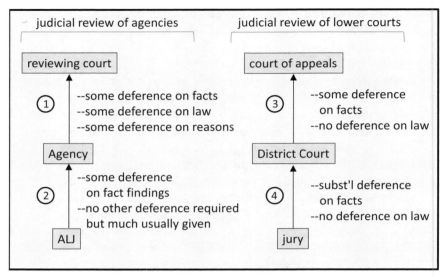

Figure 3.5   Who Defers to Whom? Agencies and Courts Compared

decision—as though it had heard the evidence itself." ATTORNEY GEN-ERAL'S MANUAL ON THE ADMINISTRATIVE PROCEDURE ACT 83 (1947). This much is thought to be required by the "mixed" model of adjudication we looked at in Figure 3.4 above. That is, routing the appeal back inside the agency is intended to assure that basic control of agency policy remains in the hands of accountable presidential appointees, not lower level employees like ALJs.

With respect to some kinds of evidence the courts may require some deference to ALJ findings. It is clear from the legislative history of the APA that at least in a case where the demeanor of witnesses is important; the ALJ findings may be "of consequence" or may be entitled to "considerable weight" on internal agency review. Senate Report quoted in ATTORNEY GENERAL'S MANUAL ON THE APA 84 (1947). As we will see, the ALJ opinion is part of the "whole record" that a reviewing court must examine for the "substantial evidence" needed to support agency fact-findings. Where the agency has disagreed with an ALJ on evidence as to which witness demeanor is important, the evidence supporting the agency decision may appear less substantial than it otherwise might. This settled rule was stated in the classic, Universal Camera v. NLRB, 340 U.S. 474 (1951). The practical outcome is that an agency may reject ALJ fact findings, but with respect to demeanor-based facts, the agency's own success on judicial review may be affected by how persuasively it explains the rejection.

Given that the agency generally has the ultimate power of decision, should a lawyer reserve the full development of the case and the best arguments for the appeal? After all, § 557(b) seems to say that on review the agency is not bound by much that the ALJ decides. For a number of reasons, that would be a disastrous way to represent a client in the administrative world. To begin with, the case must be fully developed at the hearing since evidence will not usually be taken on appeal; under the exclusive record requirement we have discussed, evidence not in the record cannot be used.

Further, as a practical matter, most reviewing bodies will grant the initial decision something like a substantial presumption of correctness. The significance of the ALJ's efforts over weeks, months or longer on full understanding of the case will not be lost on the reviewing body, nor will that body be anxious to redo that work itself. So it turns out that despite the clear power of the agency to reverse the ALJ, the vast majority of ALJ decisions are going to be affirmed. It adds up to this: as in the judicial arena, the best time to win your case is at the first instance.

Note the exceptions in the final sentence of § 557(b). The three sections, § 554(d), § 556(b) and § 557(b), operate together to insure that in most cases the presiding official will be an ALJ. A different result is authorized, however, "in [formal] rulemaking or in determining application for initial licenses" — in which case any "responsible employee" may preside and recommend a decision. As we have seen, the APA permits somewhat more relaxed procedures for these two categories of proceedings where the issues may be general, statistical, and technical. And in rulemaking and initial licensing even these relaxed procedures can be dispensed with if "timely execution" of agency business "imperatively and unavoidably so requires."

(c) Before a recommended, initial, or tentative decision, or a decision on agency review of the decision of subordinate employees, the parties are entitled to a reasonable opportunity to submit for the consideration of the employees participating in the decisions—

(1) proposed findings and conclusions; or
(2) exceptions to the decisions or recommended decisions of subordinate employees or to tentative agency decisions; and

(3) supporting reasons for the exceptions or proposed findings or conclusions.

Comment: These provisions spell out the usual understandings we would find in a typical judicial trial—parties will be able to submit proposals both as to facts (findings), applicable law (conclusions), and objections to agency rulings (exceptions)—all with the opportunity of supplying supporting reasons. This last requirement can include the opportunity to submit written briefs and oral argument if necessary. The timing and manner of making these submittals will be covered by agency rule.

(c) ... The record shall show the ruling on each finding, conclusion, or exception presented. All decisions, including initial, recommended, and tentative decisions, are a part of the record and shall include a statement of—

(A) findings and conclusions, and the reasons or basis therefor, on all the material issues of fact, law, or discretion presented on the record; and
(B) the appropriate rule, order, sanction, relief, or denial thereof.

Comment: This language insures that the initial ALJ decisions respond to the parties' proposals and address their arguments. It also assures that the agency (or judicial) reviewers will know with some clarity what the decision is based upon. When we reach the chapter on judicial review below, we will see that reviewing courts today have emphasized the importance of clear agency explanations.

The Attorney General's Manual says agencies can issue decisions in "narrative or expository form" (i.e., without separate sections for each finding and conclusion), but that a reviewing body must be able to find responses to each finding and conclusion sufficient to allow an assessment of the record and legal basis for the decision. ATTORNEY GENERAL'S MANUAL ON THE ADMINISTRATIVE PROCEDURE ACT 86 (1947).

(d)(1) In any agency proceeding which is subject to subsection (a) of this section, except to the extent required for the disposition of ex parte matters as authorized by law—

(A) no interested person outside the agency shall make or knowingly cause to be made to any member of the body comprising the agency, administrative law judge, or other employee who is or may reasonably be expected to be involved in the decisional process of the proceeding, an ex parte communication relevant to the merits of the proceeding;

(B) no member of the body comprising the agency, administrative law judge, or other employee who is or may reasonably be expected to be involved in the decisional process of the proceeding, shall make or knowingly cause to be made to any interested person outside the agency an ex parte communication relevant to the merits of the proceeding;

Comment: Section 557(d) is one of the very few major additions to the APA since its adoption in 1946. Added in 1976, it was passed after some dramatic instances of ex parte contact. Congress clearly felt that the already existing prohibition of ex parte contacts in § 554(d) needed to be strengthened or emphasized.

To what kinds of proceedings does § 557(d) apply? Its opening sentence makes clear that — like § 554(d) — these prohibitions apply only to formal proceedings. Neither section applies to informal adjudications, nor to informal rulemaking. This means, again, that there are *no* APA limits on ex parte contacts in informal rulemaking and informal adjudication. Any limits that exist will have to be found in another statute or rule. As we noted in Chapter 2, there have been occasional due process limits applied to ex parte communications in informal proceedings where those proceedings involved "conflicting private claims to a valuable privilege." Sangamon Valley v. U.S., 269 F.2d 221 (D.C. Cir. 1959). That development, after the Court's restrictions on judicial creativity in adding procedures, seems unlikely to grow. See Yankee Nuclear Power Corp. v. NRDC, 435 U.S. 519 (1978).

Recall that § 554(d) prohibits an ALJ from consulting ex parte "a person or a party" on a "fact in issue." What does § 557(d) add? It is narrower in one sense — § 557(d) only prohibits contacts from *outside* the agency. On the other hand, § 557(d) is broader in that it prohibits all communications "relevant to the merits." not just communications about "facts in dispute" which are prohibited by § 554(d). Thus, discussions of policy, law, or discretion are prohibited by § 557(d). Section 557(d) is also broader in that it explicitly reaches communications with the heads of the agency who, as we have seen, are excepted from the § 554(d) prohibitions.

The § 557(d) prohibition only reaches communications to or from "interested persons." That phrase has been very broadly interpreted by the courts to extend well beyond parties to the case and to include anyone who has more of an interest in the proceeding than a general member of the public. The phrase also covers public officials such as members of Congress or the White House. Prof'l Air Traffic Controllers Org. v. FLRA, 685 F.2d 547 (D.C. Cir. 1982). Do note, however that the definition of "ex parte communication" in § 551(14) does not include "status reports." So the section does not end the practice by which members of Congress or of the executive branch can signal their views on a pending case by the manner in which they inquire into its status.

> (d)(1).....(C) a member of the body comprising the agency, administrative law judge, or other employee who is or may reasonably be expected to be involved in the decisional process of such proceeding who receives, or who makes or knowingly causes to be made, a communication prohibited by this subsection shall place on the public record of the proceeding:
>
> (i) all such written communications;
> (ii) memoranda stating the substance of all such oral communications; and
> (iii) all written responses, and memoranda stating the substance of all oral responses, to the materials described in clauses (i) and (ii) of this subparagraph;
> (D) upon receipt of a communication knowingly made or knowingly caused to be made by a party in violation of this subsection, the agency, administrative law judge, or other employee presiding at the hearing may, to the extent consistent with the interests of justice and the policy of the underlying statutes, require the party to show cause why his claim or interest in the proceeding should not be dismissed, denied, disregarded, or otherwise adversely affected on account of such violation; and
> (E) the prohibitions of this subsection shall apply beginning at such time as the agency may designate, but in no case shall they begin to apply later than the time at which a proceeding is noticed for hearing unless the person responsible for the communication has knowledge that it will be noticed, in which case the

prohibitions shall apply beginning at the time of his acquisition of such knowledge.

Comment: These provisions provide what can be provided in the form of sanctions for violations of the section. As we have noted earlier, this is a difficult matter to legislate. As a practical matter, we cannot order the agency recipient of an unlawful ex parte communication simply to disregard it. Whether a jury under judicial instruction could disregard an improper question is doubtful enough — it is much less likely that an official serving at the pleasure of the president could be asked to "forget" a phone call from the president.

And ruling against a party on whose behalf the communication was made — authorized by the language quoted above — may not be realistic if the public interest would suffer. That leaves disclosure and the opportunity to rebut the only practical ways in which the damage from an improper communication can be minimized.

(2) This subsection does not constitute authority to withhold information from Congress.

Comment: This part of § 557(d) assures that agencies cannot use the section to refuse congressional requests for information, a protection Congress frequently includes in such statutes.

APA § 558

Imposition of Sanctions; determination of applications for licenses; suspension, revocation, and expiration of licensing.

(a) This section applies, according to the provisions thereof, to the exercise of a power or authority.

(b) A sanction may not be imposed or a substantive rule or order issued except within jurisdiction delegated to the agency and as authorized by law.

(c) When application is made for a license required by law, the agency, with due regard for the rights and privileges of all the interested parties or adversely affected persons and within a reasonable time, shall set and complete proceedings required to be conducted in accordance with sections 556 and 557 of this title or other proceedings required by law and shall make its decision.

Comment: Subsection (c) tells license applicants that the licensing agency must set any hearings on the application and decide the matter within a reasonable time. This requirement would apply whether the hearing on the license was to be formal (i.e., one required to be "on the record") or informal.

(c).... Except in cases of willfulness or those in which public health, interest, or safety requires otherwise, the withdrawal, suspension, revocation, or annulment of a license is lawful only if, before the institution of agency proceedings therefor, the licensee has been given—

(1) notice by the agency in writing of the facts or conduct which may warrant the action; and
(2) opportunity to demonstrate or achieve compliance with all lawful requirements.

Comment: An existing license cannot be terminated in any of the ways listed without giving the licensee a "second chance"—an opportunity to know the grounds on which termination is proposed and an opportunity to correct the shortfall. The notice given must be specific enough to allow the licensee to make the necessary corrections.

Note that the list of terminations does not include expiration. When a license expires according to its own terms, this section gives the licensee no special protections.

Note also the exceptions in the beginning sentence. If the agency can show that the licensee's behavior was willful (shown, e.g., by repeated violations or conduct beyond mere negligence) it need not provide notice and a second chance. The exception for "public health, interest, or safety" requires that the agency show something of an emergency or unusual situation. As Professor Asimow says, "an agency cannot dispense with notice merely because it deems that the 'public interest' requires revocation ... since that would obviously be true in every case" of license termination. American Bar Association, A GUIDE TO FEDERAL AGENCY ADJUDICATION 159 (Asimow Ed. 2003).

(c).... When the licensee has made timely and sufficient application for a renewal or a new license in accordance with agency rules, a license with reference to an activity of a continuing nature does not expire until the application has been finally determined by the agency.

Comment: An obvious rule of fairness. The agency cannot defeat a license by simply delaying action on a renewal request until the original license expires. Note, however, that the renewal application must be both timely and sufficient.

E. Informal Adjudication

At the federal level, about 90% of proceedings fitting the APA definition of adjudication are informal—i.e., are conducted under statutes which do not require a hearing "on the record" and which, accordingly, are not required to comply with the adjudicative procedures outlined in §§ 556–557. What procedural protections are available to persons involved in such proceedings? As we have seen, there are some limited requirements in § 555 and § 558 of the APA. See American Bar Assoc., A GUIDE TO FEDERAL AGENCY ADJUDICATION Chap. 9 (Asimow Ed. 2003). And, of course, there are the requirements of due process which we will examine in Chapter 4. Beyond that, there are only an agency's own procedural regulations and these are surely affected by the agency's own preference to be free of APA-type formalities, especially those that limit the agency's selection of and control over the officials who preside at such hearings.

Why are there no APA provisions governing 90% of agency adjudications? One answer is that if Congress did not want the process to be formal (hence did not require that it be "on the record") any APA-required formality would frustrate that intent. Further, it could be said that parties in informal hearings are adequately protected by the due process clause, which assures basic fairness. And there is the frequently heard argument in benefits cases that providing more formal process to the private parties involved is not helpful as the parties typically are not as able to use formal process as easily as lawyer-represented parties in other regulatory settings. Further, in these cases the government usually appears in support of the claimant rather than as an adversary. In such conditions, procedural formalities are less necessary and, by creating an adversarial atmosphere, may even be harmful.

Those are plausible but not very convincing answers. While due process is alive and well in administrative law—as we'll see in Chapter 4—due process formalities may be of limited use for the typically unrepresented parties in high-frequency adjudications. Moreover, it may not be feasible for agencies with high volume case loads to give day-to-day operational meaning to uncertain and complex constitutional doctrine. Pierce, Shapiro and Verkuil, AD-MINISTRATIVE LAW AND PROCESS § 6.4.11 (5th ed. 2009).

What is needed is some simple and flexible statutory guidance. Surely some minimal requirements for most adjudications could assure basic fairness without depriving the proceedings of the speed, low cost and informality Congress sought in not requiring record hearings. In one study, over half the informal adjudications conducted by federal agencies already involve notice, a statement of reasons, a neutral decisionmaker and some opportunity for presenting argument. Verkuil, *A Study of Informal Adjudication Procedures*, 43 U. CHI. L. REV. 739 (1976). It would be wise to add some requirements of this sort to the APA to bring the other half of the agencies into the game. Such proposals have been advanced (see Pierce, Shapiro and Verkuil, supra) and an ABA version has been drafted. See Asimow, *The Spreading Umbrella: Extending the APA's Adjudication Provisions to All Evidentiary Hearings Required by Statute*, 56 ADMIN. L. REV. 1003 (2004).

The 1981 Model State Administrative Procedure Act includes some provisions for informal adjudications and a few states have explored the option. Uniform Law Commissioners, 1981 MODEL STATE ADMINISTRATE PROCEDURE ACT § 4-502-505; Revised Code of Washington, 34.05.482-494 (1988). The Model Act sections provide that in an informal proceeding involving a sanction, the presiding official shall "give each party an opportunity to know the agency's view of the matter and to explain the party's view," and "shall give each party a brief statement of policy reasons, findings of fact and conclusions of law to justify the action." It also provides for some limited internal agency review. Model Act § 4-503(b) and § 504.

Checkpoints

- Adjudication is a special form of dispute resolution involving presentations of evidence and argument by parties, with a decision by a neutral decisionmaker.

- The APA formal adjudication procedures (§§ 556–557) apply only if another statute requires them, signaled by a statement that the hearing is to be "on the record."

- The APA uses a mixed model of adjudication in which prosecutors and final decisionmakers are inside agency personnel, while judging is initially done by independent ALJs whose independence is protected by statutory provisions limiting the agency's control over the judge's tenure or salary.

- Decisional officials may be challenged for bias if they exhibit focused antagonism toward parties or pecuniary interest in proceeding. Policy and legal predispositions of officials are not grounds for disqualification.

- Persons compelled to appear before an agency are entitled to be accompanied and advised by counsel.

- Procedural rules and rules of evidence in formal adjudications are modeled on, but more flexible than, similar rules in judicial settings.

- APA entitles parties to an adjudication to appear in person and, if needed, to cross-examine witnesses.

- The transcript and all papers filed are the exclusive record for decision.

- Ex parte communication from both inside and outside the agency are prohibited in some circumstances.

- On appeal from initial decision of the ALJ, the agency seldom needs to defer to ALJ rulings, except perhaps to ALJ findings based on demeanor. In practice, though, considerable deference may be shown to the findings and conclusions of the ALJ.

Chapter 4

Constitutional Requirements for Fair Process

Roadmap

- The Language of Due Process
- The Basic Due Process Questions:
  - Whether due process applies
  - When it applies, what procedures does it require
  - At what time must the procedure be made available
- The Interests Protected — Formal Analysis of Liberty and Property
- Determining the Process Due — Flexible Analysis of Costs and Benefits

---

A. Introduction — Due Process in the Administrative World

In Chapter 1 we considered the federal constitution as a general framework, examined how it allocated duties to (and separated the powers of) various branches of the government. We noted that the administrative process in its present scale was unanticipated by the framers and was thus not treated in this set of assignments. We suggested that modern administrative law is at bottom a series of steps to replace for regulatory agencies some of the protections that were thought to inhere in the division of government into different and separated branches. Now we come to a more specific constitutional discussion, this time focusing on specific constitutional requirements for fair procedure. Procedural due process will be elaborated in your work in constitutional law; what follows here is a brief sketch of its role in the regulatory process.

In its procedural dimension, the due process clause and its interpretive history are long and rich. But at its core is this: beginning with ancient language requiring that government must act according to procedures provided by existing law, due process has modulated into a more demanding requirement that the procedures required by law themselves be consistent with a gradually unfolding perception of what is fair procedure—a perception that is defined ultimately by the courts. Read that again and let it simmer a bit.

The governmental and jurisprudential implications of this development are enormous and have been the subject of rich discussion. For our purposes we need a feel for how courts have defined fairness in the context of the administrative process. More particularly, we need a sense of how courts have responded to increasing claims for increased procedural protections in the presence of serious problems of cost and inappropriate interference with the management or mission of the agencies.

We should start with the constitutional text itself. Referring to federal officials, the Fifth Amendment says that a person cannot be "deprived of life, liberty, or property, without due process of law ..." The 14th Amendment imposes the same limits on state officials. In the administrative law context, what is the meaning of this magisterial and cosmically broad phrase "due process"? Here are a couple of preliminary points to help keep you on track:

- Leave for popular essays the incorrect notion that due process is some kind of a shield—something that prevents the government from depriving one of life, liberty, or property. The fact is government must be able to impose such deprivations if it is to protect us from unfit airline pilots, unqualified welfare recipients, incompetent government employees, and the like. For the lawyer, it is more helpful to consider procedural due process as a path the government must follow in imposing deprivations it is authorized to impose.

- Try to think of procedural due process doctrine as basically practical. That is, while the concept is based on an elegant principle—governmental process that results in serious deprivations should be (and should seem to be) fundamentally fair—due process ultimately seeks practical solutions. Find a practical way to provide process that seems fair and you're half-way home.

- Treat due process as a last resort doctrine. Resist the temptation to jump immediately to this rhetorical high ground, no matter what personal satisfaction it generates. The fact is—and your client is entitled to the benefit of this—that much cheaper, simpler and quicker solutions may be found in statutes or agency regulations or through negotiation with agency staff. Commit to memory the couplet in Figure 4.1.

- Due process law has been almost entirely framed by lawyers and judges, so expect that the kinds of procedures that will be considered and some-

'For proud Due Process speaks in thun'drous voice
Should first we seek, perhaps, some plainer choice?

Figure 4.1   A Useful Reminder in Iambic Pentameter

times required are those associated with judicial proceedings. It is not that the methods of trial are always better or fairer than other methods for resolving disputes—they are not, and the careful analyst never forgets this. But those steeped in the judicial tradition have been the principal architects of due process jurisprudence and, as Figure 4.2 shows, the lineage is unmistakable.

• Finally, remember that radiations from the consensus about fair procedures developed in due process analysis impact many other choices of agency procedure and many judicial interpretations of agency procedural statutes. A developed sense for due process is thus a generally useful skill in the administrative legal world.

The basic questions we'll want to answer are diagramed in Figure 4.3. Spend a few minutes studying this map. It should help keep you oriented as we proceed. The diagram suggests that we need to examine the *issues* and the *interests* relevant to due process and the *cost* and *benefits* associated with its requirements.

B. What Issues Are Appropriate
for Due Process Methods?

If due process is going to require procedures of the kind we associate with trials, it is fair to ask about the kinds of issues trial procedures deal with effectively. The methods of trial in their classic form—examination, confrontation, cross-

---

due process might require some or all of these elements:

1. notice
2. opportunity to be present
3. opportunity to speak
4. opportunity to confront and cross examine
5. opportunity to submit rebuttal evidence
6. representation by counsel
7. an impartial hearing tribunal
8. a reasoned opinion
9. a decision based exclusively on the record
10. judicial review

this kind of hearing goes by a variety of labels including:

--evidentiary hearing
--due process hearing
--adversary hearing
--formal hearing
--on the record hearing
--trial hearing
--adjudicative proceeding, contested case (state)
--'fair hearing' (public assistance term)

Figure 4.2   The Language of Due Process

examination, rebuttal, etc.—would seem to be most useful in administrative settings where the legitimacy of a deprivation turns on disputed issues of fact concerning the individual being subjected to the deprivation. As we have seen, these kinds of facts are called by some scholars "adjudicative facts." 3 Pierce, ADMINISTRATIVE LAW TREATISE § 9.2 (4th ed. 2002). Thus, if the validity of a deprivation—say a license revocation—turns on conclusions about the person's own qualifications for the license, it would seem useful to give the affected individual notice of the action, a statement of the reasons it is being taken, and the opportunity to explain or rebut the factual assertions supporting the agency action. These methods can help assure the accuracy of factfinding and the neutrality of law-applying. In the bargain, they treat the individual not as a helpless victim of government power but as an individual whose dignity warrants an appropriate opportunity to participate in government decisions that specially affect him.

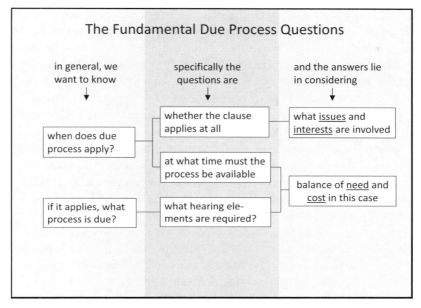

Figure 4.3   A Map of Procedural Due Process

This is not new to our discussions. In Chapter 2, we discussed the *BiMetallic* and *Londoner* cases. In BiMetallic Inv. Co. v. Colorado, 239 U.S. 441 (1915), the Supreme Court held that due process did not require any form of hearing before a judgment was made that the general tax rates in Denver were to be raised by 40%. The reason for the rate change was general (systematic under-assessment of all Denver property by local tax assessors), owed little to the shape, use, or value of any particular parcels of Denver real property. Resolving the dispute about the state's legal authority to impose such a measure could be resolved by legislative hearings, written submissions, etc. Providing individual property owners with the opportunity to examine and cross-examine assessors would add nothing but cost and delay and could, in the bargain, create inconsistency.

By contrast, in Londoner v. Denver, 210 U.S. 373 (1908), the Court said some elements of a trial hearing were required by due process before the city could levy a special assessment on Mr. Londoner's property. The amount of the assessment was special to Mr. Londoner—may have been affected by the value, shape, and use of Mr. Londoner's particular lot. Both accuracy and acceptability would be enhanced if Mr. Londoner were able to appear and discuss these particulars with the deciding body.

There is not always a bright line dividing issues of adjudicative fact from other issues (as we'll see in *Mathews v. Eldridge,* discussed below) but it is a distinction worth applying when it fits. Limiting due process protections to cases of disputed adjudicative fact reflects the wisdom that courts should not impose expensive and cumbersome procedures on government action unless those procedures generate plausible benefits in accuracy or perceptions of fairness.

Of course, this view of due process offers little solace to the citizen deprived by the government of something valuable where the deprivation turns on general facts and not on facts special to that individual. Revoking or refusing to renew a taxi license because of a judgment that there are too many taxis in town does not under this analysis offer any due process protections. While the impact on affected drivers may still be catastrophic—and while the issue about the correct number of taxis in town may be hotly disputed—most would agree that concerns about accuracy and perceptions of fairness would be largely met by public meetings and written submissions rather than the considerably more expensive individualized and personal hearings called for by due process.

Finally, note that due process doctrine should never require trial methods to resolve disputed issues of adjudicative fact where better methods are available. As we saw in some of the exclusions from APA formal hearing requirements (APA §554 discussed in Chapter 3), factual disputes that can more accurately and cheaply be resolved by tests or measurements should not be encumbered with more formal methods. Measurements and tests are not, of course, perfect, but most would agree that for some kinds of factual disputes they are superior to the use of trial methods; in such cases, due process should not require more.

C. What Interests are Protected by Due Process?

Assume, then, that we have identified an *issue* that is appropriate for due process resolution; the next question is whether the *interest* affected is of sufficient importance to warrant due process protection. There are many types of interests that the government may be in a position to restrict, limit or terminate and in many cases the impact on individuals may be serious. One might think, e.g., of businesses depending on government licenses, manufacturers doing business with government agencies, those on public assistance programs, government employees, public school students, those purchasing direct government services such as utilities, etc.

Within that range of government operations, one might suppose that any serious governmental deprivation would warrant due process protections. This view is attractive to many. After all, if a governmental deprivation is grievous and if it turns on disputed facts about the individual citizen, shouldn't that citizen have an opportunity to participate meaningfully in the determination? Wouldn't that promote both accuracy and acceptability? If the *magnitude* of the loss is severe in this sense, why should the *nature* of the interest matter? Some thoughtful commentators have felt that the phrase "life, liberty or property" should be regarded as an aggregate general reference to the conditions of life in a political community, not as an exclusive list of specific interests that alone are to be protected. Pierce, Shapiro and Verkuil, ADMINISTRATIVE LAW AND PROCESS 241–43 (5th ed. 2009). On a broad reading of that kind, *any* serious loss to a citizen caused by governmental action would trigger the protections of the clause. As we will see, that view prevailed for a short time in the early 1970s, but has given way to a much narrower reading since then. Two explanations have been given for this narrowing.

1. As a matter of doctrine, it is said that the claimant's interest must fit the constitutional text more precisely — i.e., the interest must be within the constitutionally enumerated classes for which due process is guaranteed: they must be either property or liberty interests. Current doctrine is a development of this notion.

2. At the practical level, it turns out that due process is not free; it is usually not even cheap. There are the costs of providing the proceeding itself, which can be considerable in agencies with many thousands of disputes to resolve. And if deprivation cannot be imposed until after the hearing (the usual case, discussed below) there is also the cost of providing benefits or services to allegedly unqualified claimants, while the hearing to establish disqualification continues. Finally, there is the cost associated with the intrusion of formal process into the day to day operations of the acting government unit — an especially high cost in the case of government institutions that have special relationships with their clientele such as hospitals, prisons, and public schools.

Let's see what luck the courts have had in defining property and liberty interests.

1. Property Interests

It was once said that a citizen did not have a property interest in something unless he had a "right" to it. As a result, the deprivation of something to which the citizen had a right would be a deprivation of a property interest and would come within the constitutional protection. On the other hand, deprivation of something the citizen was merely privileged to enjoy was not protected — the deprivation could take place without any constitutionally required procedure. This historic right/privilege doctrine was criticized both because it was too restrictive and because it often served as a screen for judgments of relative social status—a pool hall license was only a privilege while a doctor's license was a right.

In 1970, the Court explicitly abandoned the right/privilege doctrine. In Goldberg v. Kelly, 397 U.S. 254 (1970), a welfare recipient's benefits had been terminated without a prior hearing, and the Court held this a violation of due process. The Court said that Mr. Kelly's interest in welfare payments was "important" and the loss he suffered from its termination was "grievous." 397 U.S. at 263. Because Kelly's interest had these qualities, the Court said his interest was "more like property" and as such within the constitutional text.

Replacing the restrictive right/privilege with a generous "grievous loss" test threatened a virtual explosion of due process cases, with attendant costs and complications. Within two years the Court moved to head off such a development by sharply narrowing the class of interests protected. In Board of Regents v. Roth, 408 U.S. 564 (1972), the Court rejected a due process claim of an untenured college instructor whose annual contract had not been renewed and who had been given no hearing on the question. Surely, this was a "grievous" loss in the Goldberg sense. But the Court said:

> To have a property interest in a benefit, a person clearly must have more than an abstract need or desire for it. He must have more than a unilateral expectation of it. He must, instead, have a legitimate claim of entitlement to it. It is a purpose of the ancient institution of property to protect those claims upon which people rely in their daily lives, reliance that must not be arbitrarily undermined. It is a purpose of the constitutional right to a hearing to provide an opportunity for a person to vindicate those claims. 408 U.S. at 577.

The new phrase here is "legitimate claim of entitlement." To have a constitutionally protected property interest in a government benefit, service or position, one must have a "legitimate claim of entitlement" to it. One's initial reaction might be that "legitimate claim of entitlement" is just a longer way of saying "right," with the Court in Roth simply returning to the discredited right/privilege doctrine. Some critics felt that way, but in context, and as explained by the Court, entitlement analysis still protects a broader range of interests than had been protected by the classic right/privilege test.

> 'Liberty' and 'property' are broad and majestic terms.... They relate to the whole domain of social and economic fact.... For that reason, the Court has fully and finally rejected the wooden distinction be-

tween 'rights' and 'privileges' that once seemed to govern the applicability of procedural due process rights.... [P]roperty interests protected by procedural due process extend well beyond actual ownership of real estate, chattels, or money.... Yet, while the Court has eschewed rigid or formalistic limitations on the protection of procedural due process, it has at the same time observed certain boundaries. For the words 'liberty' and 'property' in the Due Process Clause of the Fourteenth Amendment must be given some meaning. 408 U.S. at 571–72.

Where does one look to see if a claimant has a legitimate claim of entitlement? Importantly, the Court said the constitution was not the source of these entitlements. Instead, entitlements

are created and their dimensions are defined by existing rules or understandings that stem from an independent source such as state law—rules or understandings that secure certain benefits and that support claims of entitlement to those benefits. 408 U.S. at 577.

Roth did not overrule *Goldberg*, but explained that in *Goldberg*, Mr. Kelly met the *Roth* test. That is, Kelly had a "legitimate claim of entitlement" to his welfare payments—an entitlement grounded in the statute defining his eligibility. While there was no entitlement to have a welfare program in the first place, once such a program was in place and once Mr. Kelly had qualified for payments under statutory criteria, he had an entitlement to those payments that would be treated as property for due process purposes. Professor Roth, by contrast, had only a year-by-year contract, and no university rules or expectations promised anything about renewal. Assuming they were not violating any other constitutional requirements (e.g., First Amendment guarantees), college authorities had complete discretion to renew or not to renew Roth's contract. Roth, then, had only a unilateral expectation or hope for renewal. The complete discretion over renewal that the college officials had was simply inconsistent with any notion of "entitlement." With no entitlement to renewal of his contract, Roth's interest did not rise to the level of a property interest within the meaning of the 14th Amendment.

The required legitimate claim of entitlement does not always require a specific statutory guarantee or a formally signed contract. In Perry v. Sinderman, 408 U.S. 593 (1972), a case considered at the same time as *Roth*, the Court refused to grant summary judgment to a college sued by an untenured professor whose contract (like Roth's) had not been renewed. In his complaint, Professor Sinderman had alleged that he and others reasonably relied on statements in the college's Faculty Guide that implied the presence of a de facto tenure system. The presence of these rules and understandings limited the discretion of the college in nonrenewal and could have created an entitlement in Sinderman's favor. The Court held that a legitimate claim of entitlement might arise from such "rules or mutually explicit understandings that support [the] claim of entitlement." 408 U.S. at 601; hence, Sinderman should have been allowed to prove the existence of such understandings—summary judgment for the college was thus error. The Court was very clear that finding such an entitlement would not grant Sinderman reinstatement; but it would obligate college officials to provide him due process—presumably some kind of hearing at which he could be informed of the grounds for the nonrenewal and through which he could challenge their sufficiency. 408 U.S. at 603.

Current entitlement analysis seems to focus, then, on the degree of discretion public officials have over the continuation of a benefit. As shown in Figure 4.4, where that discretion is great, the due process claim is less likely to succeed.

The presence or absence of discretion is not always easy to calculate. In Castle Rock v. Gonzales, 545 U.S. 748 (2005) the Court was faced with a statute the text and history of which seemed to express an intent that restraining orders in domestic abuse cases be promptly enforced—that officers with such orders had no discretion to disregard them or to delay their enforcement. In this

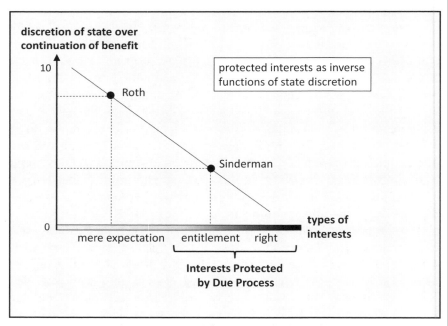

Figure 4.4   Entitlement and Discretion

case, such a disregard or delay resulted in the tragic murder of plaintiff's three children. Plaintiff filed an action under 42 U.S.C.1983, claiming a violation of procedural due process under the 14th Amendment. The argument was essentially that a statute that denies an official any discretion in carrying out an order (i.e., that compels enforcement of the order) confers an entitlement on plaintiff in the same sense that the rules and understandings limiting the college's discretion in *Perry* created an entitlement in Professor Sinderman. The § 1983 action was for damages for failure of the officers to provide the police conduct to which plaintiff was entitled.

In a divided opinion, the Court ruled there was no entitlement here. The Court said that even if the statute did not explicitly confer discretion — indeed, even if it denied discretion — there was a well established tradition of police discretion in enforcement settings. This discretion meant — under the *Roth/Perry* analysis — that plaintiff had no entitlement to prompt enforcement, thus no property right to which due process could attach and thus no constitutional violation that could ground an action under § 1983.

Of course, *Castle Rock* was not quite the same case as *Roth*. In *Castle Rock*, plaintiff alleged damage as a result of official failure to act (promptly enforcing the restraining order). In *Roth*, strictly read, plaintiff was not complaining about the failure to renew his contract but about the absence of an adequate hearing before the decision on renewal was made. But *Castle Rock*, in finding "inherent" discretion in some governmental functions, narrows the reach of protectable entitlements still further.

Entitlement analysis has been widely criticized and one thread of that criticism is that it seems to give the legislature practical control over the meaning of the due process clause. In theory, a legislature could render the clause meaningless with respect to any given benefit by the simple expedient of granting public officials complete discretion over the continuation of the benefit. Yet surely the goals of accuracy and acceptability in government decisions about individuals remain even where discretion must be substantial, perhaps especially so in such cases. You might be interested in knowing that Congress has passed some statutes seeming to give unlimited discretion to agencies. See, e.g., the 1997 welfare reform statutes which state that "this part shall not be interpreted to entitle any individual or family to assistance under any State program funded under this part." 42 U.S.C. § 601 (1997). It remains to be seen how the Court will react to such efforts to expand agency discretion — and thus to further limit the reach of due process.

Finally, it is worth noting that even where courts agree that some process is due before an *existing benefit is terminated*, there has been no really satisfactory answer to the question of whether any process is due before an *appli-*

cation for a benefit is denied. On its face, entitlement analysis makes an applicant's case difficult, since there would appear to be nothing at the application stage to which the applicant is entitled, only the possibility that if the applicant's qualifications can be shown, an entitlement may be conferred in the future. Still, there is no persuasive reason why our goals of accuracy and acceptability should not be sought in application cases as well as in revocation cases; very similar issues about the applicant's qualifications might have to be resolved before either determination is made, suggesting the value of some kind of hearing. Perhaps this logic has not gained purchase because of the relatively larger number of denials than revocations, or the courts' tendency over the years to be "more solicitous of established relationships than expectations." Strauss, ADMINISTRATIVE JUSTICE IN THE UNITED STATES 59 (2d ed. 2002).

The Supreme Court has not ruled on the general question and the lower courts have struggled with it with conflicting results, though even courts that do not accept the application/revocation distinction nevertheless impose more exacting standards for creating an entitlement in the context of applicants. Shapiro and Levy, *Government Benefits and the Rule of Law: Towards a Standards-Based Theory of Due Process*, 57 ADMIN. L. REV. 107, 116 (2005). In a particularly well-reasoned opinion, the Second Circuit has said that the result should turn on the amount of discretion the agency has in considering the application. If statutory standards are relatively objective, the applicant's interest in procedural protections is greater. The court said:

> [W]e have explained that whether a benefit invests the applicant with a 'claim of entitlement' or merely a 'unilateral expectation' is determined by the amount of discretion the disbursing agency retains.... Statutory language may so specifically mandate benefits awards upon demonstration of certain qualifications that an applicant must fairly be recognized to have a limited property interest entitling him, at least, to process sufficient to permit a demonstration of eligibility. Kapps v. Wing, 404 F.3d 105, 115–16 (2d. Cir. 2005) (opinion by Calabresi, J).

Note that this analysis doesn't necessarily guarantee an applicant a full scale hearing, only "process sufficient" to demonstrate eligibility.

The uncertainty will continue until the Supreme Courts ends it. In the meantime, plaintiffs who believe an application has been arbitrarily denied might explore any internal or external appeal processes that are available and, failing that, might consider constitutional options other than entitlement analysis. Vance, *Applications for Benefits: Due Process, Equal Protection, and the Right to Be Free From Arbitrary Procedures*, 61 WASH. & LEE L. REV. 883 (2004).

2. Liberty Interests

The *Roth* Court's definition of liberty was stated in broad terms — due process protects an individual's right to "enjoy those privileges long recognized as essential to the orderly pursuit of happiness by free men." 408 U.S. at 572. But the Court applied the concept very narrowly in the case. The Court said that in the case of nonrenewal of a public employment contract one's liberty interests are threatened only if the manner of nonrenewal imposed a stigma on Professor Roth that threatened his reputation or his opportunity to be employed elsewhere. The Court found no stigma in a seemingly neutral failure to renew an annual contract.

Later cases have not clarified the concept of liberty, and some of them are very hard to reconcile. Early, *Goldberg*-era cases seemed generous, but later cases have moved in the opposite direction. The opinions are in disarray, the Court is divided and the resulting doctrine is not helpful. One needs only to compare two similar cases with opposite results to get a sense of the doctrine's difficulty. In Wisconsin v. Constantineau, 400 U.S. 433 (1971), the Court held that reputational harm caused by public posting of a claim that plaintiff was a habitual drunkard *did* infringe a protected liberty interest. By contrast, in Paul v. Davis, 424 U.S. 693 (1976), the Court held that public distribution of plaintiff's name as an active shoplifter did *not* infringe a liberty interest. One thread to remember: the Court has shown concern about thousands of cases a year from prisoners claiming protected liberty interests in relatively minor deprivations. In Sandin v. Connor, 515 U.S. 472 (1995), the Court sought to limit that development by imposing a filter to eliminate less important deprivations. The Court said that a liberty interest was not infringed within the meaning of the due process clause unless the deprivation was "atypical" or "substantial."

In your constitutional law courses you can trace these developments further. For our purposes the bottom line is this: if a due process claim is being based on invasion of a liberty interest, a plaintiff must show a deprivation that is really unusual or substantial, or one that imposes a reputational harm beyond embarrassment and that plausibly affects one's employment prospects.

3. A Concluding Note on Interests Protected by Due Process

In trying to identify the interests due process protects, remember that there is one class of interests that is usually protected — one's interest in exercising other constitutional rights. The so-called doctrine of unconstitutional conditions is developed further in courses on constitutional law, but it was reflected in *Perry v. Sinderman*, supra, as an additional ground of decision. In the district court, Professor Sinderman had claimed his nonrenewal was in part because of speeches he had given that were critical of the Odessa Junior College's Board of Regents. The Court said:

> For at least a quarter-century, this Court has made clear that even though a person has no 'right' to a valuable governmental benefit and even though the government may deny him the benefit for any number of reasons, there are some reasons upon which the government may not rely. It may not deny a benefit to a person on a basis that infringes his constitutionally protected interests — especially, his interest in freedom of speech. For if the government could deny a benefit to a person because of his constitutionally protected speech or associations, his exercise of those freedoms would in effect be penalized and inhibited. This would allow the government [indirectly] to 'produce a result which (it) could not command directly. 408 U.S. at 597.

So while Odessa Junior College may have had otherwise complete discretion as to the renewal of Professor Sinderman's contract, it couldn't fail to renew because he had exercised his rights under the First Amendment. (Professor Roth had also claimed that his nonrenewal was punishment for protected speech, but the Court found inadequate support for the claim. 408 U.S. at 546 n.14.)

Notice the relationship between due process and the doctrine of unconstitutional conditions. Without the kind of hearing or statement of reasons that might be required by due process, it might be impossible for a plaintiff to discover the real motivation behind the agency action. It appears that a plausible claim that the deprivation was intended to infringe other constitutional rights might get a plaintiff a hearing to explore the foundation for such a claim, but a court might not call it a due process hearing. See Monaghan, *First Amendment Due Process*, 83 HARV. L. REV. 518 (1970).

On the whole, the Court's current opinions on what kinds of interests are subject to due process protection are not always clear and are usually sharply divided. At some level, the individual Justice's own views about the importance of a particular interest can affect a vote. As unfortunate as this is from the standpoint of a fully principled doctrine, it may be inevitable so long as the accepted doctrine requires that interests be subsumed within vague terms like liberty and property. The difficulty would be greatly diminished if the Court were to adopt the pre-*Roth* view mentioned above — that all interests threatened with serious or grievous losses should trigger the clause's protections. Questions of scope and magnitude could then be addressed in deciding what process was due, a very flexible set of doctrines to which we now turn.

D. What Process Is Due?

Assume now that we have the correct *issues* and the correct *interests* and that due process therefore attaches to the case. The two questions that remain are (1) what process is due and (2) at what time (i.e., before or after the deprivation) must it be made available? The essential doctrine here is easy to state, but since it inevitably requires a case by case appraisal is devilishly hard to predict. Still, the doctrine seems to focus analysis on correct factors so that it may be ultimately helpful as doctrine.

In deciding exactly what process is required by due process, it is useful to remember that we are dealing here with a flexible list of procedures. Don't think that if due process applies you will be entitled to a set list of procedures such as those identified in Figure 4.2 above. We have said that procedural due process is a matter of practical accommodation, and this is nowhere more true than when considering which procedures will be required in a given case. There will be cases where only a relatively full formal process will be required, with full opportunities to rebut, to cross-examine, and to have an impartial decisionmaker. There will be other cases where all that is required is the ability to explain briefly one's own side of the dispute. Goss v. Lopez, 419 U.S. 565 (1975). Flexibility and appropriateness are the keys.

In deciding where on this continuum of formality a given case lies, the beginning point for the past three decades has been the Court's opinion in Mathews v. Eldridge, 424 U.S. 319 (1976). In this case, Mr. Eldridge's social security disability benefits had been terminated because of an agency judgment that his disability had ended. The agency had sent him a questionnaire and on the strength of that, and written reports from other doctors (including his own), the agency advised him of a tentative determination of ineligibility, invited him to supplement the record. That invitation not being accepted, the agency terminated Eldridge's disability payments. The process in place provided for a full evidentiary hearing *after* termination, with any sums improperly withheld to be paid retroactively. Eldridge did not seek such a hearing but filed an action challenging the constitutionality of the process in that it did not provide him a hearing *before* the benefits were terminated. So the narrow question was not *whether* due process applied (it did, as the issues were clearly adjudicative and the interests qualified under *Roth*) or *what* procedures were due (as the full evidential hearing Eldridge would get would more than satisfy any due process requirement) but *when* those procedures had to be made available (before or after the termination of the benefits). Both the district court and the court of appeals, relying on *Goldberg*, held that a pre-deprivation trial hearing was required. The Supreme Court reversed.

In addressing the timing question, the Court set out a broad three-factor test that has been used ever since to determine both the procedures that are required and the time at which they must be provided. Look again at the list of possible procedures in Figure 4.2 above. The task of the courts is to pick out those that should be required in light of the three *Mathews* factors. Here is the Court's description of the factors:

> [O]ur prior decisions indicate that identification of the specific dictates of due process generally requires consideration of three distinct factors: First, the private interest that will be affected by the official action; second, the risk of an erroneous deprivation of such interest through the procedures used, and the probable value, if any, of additional or substitute procedural safeguards; and finally, the Government's interest, including the function involved and the fiscal and administrative burdens that the additional or substitute procedural requirement would entail. (424 U.S. at 334–35).

Let's consider the three factors separately.

1. The Private Interest

The first factor to consider is the private interest affected by the deprivation. We saw that in deciding whether due process applied today's Court does *not* look at how grievous was the harm inflicted but only at the nature of the interest affected—grievous or not, the harm must affect a property or liberty interest. By contrast, when the "whether" question is settled and the question becomes "what" process is due, the Court *will* look at the magnitude of the loss a plaintiff in this situation is likely to suffer. It will ask exactly what harm such a person would suffer because of the particular procedural shortfall which is complained of. In *Mathews*, that shortfall was the timing of the hearing, so the question was, what harm would someone in Eldridge's situation suffer from termination of disability benefits before the full hearing that was available. *Goldberg* had held that a pre-deprivation hearing was essential and the district court and the court of appeals applied that rule, only to be reversed by the Supreme Court. The Court said the timing of the termination did not impact those in Eldridge's situation as much as it had the plaintiff in *Goldberg*. Since disability payments were not paid on the basis of need (as was the case of the welfare payments in *Goldberg*) one could not automatically assume termination of disability would cause immediate financial hardship. Actual evidence in the case showed that Eldridge was, in fact, in serious financial need, but the Court said one didn't ask whether *this* plaintiff was impacted but whether disability claimants generally were impacted by the loss of their benefits for a period. The Court concluded that disability beneficiaries were less likely than welfare recipients to suffer from the typical year-long wait for a hearing. So Mr. Eldridge didn't score highly on the first *Mathews* factor.

2. The Risk of Error

The second element of the *Mathews* test is the question of whether the procedures available to Mr. Eldridge were likely to produce unacceptably high rates of error. Stated otherwise, would the additional procedures plaintiff claimed have significantly improved the accuracy of the decision. While *Mathews* was focused on the timing of the hearing not its quality, one might suppose that this factor was less critical. But timing would be implicated if the absence of procedures before the benefits were terminated was manifestly likely to produce high rates of error. In such a case, this factor would suggest the need for continuation of the benefits until the more careful hearing available later was completed. The parties showered the Court with various reversal rates—they ranged, depending on the base used—from 3% to over 50%, but the Court found them not of dispositive value.

More important to the Court was the nature of the issues at dispute and the kinds of evidence on which conclusions would turn. If the issues involved disputed testimony of witnesses, for example, cross-examination might have been useful. The issues here, however, were what the Court characterized as technical medical issues turning on what it called "routine, standard and unbiased medical reports by physician specialists." It has been said that while much of the evidence was "scientific" and most of the medical tests were "routine" and "unbiased," the real issue was disability—a much more complex determination and one for which some cross-examination and some opportunity for rebuttal could have added to the accuracy of the agency determination. But with the Court's characterization of the issues as purely medical, Mr. Eldridge didn't score highly on this factor either. The process was error free enough to make it acceptable to cut off the benefits now and let Mr. Eldridge try to get the result reversed in the later full hearing.

3. The Public Interest

The final element of the *Mathews* test asks about the impact of the case on the public. Here, the Court focused mostly on dollar costs to the government. In high volume settings, these costs can be substantial. To get a sense of the volume involved, consider that as of December 2008, there were 7.4 million disabled workers receiving benefits and that the Social Security Administration gets 2.5 million new applications each year. If an application goes into the hearing stage, delays can be substantial. In 2008, there were 765,000 cases pending at the hearing level and 53,000 cases pending at the internal appellate stage. The average time to receive an award after hearing was 535 days. See http://www.allsup.com/about-us/news-room/resources-for-journalists/general-statistics.aspx.

If relatively highly paid officials need to be employed to preside at such hearings, the costs can be staggering. The Court also noted that formal hearings would be much more numerous if disability payments continued until their completion. Why would any claimant not appeal if it meant their payments would continue for another year and a half ? True, the statute provided that overpayments to beneficiaries could be recouped if the hearing showed that the beneficiary was unqualified, but recoupment did not seem to the Court to be practical with this particular group of claimants. The Court was also concerned about the costs associated with the intrusion of adversary procedures into special settings and special relationships.

4. Concluding Note on Due Process Procedures

The *Mathews* analysis is functional. It focuses the courts' attention on the important questions: how much is at stake for the claimant and how valuable would additional procedures be compared to their costs. Moreover, the test is holistic. That is, courts are to consider not just the three functional factors in isolation but as interdependent parts of the whole.

There has been extensive criticism of how the Court actually applied the three factors in *Mathews*, an early classic being Mashaw, *The Supreme Court's Due Process Calculation for Administrative Adjudication in* Mathews v. Eldridge: *Three Factors in Search of a Theory of Value*, 44 U. CHI. L. REV. 28 (1976). But the *Mathews* formula seems a mature way of proceeding, even conceding its difficulty and its unpredictability. It does two things administrative law doctrine should always do. First, it encourages parties to take their own steps to reduce the incidence of the problem. For example, *Mathews* factor 2 — the "risk of error" factor — provides incentive for agencies to explore internal quality control measures (better training, more effective supervision, etc.) to keep the error rate low. Mashaw, *The Management Side of Due Process: Some Theoretical Notes on the Assurance of Accuracy, Fairness, and Timeliness in the Adjudication of Social Welfare Claims*, 59 CORNELL L. REV. 772 (1974). Not only does a lower error rate reduce appeals and litigation, it is of obvious value in better meeting the agency's mission and in making correct initial decisions about beneficiaries.

Second, the *Mathews* formulation enriches the process of judicial review by insuring briefs and arguments that present the court with functionally rele-

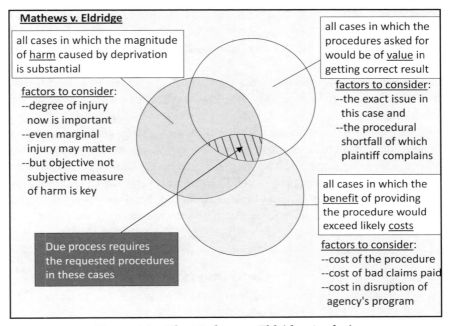

Figure 4.5   The Mathews v. Eldridge Analysis

vant facts and considerations. Think of it this way: if you were a judge having to decide whether a given procedure was appropriate, what would you want briefs and arguments of counsel to inform you about? Chances are the *Mathews* factors—the hardship to the plaintiff and the value and cost of additional procedures—would be central to your analysis.

Figure 4.5 shows a schematic of the *Mathews* analysis.

You might want to compare this kind of functional doctrine with the more formalistic analysis we will now and then see in Chapter 5 (especially in doctrines concerning standing) and Chapter 6 (especially in our discussion of *Chevron*).

E. Concluding Note on Due Process

We have seen that the first issue in a due process case is whether the clause applies at all. Under current doctrine, courts do not resolve this question by asking about the *weight* of the loss to the plaintiff (how grievous is it?) but instead on the *nature* of the plaintiff's interest (is it a property or a liberty interest?). The courts have not been successful or even consistent in defining these interests. But there is an undeniable sense that some limits are needed on due process protections because of the magnitude of the costs that would be incurred if protection were extended to every grievous loss citizens might experience at the hands of the state.

Mathews teaches how flexible due process protections can be — how the level of formality can be adjusted up or down as the issues, the impact, and the costs are considered. As we have suggested above, it would seem that *Mathews* contains within it enough flexibility to deal with any problems of scope or magnitude that might arise from use of the "grievous loss" test to determine whether due process applies. The entire due process calculus would make more sense to this viewer if due process conditioned *all* government action that produced serious deprivation, with the understanding that the nature, extent and timing of any required procedures would be determined by a consideration of the *Mathews* factors.

Checkpoints

- Procedural due process is an ancient doctrine aimed at assuring basic fairness in government action that injures individuals.

- Due process has been nursed and cultivated by lawyers and judges, retains that outlook and that nomenclature.

- The three questions in a due process case are

  (1) does the clause apply at all?

  - The clause applies if the issues in dispute are adjudicatory and

  - The interests of claimant warrant the clause's protection, viz

    - property interests — matters to which the claimant has a legitimate claim of entitlement

    - liberty interests — definition is subject to wide and unpredictable swings, includes harm to reputation serious enough to affect employment prospects

  (2) if it applies, what process is due?

  - what process is due determined by consideration of three *Mathews* factors

    - how seriously are people in claimant's class injured by action?

    - how helpful in avoiding error would additional procedures be?

    - how is the public affected (e.g., by the cost of additional procedures)?

  (3) and at what time must the procedure be made available (before or after the hanging — also determined by the three *Mathews* factors)?

Chapter 5

The Availability of Judicial Review

Roadmap

- Why there are restrictions on the availability of judicial review?
- Whether judicial review is available
- Who is entitled to judicial review?
- When is judicial review available?
- How is judicial review obtained?
- A note on Primary Jurisdiction

A. Introduction: The Whether, Who, When and How of Judicial Review

In Chapter 1, we suggested that much of U.S. administrative law could be understood as a body of workable corrective devices to minimize the harms caused by separation of powers shortfalls. In the next two chapters we will consider judicial review of administrative action — from our special perspective, one of the chief mechanisms through which these correctives are defined and applied. In these chapters, we will see an effort to employ traditional judicial review in a most challenging new setting rife with scientific and technical details and beset with political and policy conflicts. This is not a project easily managed by an institution designed centuries ago to permit a citizen to replevy a cow or determine the owner of Blackacre.

The doctrines we will consider answer questions such as *whether* there should be judicial review of administrative action at all, *when* it should be available, *who* should be able to invoke it, *how* the invoking is done and, finally, *what* the nature of that review should be. These questions require us to examine closely the nature of the administrative process and, equally important, the nature of the U.S. judicial process. This chapter will focus on the whether, when, who and how questions, leaving for the next chapter the ultimate question of what that review should consist of.

Let us begin with a reminder of why judicial review of administrative action is so critical. The answer may not be altogether obvious; after all, if a strict separation of powers is the hallmark of our system, shouldn't we insist that the judicial branch leave the other branches to their constitutionally assigned tasks? Supporting such a view are the obvious facts that the executive and legislative branches have substantial advantages over the judicial branch in efficiency, staff resources, ability to innovate, currency, scientific and technical expertise and, of course — as elected instead of life-appointed officials — accountability. If these considerations have weight, why should we assign to the judicial branch *any* important role in the regulatory process?

Consider the wisdom in this:

> The guarantee of legality by an organ independent of the executive is one of the profoundest, most pervasive premises of our system. Indeed, I would venture to say that it is the very condition which makes possible, which makes so acceptable, the wide freedom of our administrative system ... It is, of course, true that the agencies make positive contributions ... which ... courts could not make. It is also true that the good public servant is devoted to the law ... [and that] the risks of judicial sabotage under the guise of protection are considerable. But ... there is in our society a profound, tradition-taught reliance on the courts as the ultimate guardian and assurance of the limits set upon executive power by the constitutions and legislatures. Jaffe, JUDICIAL CONTROL OF ADMINISTRATIVE ACTION 321–24 (1965).

Legitimacy is a basic premise of our government. The rule of law requires that all exercises of governmental power must be within legal limits; agencies must be kept within the powers assigned to them by the legislature and the executive. And when legislators empower agencies, they themselves must be kept within bounds set by the constitution. It is not that judges are pure of heart while executives and legislators are lawless rogues — after all, executive and legislative officials, just like judges, take and honor an oath to support the nation's constitution and laws. And it is not that there is no other way to assure that government stays within its bounds — other cultures have devised perfectly satisfactory means of controlling government that do not require heavy use of the courts.

In our history, however, we have long tradition of assigning important roles to judges. We have Lord Coke's 17th Century assertion in Dr. Bonham's case,

77 Eng. Rep 646 (C.P. 1610); we have John Marshall's opinion in Marbury v. Madison, 5 U.S. 137 (1803); we have Madison's insight about the dangers of majority factions in The Federalist No. 10 and Hamilton's follow-up in The Federalist No. 78 that judicial officers are a "barrier to the encroachments and oppressions of the representative body"; and we have America's 19th Century frontier experience in which judges were often the most visible embodiments of law and justice in a barely civilized community. Whatever the causes, it is clear that the institution of judicial review is firmly settled in our system: we have historically asked courts to serve as one of the important checks on the legitimacy of government action.

You can take it as given, then, that in our culture there *will* be some type of judicial review of almost all administrative action. It will be a rare legislative delegation that does not contain a specific judicial review provision or provide for judicial review under the general provisions of the APA. Even when Congress seeks to limit or preclude judicial review, the congressional limits must be interpreted and applied by courts that, as keepers of the tradition, have taken their role seriously, have not been overly generous in interpreting preclusive language. And when Congress has been silent — neither providing nor precluding judicial review — we will see below that in most cases there will be a strong presumption that most agency action is judicially reviewable.

If we are going to have judicial review, if we are to use traditional courts to monitor legality in the technical, scientific and political work of administrative agencies, how can courts perform that function? Remember that courts are highly specialized instruments. Like violins, they are exquisite in performing the job for which they were designed, but less effective — even clumsy — when asked to perform other tasks. Consider the following characteristics of the judicial process which are of particular relevance to us here:

- The core function of the courts is the resolution of individual disputes; they are not designed for general policy-making or management of large institutions.
- Courts can only provide and enforce limited types of relief.
- While policy views of judges may, at the margins, affect decisions, judicial decisions are not intended primarily to reflect judicial political preferences. The classic judicial dispute resolution process instead involves a passive, neutral tribunal responding to legal arguments of adversary parties leading to a reasoned decision applying accepted legal principles.
- The judge is a generalist not an expert in the regulatory field.
- Federal judges have life tenure, are not directly accountable to the public.

- Courts are very few in number compared to the millions of agency actions that might need review.

Besides these qualities internal to the judicial process, there are external factors that suggest practical and legal limits on judicial review. This will turn out to be a very complex and difficult body of law; the reasons for limiting review can overlap, can appear in many variations and many levels of persuasiveness, can be devilishly difficult to define and can change over time. Think of the law in this chapter as efforts to permit courts to contribute what they can to assuring the legality and legitimacy of the regulatory process, without imposing on judges tasks that are fiscally wasteful, functionally infeasible or politically inappropriate.

B. Whether Judicial Review Is Available

Historically, United States courts were reluctant to intrude on the executive function. At the beginning of the 20th century, however, and picking up considerable speed in the 1930s, courts became more comfortable in reviewing executive and administrative action. By 1967, the Supreme Court was ready to state that there was a general presumption of judicial review. Abbott Laboratories v. Gardner, 387 U.S. 136 (1967). The Court also made it clear that rebutting the presumption of reviewability would not be easy, would require "clear and convincing evidence" of a contrary legislative intent. It seems generally agreed that the availability of judicial review is not always required to satisfy due process, but the Court found support for a presumption of reviewability in what it called the "generous review provisions" of the APA which, the Court said, " must be given a hospitable interpretation." 387 U.S. at 141.

1. Express and Implied Preclusion

Section 701(a)(1) of the APA recognizes the possibility that statutes can rebut the presumption of reviewability by explicitly precluding review but, as you would expect, courts usually construe preclusion statutes narrowly. Section 701(a)(1) says review is precluded only "to the extent that" statutes so provide and courts have sometimes been creative in disentangling from the entire dispute purely legal or constitutional issues which can be reviewed despite general preclusive language. Of course, Article III, Section 2 of the constitution grants the Congress considerable power to regulate the business of the courts, but neither the Congress nor the courts have tried to define the extent of those powers with any precision. You will consider this in more detail in your courses in Federal Jurisdiction and Constitutional Law, and we touch it again below in our discussion of standing. For now, remember that if Congress has the will—and can find clear words to express it—it can reduce to some degree the extent to which administrative action can be subjected to review by the courts.

Absent *express* preclusion language, courts have sometimes found a particular type of review *impliedly* precluded. Given the strength of the presumption of reviewability, such cases will be relatively infrequent and are usually explained by something special in the nature of the case. Dalton v. Spector, 511 U.S. 462 (1994) (preclusion inferred from statements in legislative history, though Court relies more on lack of finality than preclusion); Thunder Basin Coal Co. v. Reich, 510 U.S. 200 (1994) (comprehensive enforcement scheme signals Congress intended to preclude some kinds of judicial review).

At the doctrinal level, the Court has not always sent consistent signals. In Block v. Community Nutrition Institute, 467 U.S. 340 (1984) the Court considered a complex administrative scheme aimed at supporting milk prices. A unanimous Court found milk consumers impliedly precluded after an analysis of the statute's language, its structure, its objective, and the particular kind of agency action that was involved. This analysis persuaded the Court that when Congress authorized review of a complex scheme by some participants (e.g., milk handlers), it intended to preclude review by others. Of the *Abbott Laboratories* principle that review was always available absent "clear and convincing" evidence to the contrary, the Court said it had never used that test in a strictly evidential sense. Instead, the test was whether congressional intent to preclude was "fairly discernible in the detail of the legislative scheme." 467 U.S. at 351. Two years later, the Court permitted review in the face of statutory preclusion language, citing the *Abbott Laboratories* presumption, which it described as a "strong presumption" that imposed a "heavy burden" on one trying to rebut it, and that rebuttal was possible only with "persuasive reasons to believe that such was the purpose of Congress." Bowen v. Michigan Academy of Family Physicians, 476 U.S. 667 (1986). We can conclude then that the *Abbott Laboratories* presumption is alive and well, though the Court's enthusiasm for *Abbott Laboratories*' "clear and convincing" language sometimes wavers.

Finally, there are a few cases where the presumption of reviewability is not used and, indeed, is reversed. In Heckler v. Cheney, 470 U.S. 821 (1985) plaintiffs sought to compel the Food and Drug Administration to take enforcement action against certain drugs. The Court found the agency's refusal unreviewable since the decision seemed to the Court like an exercise of prosecutorial discretion — action which had historically been unreviewable. The Court said that in such cases, there is a presumption of *un*reviewability. Similar holdings have occurred with respect to issues traditionally thought best left to the exercise of agency discretion, such as fund allocations from a lump-sum appropriation, Lincoln v. Vigil, 508 U. S. 182 (1993); the decision of the CIA to terminate an employee, Webster v. Doe, 486 U.S. 592 (1988); in litigation, an agency's decision not to appeal, Didrickson v. U.S. Department of Interior, 982 F.2d. 1332 (9th Cir. 1992); or an agency's denial of reconsideration, AAPC v. FCC, 442 F.3d 751 (D.C. Cir. 2006).

2. Commitment to Agency Discretion

A special kind of limit on judicial review is captured in the language of the APA § 701(a)(2) which excludes judicial review "to the extent that agency action is committed to agency discretion by law." Of course, under the preclusion language we have just looked at in § 701(a)(1), Congress effectively commits a matter to agency discretion to the extent it explicitly precludes judicial review. But § 701(a)(2) has been seen by some as an invitation for *courts* to decide as a matter of judicial self restraint whether review was appropriate, leaving § 701(a)(1) as a provision requiring the courts to defer to a *legislative* signal not to intervene. A good review is Levin, *Understanding Unreviewability in Administrative Law*, 74 MINN. L. REV. 689 (1990).

In thinking about the degree to which agency discretion is reviewable, we need to compare the seemingly contradictory provisions of sections 701(a)(2) and 706(2)(A).

§ 701(a)(2)	§ 706(2)(A)
No review under APA	Court can set aside agency
"to the extent that agency action is	action "found to be …
committed to agency discretion"	an abuse of discretion"

Since Congress included both sections, orthodox statutory interpretation theory obliges us to see if they can both be given meaning. You might begin by noting that in every administrative decision for which review is sought there will be some legal *standard* according to which the decision was made, and the violation of which is at the heart of the petition for review. There will also be an inevitable degree of *discretion* in applying that standard to the case at hand. So every agency decision involves *both* the application of legal standards and the exercise of discretion. It is also plain that, depending on the specificity of the standard, the proportion of the decision which is controlled by discretion will vary from case to case. Consider Figure 5.1.

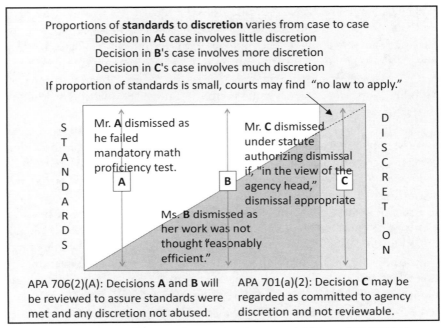

Figure 5.1   Working With APA Sections 701(a)(2) and 706(2)(A)

In the cases pictured in Figure 5.1, suppose we had only § 706(2)(A)'s pro-hibition of "abuse of discretion" to contend with. At least in cases like **A** and **B** there appear to be sufficient legal standards so that the agency action could be reviewed to assure that those standards had been met. And part of that re-view certainly includes whether the agency abused its discretion in applying the legal standard.

What is added when we stir in § 701(a)(2) language about commitment to agency discretion? The problem has been seen from several perspectives. Some-times the courts simply conclude that when the proportion of discretion to standards reaches a certain point, the court will treat the matter as having been wholly "committed to agency discretion" and not reviewable at all. This is de-scribed variously by the decisions, but its essence is a sense that when Con-gress has conferred very broad discretion on the agency there is no useful role left for the courts. In the example in Figure 5.1, if in fact **C** was viewed as a se-curity threat by the agency head the statutory terms have been fully met. What can judicial review add? Do you think the statute invites the court to second-guess the agency head on how serious a threat to national security **C** was? Prob-ably not.

The Court has extracted a phrase from the legislative history of the APA, and said review is excluded under § 701(a)(2) when there is "no law [i.e., no legal standards] to apply." Citizens to Preserve Overton Park v. Volpe, 401 U.S. 402, 410 (1971). *Overton Park* went on to find "law to apply" in the form of factors the agency was to use in exercising its discretion. Review was possible, said the Court, since a court could usefully examine the question of whether the factors were properly weighted and considered.

Even here, however, the matter is not free from dispute. The Attorney General's Manual listed as matters that should be committed to agency discretion some matters for which there may have been law to apply but for which judicial review would be too intrusive into agency management of priorities and resources, such as denial of petitions for rulemaking, denial of loans, refusing to issue an enforcement complaint, etc. ATTORNEY GENERAL'S MANUAL ON THE APA 95 (1947). And in a spirited dissent in Webster v. Doe, 486 U.S. 592 (1988) Justice Scalia argued for unreviewability of action even when there was "law to apply," in aid of protecting inherently discretionary agency action, action which was traditionally not reviewed by courts, and action for which judicial review would be disruptive. Justice Scalia said that the " 'no law to apply' test can account for the nonreviewability of certain issues, but falls far short of explaining the full scope of the areas from which the courts are excluded." 486 U.S. at 608. See Figure 5.2.

Another perspective is that in a system operating under the rule of law there are always foundational legal principles with which agencies must comply, no matter the degree of discretion that appears in the statutory delegation itself. Thus, if Congress authorizes an agency to grant a competitive license to whichever applicant the agency "deems" most qualified, an agency decision to choose among applicants by a flip of the coin would be reviewable as arbitrary. Fundamental requirements that agency action not be arbitrary become "law to apply" though there may be no standards set out in the agency's statute itself. In this view, the court's task under § 706(2)(A) is to examine every exercise of agency discretion for its rationality, its evidential support, and the overall quality of its judgment. Pressed to its extreme, this view of § 706(2)(A) would seem to make § 701(a)(2) redundant.

A third perspective arises from the way § 701(a)(2) is worded. The statute says review is not available "to the extent that" a matter is committed to agency discretion. This language permits a court to disaggregate the agency action into components, some of which are committed to agency discretion and some not. An example is Webster v. Doe, 486 U.S. 592 (1988), discussed above, where the statute authorized the agency to dismiss an employee when the Director "shall deem such termination necessary or advisable in the interests of

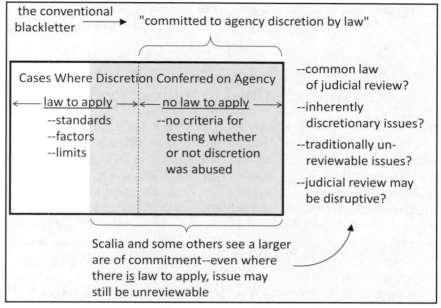

Figure 5.2   How Broad is the Commitment to Agency Discretion?

the United States." A gay employee was terminated under this section and raised both statutory and constitutional claims objections to the termination. The Court held his *statutory* claim had been committed to agency discretion; hence he was not able to argue that his dismissal was not "necessary or advisable in the interest of the United States." But the Court held that the employee's colorable *constitutional* claims survived. The Court found that any other interpretation would raise serious constitutional questions. The commitment to agency discretion, in other words, only went "to the extent that" statutory claims were raised. For a similar decision, see Johnson v. Robison, 415 U.S. 361 (1974).

With so many perspectives, this is difficult doctrine to parse and predict. In evaluating a case in this area, perhaps one can do no better than to consider a range of functionally relevant factors, such as those proposed by Saferstein:

- how broadly is the agency's statute drawn?
- how much expertise is required for a sound decision? how "managerial" is the decision or its consequences?
- how effective can a court be in framing and enforcing relief?
- how important is prompt (i.e., agency) resolution?
- what quantity of these decisions need review?
- are there ways of limiting abuse other than by judicial action?

Saferstein, *Nonreviewability: A Functional Analysis of "Committed to Agency Discretion,"* 83 Harv. L. Rev. 367 (1968). Briefs, arguments and predictions will be improved if they reflect considerations of this type.

C. Who Is Entitled to Judicial Review?

In the usual administrative law case, standing is not a problem. When an agency takes action against a particular individual—such as revoking the individual's license—that individual will have standing to seek judicial review of the revocation. But it is a peculiarity of the administrative process that administrative action aimed directly at one individual will sometimes have serious impacts on others. If there is a plausible claim that the action is illegal, shouldn't anyone affected by it be allowed to raise the question of its legality? Even more broadly, since illegal agency action harms everyone in some sense, shouldn't anyone—directly affected or not—be allowed to stop the illegal action?

Suppose a private school that discriminates on the basis of race seeks charitable status from the Internal Revenue Service in order that contributions to the school can be deducted on the donor's tax return. If the IRS grants that status to such a school—an act subject to a plausible legal challenge—shouldn't anyone be able to challenge the act? The private school itself, of course, would have little interest in challenging the action since it benefits from it. Nor would the school's donors challenge the act. Even the parents of students in the school are unlikely challengers as their tuition costs are kept low by reason of outside donations, and they may not have ideological objections to the discrimination. Could a civil rights organization sue the IRS? Or what about a parent in a *public* school, alleging that the IRS policy encouraged white-only private schools, reducing the likelihood of a truly integrated public school system?

If our system is truly operating under the rule of law, one might suppose that any challenger would be welcome in aid of stopping unlawful action. But it will turn out that in a variety of ways courts have been reluctant to extend the opportunity to challenge alleged unlawful action very far beyond plaintiffs who are most directly affected by it. Why should this be the case?

As a purely practical matter, it might be that courts need to protect the limited resources they have. Opening up the courthouse doors to anyone who has a plausible challenge to the legality of agency action might swamp the courts.

In addition, if the agency action affects people broadly, couldn't correction for undesirable behavior more effectively be addressed by the legislative branch than the judicial? The legislative branch would presumably respond to concerns of broad groups in the community and the legislative tools (research, wide discussion, solution by general rule) would have advantages over the typical tools available to courts. To the extent that the agency action involves difficult and controversial policy choices — as it usually will — perhaps the accountable legislative branch is the more appropriate venue for resolution.

Apart from such practical and theoretical considerations, are there legal reasons why standing to challenge agency action should not be extended infinitely? The first legal impediment to the extension of standing is the constitutional doctrine that the judicial power of the United States extends only to "cases and controversies." While these words do not in terms rule out a suit by public school parents against an IRS regulation concerning discriminating private schools — i.e., it could be called a "case" and without doubt there is a "controversy" — by long standing interpretation these words are construed to refer to the kind of dispute which was typical in the common law courts at the time the Constitution was drafted. There is a case or controversy in this sense when the owner of Blackacre has a boundary dispute with the owner of adjoining Whiteacre. If a court decides that the public school parents are not as immediately connected to the dispute as the adjoining landowners in a boundary dispute case, the court may say there is no judicial power to consider the challenge. Notice that a constitutional ruling of this kind puts the degree of judicial review beyond the reach of legislative correction in most cases. Under this reading of the constitutional language, the legislature is not permitted to open the courthouse doors to anybody with a plausible legal claim, but only to those who have a "case or controversy."

Judicial opinions on standing often advance additional rationales. Standing rules seek to keep out of the court plaintiffs without a personal stake in the outcome who for that reason could not be relied on for vigorous advocacy. Spirited advocacy, you will recall, is very important to the essentially passive American court system. This may be in large part a fiction in today's world of well financed and passionately committed interest groups. It would be hard to find a group with a deeper commitment than the public interest or environmental groups who frequently face standing barriers. But this rationale is still advanced by judges and some commentators. A variation on the theme is reflected in statements that courts do not want to deal with hypothetical matters, so will reject plaintiffs whose interests are not obviously and directly affected by the agency action. In part, this reflects the historic reluctance of federal courts to issue advisory opinions.

There is an obvious tension between the need to respect the rule of law on the one hand and the practical and legal needs of the legal system on the other. The resulting standing doctrine is made up of difficult decisions, tortuously reasoned opinions and little guidance for anyone. There are a few general labels which the courts rehearse frequently, and your reasoning and research must begin with these terms. But the terms are so subject to manipulative interpretation they will not be of much predictive help to the lawyer. In a moment of rare candor, the Supreme Court has said that "generalizations about standing to sue are largely worthless as such." Association of Data Processing v. Camp, 397 U.S. 150, 151 (1970). To see an academic debate over efforts to present a principled justification of standing doctrines, see Brilmayer, *The Jurisprudence of Article III: Perspectives on the "Case or Controversy" Requirement*, 93 HARV. L. REV. 297 (1979); Tushnet, *The "Case or Controversy" Controversy*, 93 HARV. L. REV. 1698 (1980).

It is common to distinguish the *constitutional* requirements for standing from other requirements that have their base in practical matters — the so-called *prudential* considerations.

1. Constitutional Considerations

The constitutional case or controversy requirement is said to require three showings:

1. That plaintiff must have suffered (or is about to suffer) an *injury in fact*. An injury in fact can be an injury of any type (economic, recreational, aesthetic, etc.) and in theory can be of any magnitude (an "identifiable trifle" is said to be enough), but a fair reading of the cases suggests that standing is much more likely to be granted (and the opinions will be much less divided) when the injury is economic and is substantial.

2. That the injury was *caused by* (or *fairly traceable to*) the agency action challenged.

3. That a victory for the plaintiff in the case will likely *redress* the injury identified.

The first condition — that the petitioner must have suffered an injury in fact — is fairly new to the law of standing, having made its first appearance in Supreme Court jurisprudence in 1970. Association of Data Processing v. Camp, 397 U.S. 150 (1970). It was probably not intended to be a particularly onerous burden to a petitioner. As it was used in *Data Processing* the injury in fact test was merely a way of modifying the rigor of an earlier standing doctrine that required petitioners to show a "legal" injury. Justice Douglas said the question of whether there was a legal injury goes to the merits. To get a court to review the merits, a plaintiff need only to show that it suffered an injury in fact (Justice Douglas added other requirements that we'll discuss below).

As the Court has now and then felt the need to restrict the size of the class of those who could challenge agency action, it has embroidered the injury in fact test with a variety of poorly defined, vague and easily manipulated qualifiers. Justices and judges seeking to limit access to the courts today ask such questions as

- how likely is it to occur (is the injury certain, probable, possible?)
- how soon will it occur (will it happen imminently, soon, later?)
- how specially is plaintiff affected (the only sufferer, or is injury widely shared?)
- with what specificity can injury be described (concretely, vaguely?)

Plaintiffs seeking relief before "tough" standing judges will seek to prove injuries that are certain to occur, imminent, special to the plaintiff and capable of description in concrete terms.

The generality of these terms makes a standing decision difficult to predict. Some have noted that the inquiry into whether or not there has been an injury in fact is itself a value laden inquiry, not a simple empirical question. Sunstein, *What's Standing After Lujan*, 91 MICH. L. REV. 163, 167 (1992). One probably can do a better job of predicting if one examines the tendencies of individual members of the bench, tendencies which vary as a function of sympathy with plaintiff's claim on the merits, or of the judge's willingness to interfere with executive branch operations.

Some examples from recent cases can give you a feel for the problem, recognizing that in most of the cases discussed below there were vigorous dissenting opinions on the standing question.

First, consider a couple of cases in which standing was found with minimal injuries in fact. In U.S. v. Students Challenging Regulatory Agency Procedures (SCRAP) 412 U.S. 669 (1973) plaintiffs (law students engaged in a project for their Administrative Law class!) alleged environmental injury as a result of increased rates the ICC had permitted railroads to charge for transporting goods for recycling. The complaint alleged that the higher rates discouraged the reuse of recycled materials and this led to a number of harmful effects including an increase in the litter and trash in the parks used by the plaintiffs. The majority of the Court found SCRAP had standing based on these injuries. Conceding that pleadings "must be something more than an ingenious academic exercise in the conceivable," and admitting that the connection between agency action and the alleged harm was "attenuated," the majority found the requisite injury. The Court brushed off the notion that the injury was too widely shared to be "individual" with the statement that "standing is not to be denied simply because many people suffer the same injury." Three Justices did not agree with the standing ruling. (For what it is worth, plaintiffs lost on the merits. Remember, standing only gets you into court, it doesn't mean you win.)

Another generous standing holding came in Duke Power Co. v. Carolina Environmental Study Group, 438 U.S. 59 (1978), where the constitutionality of the Price-Anderson Act was tested. In an effort to encourage private companies to build nuclear power plants, the Act imposed liability limits for nuclear accidents. Plaintiffs challenging the constitutionality of the Act included persons living near potential nuclear plants. While no one had yet been injured as a result of a nuclear accident, the Court found injury in fact. The Court said the construction and safe operation of the plants would themselves cause plaintiffs injury—such as increased water temperature in lakes used for cooling the plant and small amounts of radiation that would inevitably be present even in safe facilities. While these injuries were not the injuries about which plaintiffs were principally concerned—the presence of liability limits should there be a nuclear accident—they were sufficient for standing purposes.

As to the second and third elements of standing (causation and redressability) it is clear that the Price-Anderson Act didn't cause the injury—it didn't require construction of nuclear plants, it only provided a liability limit in favor of anyone who constructed one. But the Court affirmed a finding that plants would not be built without the liability limit in the Act; hence, the Act could be seen as the "but for" cause of plaintiff's injury. On that assumption, too, a victory for the plaintiff would redress the injury.

It is speculated that the Court in *Duke Power* was generous with the standing issue as it wanted to settle questions about the constitutionality of the Act. Again, plaintiffs lost on the merits; after affirming plaintiffs' standing to challenge the Act, the Court ruled the Act constitutional.

At the other end of the generosity spectrum are cases such as Allen v. Wright, 468 U.S. 737 (1984) where the Court held that parents of black children attending public schools did not have standing to challenge an IRS practice that they alleged supported racially discriminatory action by private schools. Plaintiff's claim of injury was that the IRS practice facilitated discriminatory private schools, drawing off white students who would otherwise be part of the integrated public education to which plaintiff's children were constitutionally entitled.

The Court conceded that deprivation of the right to attend an integrated school was a legitimate claim of injury, indeed, "one of the most serious injuries recognized in our legal system." 468 U.S. at 756. The problem here, said the majority, was that the second and third components of standing were missing: the injury could not be fairly traced to the action challenged, and the elimination of the action would not likely redress plaintiff's injuries. The Court found in the record no information about the number of private discriminatory schools in plaintiff's communities—if there were few, changing their policies would have made no appreciable difference in overall public school integration.

Moreover, the Court found it "entirely speculative" whether a withdrawal of the tax exemption for a private discriminating school would lead the school to change its policies. Such schools might continue their discriminatory policy even it meant the loss of some donor support. It was "just as speculative," said the Court, whether any parents—faced with perhaps increased tuition at a private school now unable to have the benefits of the tax exemption—would decide to enroll their children in public schools. Thus plaintiff's injury "results from the independent action of some third party not before the court." 468 U.S. at 757. Overall, the majority felt it was "pure speculation whether, in a particular community, a large enough number of the numerous relevant school officials and parents would reach decisions that collectively would have a significant impact on the racial composition of the public schools." 468 U.S. at 758.

Needless to say, the strong dissents of Justices Brennan and Stevens saw the standing issue differently. Justice Brennan called the majority opinion "misguided decision making" which shows "a startling insensitivity to the historical role played by the federal courts in eradicating race discrimination." 468 U.S. at 767. Justice Brennan read the second traceability element of the doctrine not to require cause in any strict sense; it is enough if the plaintiff's interests are "adversely affected" by the challenged action." Id at 774.

A virtual laboratory case study of these difficulties is presented by Lujan v. Defenders of Wildlife, 504 U.S. 555 (1990), a clear example of how Supreme Court opinions on standing can be so fragmented as to make doctrinal factors of limited value in predicting outcomes. The Endangered Species Act requires that before funding certain projects, federal funding agencies must confer with the Secretary of the Interior or the Secretary of Commerce to insure that the funded projects are not likely to jeopardize the habitat or the existence of an endangered or threatened species. In 1978, a regulation was issued making it clear that the obligation to consult extended to federally funded projects anywhere in the world. In 1986, the regulation was changed so that the obligation to consult was required only for projects built in the United States or on the high seas. Environmental groups sought to challenge the legality of this interpretation since the interpretation meant that there was no obligation to consider the impact on endangered or threatened species of U.S-funded projects in foreign countries.

The Court found that plaintiffs had not satisfied the first standing test, having suffered no injury in fact. It conceded that the interest of several plaintiffs in observing various animal species for purely aesthetic purposes was an appropriate interest, but concluded that plaintiffs had not shown a concrete, imminent and individual injury to that interest. While the plaintiffs testified that they might visit Egypt (where threatened crocodiles lived) or Sri Lanka (where threatened leopards and elephants lived), plaintiffs had no specific plans or dates for these visits. The Court said "such 'some day' intentions—without any description of concrete plans, or indeed even any specification of *when* the someday will be—do not support a finding of the 'actual or imminent' injury that our cases require." 504 U.S. at 564.

Justices Kennedy and Souter concurred with the Court on the injury in fact issue, but noted that it wouldn't have taken much in their view for plaintiff to have established the requisite injury. Purchase of airline tickets or the announcement of a date certain for their return to the area might have been enough. All that was required in their view was evidence that makes it "reasonable to assume that the affiants will be using the site on a regular basis." 504 U.S. at 579.

A plurality also found that plaintiff had not met the third standing test—redressability. These Justices felt that even if the district court had ordered the Secretary to amend its regulation so that consultation was required in connection with foreign projects—that is, even if plaintiff won this law suit—it was not clear that the agencies would comply with the regulation. (There was dispute about whether the regulation was binding.) The district court and the dissenting justices urged that the agencies would surely comply if the Court ruled that the regulation was binding, but the plurality was not ready to reach that legal question in the present case. The plurality also noted that since the U.S. funds in question represented less than 10% of the cost of the projects, the project might be completed by the foreign governments even without the U.S. grants—another redressability problem for plaintiffs.

Justice Stevens was clear that the requirements of the standing doctrine (injury in fact and redressability) were fully met in this case and that plaintiffs were thus entitled to a ruling on the merits. He concurred with the majority, nevertheless, as he felt that plaintiffs should have lost on the merits—in his view the regulation, properly interpreted, did not require consultation for projects in foreign countries.

Another element to the plaintiff's case was a statute authorizing "any person" to "commence a civil suit ... to enjoin any person ... who is alleged to be in violation ... of this chapter." 16 U.S.C. § 1540(g). The majority found this citizen suit provision in violation of Article III of the constitution which permits, as we have seen, the exercise of judicial power only where "cases and controversies" are present. The case and controversy requirement being constitutional, it cannot be obviated by statute. Again, Justices Kennedy and Souter concurred, but made it clear that in their view Congress could define injuries in a way that would clearly give rise to a case or controversy where one didn't exist before passage of the statute. If such a statute identified the injury and related it to the class of persons authorized to bring suit—conditions they felt were not met in this case—it would be well within the power of Congress to confer standing.

Finally, Justices Blackmun and O'Connor wrote a spirited dissent on the standing question, stating forcefully that there had been a serious injury in fact, that it had clearly been caused by the action complained of and that victory for the plaintiff in this case would redress the injury. These Justices also felt that the citizen suit provision was clearly within the regulatory power of Congress under Article III, Section 2.

A reading of all these opinions will no doubt make you a more impressive speaker at a CLE seminar on standing, but it is not likely to increase your ability to predict outcomes by the use of the doctrinal criteria stated. Pretty clearly the Court is divided at many levels on those criteria and you will have to look further for predictive help. Figure 5.3 shows the almost bewildering array of opinions on the issues in *Lujan*.

The cost of this sort of judicial fracturing is serious. Notice that if plaintiffs had purchased airline tickets to Sri Lanka, the two "soft" votes for no standing (Kennedy, Souter) could have been changed and the case would have been

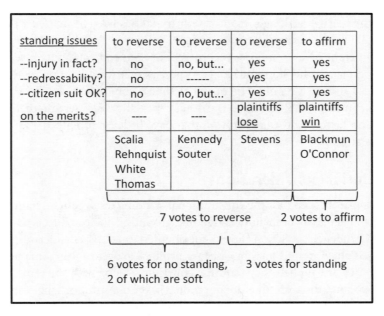

standing issues	to reverse	to reverse	to reverse	to affirm
--injury in fact?	no	no, but...	yes	yes
--redressability?	no	------	yes	yes
--citizen suit OK?	no	no, but...	yes	yes
on the merits?	----	----	plaintiffs lose	plaintiffs win
	Scalia Rehnquist White Thomas	Kennedy Souter	Stevens	Blackmun O'Connor

7 votes to reverse   2 votes to affirm

6 votes for no standing, 3 votes for standing
2 of which are soft

Figure 5.3   Issues and Votes in Lujan v. Defenders of Wildlife,
504 U.S. 555 (1990)

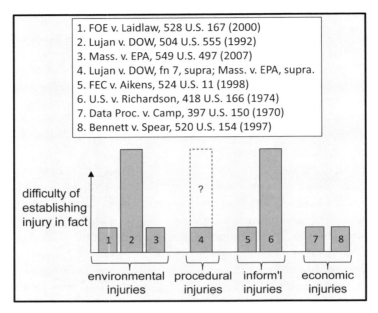

Figure 5.4   Principal Standing Cases by Type of Injury

heard on the merits. Making a case turn on trivialities like airline ticket purchases hardly seems a triumph of reasoned analysis.

In the different types of injuries plaintiffs have claimed in standing cases, is there any pattern in the Supreme Court responses that would aid prediction? As Figure 5.4 shows, the only type of injury that is consistently easy to show is economic injury. With respect to the other types, the cases defy prediction. They turn on factors and consideration that have little to do with the law or theory of standing.

2. Prudential Considerations

Even if a plaintiff can pass the constitutional standing tests, courts retain the discretion to dismiss a complaint on standing grounds if the court feels that as a matter of prudence the action should not be entertained. Not being constitutionally based, these grounds may be easier for plaintiffs to overcome in some cases, but where they are applied they slam the courthouse door with the same authority. Also, since these grounds are not rooted in the constitution, they can be altered somewhat by legislative action. There are three of these prudential considerations to which the student of administrative law needs an introduction.

a. The Zone of Interest

In addition to meeting the constitutional tests described above, a plaintiff's interest must be "arguably within the zone of interests to be protected or regulated by the statute or constitutional guarantee in question." Association of Data Processing v. Camp, 397 U.S. 150, 153 (1970). This might be read to require plaintiff to show that it was an intended beneficiary of the legislative action — essentially a requirement that plaintiff show a statutory cause of action. But the whole tenor of the opinion in *Data Processing* would not support that strict reading. The Court spoke of the trend to enlarge the class of plaintiffs — reflected in the permissive language of § 702 of the APA — and was at pains to assure us that the standing issue was different from a decision on the merits of plaintiff's claim. The "arguably within the zone of interest" formula quoted above seems only to require that there be *some* relationship between the injury of which plaintiff complains and the statutory purpose. As applied in the case, that relationship did not have to be explicit in the statute — plaintiff competitors had standing to complain about new authority given to the regulated party even though there was little or no mention of plaintiffs' interests in the statute or its history. The Court said simply, "We think Congress has provided the sufficient statutory aid to standing even though the competition may not be the precise kind Congress legislated against." 397 U.S. at 155.

In the 40 years since *Data Processing*, the Court has applied the zone of interest test with remarkably different levels of intensity. An interpretation very generous to plaintiffs is seen in Clarke v. Securities Ass'n, 479 U.S. 388 (1987), where securities brokers challenged a regulation that allowed banks to compete in the securities broker market. The Court concluded that the security brokers had standing, indicating that the zone of interest test was "not meant to be especially demanding" and that it excludes plaintiffs only where their "interests are ... marginally related to or inconsistent with the purposes implicit in the statute." "In particular, there need be no indication of congressional purpose to benefit the would-be plaintiff." 479 U.S. at 399–400.

Suppose you faced this examination problem: a regulation under the Endangered Species Act (ESA) provides that water in certain reservoirs be kept at levels sufficient to protect the habitat of certain endangered species. Farmers who wish to draw more water from the reservoir challenge the regulation on several legal grounds. Will the court hear their case? Are farmers "arguably within the zone of interests" sought to be protected by the ESA? Would it make a difference that the ESA has a citizen suit provision allowing suit by "any person" to enforce the Act?

The Ninth Circuit ruled that the farmers had no standing, that their interests were not only not within the purpose of the act, but were in fact "plainly inconsistent" with those purposes since drawing out the water they needed could threaten the habitat of endangered species. The court said that "only plaintiffs who allege an interest in the preservation of endangered species fall within the zone of interest." Bennett v. Plenart, 63 F.3d 915, 919 (9th Cir. 1995). Would you have gotten a passing grade on the exam?

The Ninth Circuit flunked. In a unanimous opinion, the Supreme Court reversed. The Court held that a generous interpretation of the zone of interest test was indicated here, because (a) the overall interest of the statute was the environment in which all have an interest, (b) the statute provided that "any person" may commence a lawsuit, and (c) the statute eliminated the usual diversity of citizenship and amount in controversy requirements and provided for recovery of litigation costs—all of which suggested that Congress intended wide availability of judicial review. Bennett v. Spear, 520 U.S. 154 (1997). (The opinion of the Court was written by Justice Scalia. Is this the same Justice Scalia who wrote the plurality opinion in *Lujan v. Defenders of Wildlife*, supra? Do the economic interests of these plaintiff farmers somehow weigh more than the aesthetic/environmental interests of the plaintiffs in *Lujan v. Defenders of Wildlife*?)

Despite these two very generous treatments of the zone of interest test, the Court now and then seems in a much less generous mood. For example, in Block v. Community Nutrition Institute, 467 U.S. 340 (1984), discussed earlier, the Court considered whether milk consumers could review an agency order affecting milk producers (dairy farmers) that had the intended purpose of benefiting those producers by increasing the price consumers had to pay for milk. The D.C. Circuit held that milk consumers had standing: they were clearly injured by the increase in milk prices and were arguably within the zone of interests of the statutory scheme.

Would you have gotten a passing grade on an exam question presenting this case? The D. C. Circuit flunked. A unanimous Supreme Court reversed, finding in the process set out in the statute an intent of Congress to restrict judicial review to milk handlers (processors). Those parties had first to present their complaints to the agency and, after exhausting those remedies, were then specifically authorized to seek judicial review. The Court felt that this way of assuring that the expert agency would first rule on any claims of illegality was preferable to allowing consumers to go directly to court, a process that would "severely disrupt this complex and delicate administrative scheme." Id. at 348.

In Air Courier Conference v. American Postal Workers Union, 498 U.S. 517 (1991), the Court was faced with a challenge by postal employees of an agency order permitting some foreign mail to be handled by private carriers, an arrangement that threatened job opportunities of postal workers. The D.C. Circuit, citing the *Clarke* case, supra, held that the employees had standing and, on the merits, the agency decision was unlawful.

Would you have passed that examination? The D.C. Circuit flunked. A unanimous Supreme Court reversed (six of the votes on standing, three on jurisdiction). On the standing question, the Court held that the so-called monopoly provisions of the postal act (which, subject to some exceptions, precluded private carriage of the mail) were intended to protect the revenues of the postal service, not the job opportunities of postal employees. Hence, the employees were not in the zone of interest protected by the act.

Incidentally, what is the relevant statute within which one looks for the zone of interest? *Clarke*, supra, had said that in zone of interest analysis "we are not limited to considering the statute under which respondents sued, but may consider any provision that helps us to understand Congress's overall purposes in the … Act." 479 U.S. at 401. In *Air Courier*, other provisions of the postal acts *did* directly affect employees, and plaintiffs claimed those sections were clearly intended to benefit employees. The Court was unmoved. The labor provisions of the act were wholly unrelated to the sections challenged except that they happened to be in the same chapter of the U.S. Code. The Court said "to accept this level of generality in defining the "relevant statute" could deprive the zone-of-interests test of virtually all meaning." 498 U.S. at 529–30.

The courts of appeal don't always flunk. In National Credit Union Administration (NCUA) v. First National Bank and Trust, 522 U.S. 479 (1998), the court of appeals had granted standing to banks to challenge an order of the agency that expanded the reach of credit unions, essentially creating more competition for banks. A five-person majority affirmed the court of appeals, noting that in *Data Processing* and *Clarke*, supra, the Court had usually held that competitors of the regulated party were within the zone of interest protected by the regulatory statute. The Court emphasized again that plaintiff does not have to show explicit recognition of its interests in the statutory text or in the legislative history. Justice Thomas said:

> in applying the "zone of interests" test, we do not ask whether, in enacting the statutory provision at issue, Congress specifically intended to benefit the plaintiff. Instead, we first discern the interests "arguably … to be protected" by the statutory provision at issue; we then inquire whether the plaintiff's interests affected by the agency action in question are among them. 522 U.S. at 492.

Of course, that merely restates the question (were plaintiff's interests arguably protected by the statute?). But the implication is that in some cases, the Court will not demand much in the way of a connection between plaintiff's interests and the statutory scheme. Justice Thomas found the necessary connection in the fact that limiting the reach of credit unions (whatever reason motivated Congress) would have necessary effects on plaintiff's business. He concluded:

> Thus, even if it cannot be said that Congress had the specific purpose of benefiting commercial banks, one of the interests "arguably ... to be protected" by [the Act] is an interest in limiting the markets that federal credit unions can serve. This interest is precisely the interest of respondents affected by the NCUA's interpretation of [the Act]. 522 U.S. at 493.

So, how seriously is the zone of interest test to be taken? It is impossible to say with much confidence. Plaintiffs for whom this may be a stumbling block need to examine the text and the history of the statute as well as the interrelationships of the players in an attempt to show that the statute under which the agency acted could negatively impact plaintiff, whether or not that impact was considered or intended by the drafters. That will usually satisfy the Court unless it is overwhelmed by process considerations. Cf. *Block v. CNI*, supra.

b. The Generalized Grievance Problem

Scattered through these opinions is a concern — now and then central to the outcome — that courts should not redress injuries that are shared by many citizens in the same way; i.e., injuries that are not in some way individualized. For example, all citizens are injured by an illegal public expenditure since the money comes from a treasury to which all citizens contribute. Nor would it violate conventional word usage to say that all citizens are injured by the government's refusal to follow the law in general. But courts have been reluctant to use such widely spread and generally shared injuries as the basis for standing decisions.

One of the difficulties with the generalized grievance concept is that on its face it is counterintuitive. That is, most would agree with the Court's statement that "[t]o deny standing to persons who are in fact injured simply because many others are also injured, would mean that the most injurious and widespread Government actions could be questioned by nobody. We cannot accept that conclusion." U.S. v. Students Challenging Regulatory Agency Procedures, 412 U.S. 669, 687–88 (1973), quoted in Massachusetts v. EPA, 549 U.S. 497, 525 (2007). A mass tort, after all, is still a tort.

The underlying rationale of the generalized grievance limit is hard to pin down. Consider some of the possible justifications for such a limit.

- It may be a matter of the volume of cases that, without the limit, would deluge the courts.

- It may be a concern that the claimed injury will not occur at all, or will not occur in magnitudes that make it worth judicial time.
- It may be a matter of finding a plaintiff who is specially hurt (and thus specially vigorous in prosecution of the case) rather than one with a merely ideological complaint.
- It may be a matter of finding an issue focused enough to be addressed by a judicial body.
- It may be a concern that without the limit important separation of powers breaches could occur, allowing private groups or judicial officers to interfere with executive operations.
- It may be a constitutional constraint. In a recent dissenting opinion, Justice Scalia expressed the view that the generalized grievance limit is really part of Article III's requirement that plaintiff's injuries must be concrete, specific, and individual rather than abstract and indefinite— in which case, note, the generalized grievance limit moves out of the prudential category of limits on judicial review and into the constitutional category, where its modification by legislative action is limited. FOE v. Laidlaw, 528 U.S. 167, 203 (2000) (Scalia, dissenting).
- Or it may be, as we have suggested earlier, that these kinds of injuries— which by definition affect enough people to have some political salience— can more safely be left for treatment by the political branches of our government.

Given these diverse theoretical bases for the doctrine, prediction is going to be difficult. The most recent case, Massachusetts v. EPA, 549 U.S. 497 (2007), was a stunning surprise to many. The state of Massachusetts sought to force the EPA to regulate greenhouse gas emissions from motor vehicles in an effort to reduce global warming. Global warming affects every person on the planet— a more generalized grievance would be hard to find—yet the Court found that Massachusetts had standing to raise the issue and, indeed, ruled for plaintiffs on the merits.

The result is said by some to rest on solicitude for the sovereignty of the plaintiff, and the Court's generosity may be limited to cases involving states as plaintiffs. More broadly, however, it has been suggested that generalizing the Court's approach might be a way to clarifying the muddled generalized grievance doctrine, so long as the rule is carefully limited to settings like Massachusetts where (1) plaintiff's potential loss of coastal land represented a particular injury (the plaintiff state was not a purely ideological plaintiff), (2) plaintiff claimed the EPA had violated a procedural right (even Justice Scalia has suggested that claims of procedural error did not require application of a rigorous standing rule, *Lujan v. Defenders of Wildlife.* supra (Court's note 9) and (3) Congress had explicitly authorized the suit. See Brown, *Justiciable Generalized Grievances,* 68 Md. L. Rev. 221 (2008).

c. Third Party Standing

Can a party have standing to redress an injury done to someone else? A couple of introductory points. First, associations can have standing to represent their members, but they must allege that some of their members were in fact injured by the action challenged, that the interests involved are germane to the association's purpose, and the presence of individual members themselves is not needed in the litigation. Hunt v. Washington Apple Adv. Comm'n, 432 U.S. 333 (1977). See, Comment, *The Rights of Others: Protection and Advocacy Organizations' Associational Standing to Sue,* 157 U. Pa. L. Rev. 237 (2008). Second, although a general interest in the problem may not get a plaintiff into court, once he is properly in court—i.e., once he has established some personal injury to himself—he can "argue the public interest in support of his claim that the agency has failed to comply with its statutory mandate." Sierra Club v. Morton, 405 U.S. 727, 737 (1972). Finally, nothing in the association standing cases affects the viability of class actions—actions in which those properly in court are under certain circumstances allowed to represent others.

Turning to the main question, can third parties sue to vindicate rights of others? The general answer is, "no." While suits by third parties were not uncommon in either English or early American legal experience, Sunstein, *What's Standing After Lujan,* 91 Mich. L. Rev. 163, 171 (1992), the general rule today is that a plaintiff cannot represent the interests of others who have been injured by agency action. The plaintiff itself must be among the injured. Thus, when the Sierra Club sought to bring a "public interest" law suit to stop the allegedly illegal construction of a ski resort in a national forest in California, the Club urged that its historic interest in the environment gave it standing to represent the public interest. The Club did not claim that the ski resort would affect it as an organization. And though it had 27,000 members within driving distance of the forest, the Club did not plead that any of its members used the area.

Over three dissents, the Court dismissed the action for want of standing. Sierra Club v. Morton, 405 U.S. 727 (1972). The Court felt that with no interest of the Club affected, and no claim that Club members used the area, the Club's argument came down to an assertion that its "interest in the problem" qualified it to sue. The opinion clearly reflected a slippery slope concern.

> But a mere 'interest in a problem,' no matter how longstanding the interest and no matter how qualified the organization is in evaluating

the problem, is not sufficient by itself to render the organization 'adversely affected' or 'aggrieved' within the meaning of the APA ... [I]f a 'special interest' in this subject were enough to entitle the Sierra Club to commence this litigation, there would appear to be no objective basis upon which to disallow a suit by any other bona fide 'special interest' organization [and] ... it is difficult to perceive why any individual citizen with the same bona fide special interest would not also be entitled to do so. 405 U.S. at 739.

3. Can Congress Expand or Restrict Standing?

The general question of the ability of Congress to control the jurisdiction of the courts has been controversial since Marbury v. Madison, 5 U.S. 137 (1803). In the area of standing, are there constitutional limits on how broadly Congress can authorize plaintiffs to sue? Section 702 of the APA is one kind of congressional expression. It authorizes judicial review by any person "adversely affected or aggrieved by agency action." Another type of congressional expression is the "citizen suit" provision included in many of today's regulatory statutes, especially in the environmental area. As we have seen, these kinds of provisions have resulted in somewhat more liberal standing opinions, but the current view is that plaintiff must still show an Article III-qualifying injury in fact. Lujan v. Defenders of Wildlife, 504 U.S. 555 (1992) (plurality opinion). It is obvious that Congress cannot by statute override Article III of the Constitution. But it is just as obvious that Congress can create rights, the violation of which would be redressable through judicial action. As Justice Kennedy (concurring) said in *Lujan*, "as government programs and policies become more complex and far-reaching, we must be sensitive to the articulation of new rights of action that do not have clear analogs in our common-law tradition." 504 U.S. at 580.

On the other hand, there is opposition on the Court to this kind of generosity in describing the powers of Congress. This view—of which Justice Scalia is the most vigorous proponent—seems rooted in separation of powers concerns, the fear being that permitting Congress too much leeway in opening courthouse doors to suits against agencies will interfere with the full performance of executive functions. This notion percolates through the Scalia plurality opinion in *Lujan*, supra, and is elaborated in a piece by then-Judge Scalia, *The Doctrine of Standing as an Essential Element of the Separation of Powers*, 17 SUFF. L. REV. 881 (1983).

The subject is more fully developed in your courses on Constitutional Law and Federal Jurisdiction; it remains a battle ground in Administrative Law. It

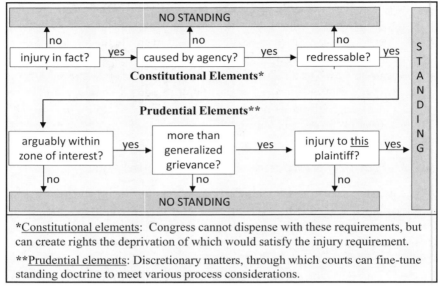

Figure 5.5   The Standing Roadmap

might interest you to note that one prominent commentator has proposed a simple way out of the citizen-suit quagmire: have Congress authorize citizen suits with a cash bounty to be paid to the winning plaintiff. A potential cash award would give any plaintiff a concrete stake in the outcome, overcoming all the doctrinal objections to citizens' suits. "A bounty system would ... also be more straightforward than the principal alternative strategy now available to Congress, involving restructured property rights." Sunstein, *What's Standing After Lujan*, 91 MICH. L. REV. 163, 232 (1992).

4. Summary of Standing

Standing law is the poster child of difficult doctrine. Figure 5.5 shows one way of mapping the various components.

D. When Is Judicial Review Available?

We have now established "what" is judicially reviewable and "who" can invoke the review process. There remains the question of timing—i.e., "when" can review be obtained. The starting point, as we all learned in civil procedure, is that courts only review decisions that are in some appropriate sense "final." Remember, the function of courts is to "review" not to "decide" these cases; that implies that the lower level unit (the agency) has completed its work on the matter being reviewed. So refresh your understanding of the concept of finality from civil procedure. A good review of the finality doctrine in the administrative agency context is McKee, *Judicial Review of Agency Guidance Documents: Rethinking the Finality Doctrine*, 60 Admin. L. Rev. 371 (2008).

In actions brought under the APA, the finality rule is embedded in § 704 which makes "final agency action" subject to judicial review. Administrative law contains two overlapping additions to the finality concept — the sense that agency action is not final until it has reached a certain level of "ripeness," and that review is premature until the petitioner has exhausted any remedies available at the agency level. What follows here is a discussion of those two doctrines.

Ripeness and exhaustion are usually regarded as common law (or equitable) doctrines — though there may be occasional statutory requirements — while some have found an indeterminate Article III basis for the doctrines. As common law notions, ripeness and exhaustion are usually applied with a considerable range of judicial discretion — an important quality to remember.

The rules of exhaustion and ripeness are more examples of doctrines that emerge from the interaction of conflicting functional goals. On the one hand, anything that delays a would-be appellant from prosecuting an immediate appeal requires the party to continue through what could be a long and expensive administrative ordeal that may turn out to be illegal. Nor would the acting agency necessarily benefit from the delay, as a clear judicial ruling might save it wasted steps. Where everything a court needs to make such a ruling is in hand, it would seem that efficiency would require prompt judicial action.

On the other hand, there are very real values in permitting an agency to finish its work on a case before subjecting it to judicial review. Think, e.g., about *factual* issues that may be involved in a formal adjudication. If the agency hearing is allowed to run its full course, there may be important refinements of factual issues furnished by agency expertise, there may be a synthesis of raw testimony in a set of findings by an experienced fact finder in the initial decision and, on internal appeal, there may be a further filtering through agency policies to reduce them to crucial relevancies. All such steps will give a reviewing court assistance in understanding the true factual basis of the dispute, in which case, early review may be counterproductive. And even beyond findings of first order facts, agency conclusions about broader empirical questions may be based on accumulated expertise, refined discretion emerging from prior experience or articulated policies deriving from presidential or legislative sources.

If full agency development of the case will clarify the *factual* basis of the dispute, much the same can be said about *legal* questions. Full development and argument may clarify and narrow legal issues which will greatly aid the reviewing court.

Ripeness and exhaustion are in some ways quite similar doctrines: resolution of ripeness and exhaustion issues sometimes turn on the consideration of similar factors, and sometimes courts interchange the doctrines carelessly. Keep in mind that ripeness focuses on the issue to be decided on the merits and the degree to which that issue has reached the state of development and refinement that will permit a court to make a sensible judgment about it. The beneficiary of ripeness doctrines is the court—protecting it from entanglement with speculative or abstract questions. Exhaustion, on the other hand, focuses on whether there are means of review or redress available within the agency. The beneficiary of exhaustion doctrines is the agency—assuring that its internal processes will be followed before judicial intrusion into the process. Clearly, they are different doctrines; just a clearly, their resolution may require consideration of similar factors.

In the final analysis, the doctrines are ways of affirming the central authority of the legislature. The legislature gave power to decide the case to the agency in the first instance; the judge's job is not to decide the case but to assure that the agency's decision about the correct solution is defensible. As we will see in the next chapter, this delicate and subtle task involves broad respect for the agency's authority, its expertise and its accountability. And all of this may be short circuited if premature judicial review is permitted.

1. Ripeness

Let's look first at ripeness. To begin with, ripeness cases usually involve rule-making rather than adjudication. When a typical adjudication proceeds to a final order, and all internally required appeals are completed, the legal issues are as ripe as they are going to get. Moreover, the hardship to the petitioners is real—they must comply with the agency order or face sanctions. In rulemaking, however, there may be many steps along the enforcement process that must be taken before the legal issues are clear and before one knows how (or even whether) the rule will impact the parties. Most of the leading cases on ripeness, therefore, involve attempts to seek judicial review of finalized but as yet unenforced rules. See Figure 5.6.

The orthodox principles of ripeness law are encapsulated in a single, classic Supreme Court case that sets out a "simple" two part doctrinal test. In *Abbot Laboratories v. Gardner*, 387 U.S. 136 (1967), pharmaceutical manufacturers sought

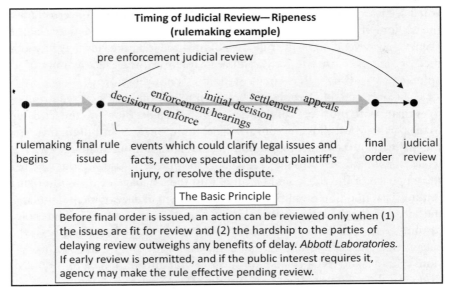

Figure 5.6   Ripeness

review of a rule promulgated by the Department of Health Education and Welfare. The rule—which was final but which had not yet been enforced against any drug manufacturer—required manufacturers to print the generic name of a drug on labels and other printed materials every time the manufacturers used the brand name of the drug in such materials. The rule's objective was to inform consumers and prescribing physicians of the availability of lower cost but equivalent medications.

The specific issue on the merits was whether the statute—which required that the generic name be "printed prominently"—authorized the "every time" regulation. Thus, on the merits, the court faced what seems a purely legal question—whether a rule was within the authority granted by the statute. There were no underlying facts in dispute, and in the district court both sides moved for summary judgment.

The Court first described the function of the ripeness doctrine, stating that its "basic rationale is to prevent the courts, through avoidance of premature adjudication, from entangling themselves in abstract disagreements over administrative policies, and also to protect the agencies from judicial interference until an administrative decision has been formalized and its effects felt in a concrete way by the challenging parties." 387 U.S. at 148. If you unpack this statement of functions in the context of a final but as yet unenforced rule, you'll see it expresses concerns we have seen before, namely concerns about the wisdom of judicial intervention when a dispute is still speculative (i.e., the agency may never enforce the rule), is not finalized (i.e., the rule may be modified or altered before enforced), and is abstract (i.e., the exact manner of its enforcement—time, place, circumstances—is not yet known).

The Court said "the problem is best seen in a twofold aspect, requiring us to evaluate both the fitness of the issues for judicial decision and the hardship to the parties of withholding court consideration." 387 U.S. at 149. In this case, the majority of the Court found both factors favored immediate review. The issues were fit for review as they raised only the pure legal issues about whether the language of the rule could be fitted into the language of the authorizing statute. That question owed nothing to further factual development. Similarly, the hardship to the parties was significant. The manufacturers faced the choice of complying with the regulation at considerable and needless expense (if the rule turned out to be invalid) or not complying with the rule and risking "serious criminal and civil penalties for the unlawful distribution of 'misbranded' drugs" (if the rule turned out to be valid). 387 U.S. at 153.

Dissenting justices in *Abbott Laboratories* noted a third consideration—the public interest—that they felt should have been included in the analysis. Preenforcement review of the regulation had the effect of delaying the effective date of the labeling requirement for at least four years (as of the date of the Supreme Court opinion), depriving the public of the benefit of information about lower cost drugs, and insuring the manufacturers the monetary benefit of "peddling plain medicine ... for fancy prices. ..." 387 U.S. at 199. The majority responded that if immediate implementation of the rule was necessary in the public interest, the agency could have made the rule immediately effective, and no judge would have granted petitioners a stay in these circumstances. How this works out in individual cases will vary with the nature of the regulation and, no doubt, the temperament of the district court judge. But thinking about ripeness should not ignore this layer of the problem. Since *Abbott Laboratories*, preenforcement judicial review of rules has become commonplace, a beneficial outcome so long as the *Abbott Laboratories* conditions are met (the issues are clear) and so long as injury to the public can be minimized by enforcement of the rule pending review.

The Court in *Abbott Laboratories* also noted that because the association petitioning for review in the case represented nearly all prescription drug manufacturers, the matter could be resolved most quickly and comprehensively by a ruling in this case—a pleading clue in a case where ripeness may be a problem. Lower courts have sometimes permitted early review of even informal agency statements when there is a clear legal question, where there is significant hardship to parties, and when a major segment of an entire industry has asked for review and will be bound by the decision made. See National Automatic Laundry v. Schultz, 443 F.2d 689 (D.C. Cir. 1971) (more than 1600 coin-operated laundry and/or dry cleaning establishments petitioned for, and got, early review of informal agency action).

The *Abbott Laboratories* principle can be seen sharply when contrasted with its companion case, Toilet Goods Association v. Gardner, 387 U.S. 158 (1967). In the *Toilet Goods Association* case, the Court refused early review of a regulation that authorized the agency to summarily suspend certification service to any manufacturer who refused agency inspectors free access to relevant facilities and records. The Court conceded that this regulation was final agency action and that its review presented a purely legal issue. But the issue was still not ripe because ancillary issues needed to be determined before the full impact of the regulation could be assessed, including the time and manner of the agency's request for access and whether a particular agency request for access provided adequate safeguards to protect trade secrets. Moreover, unlike the labeling rule in *Abbott Laboratories*, no irremediable adverse consequences flowed from delaying review in the *Toilet Goods Association* case—a refusal to admit access would lead to suspension of certification services that could then be promptly challenged through existing agency procedures. The Court thought those procedures provided an adequate forum for testing the legality of the regulation.

While *Abbott Laboratories* continues to be the principal case cited, later decisions have raised some questions. In National Parks Hospitality Association v. Dept. of Interior, 538 U.S. 803 (2003), the Court found unripe a "regulation" promulgated by the Parks Service stating that the Contract Disputes Act of 1978 (CDA) did not govern concessionaire contracts. An association of concessionaires challenged that interpretation of the CDA. The majority of the Court conceded that the Service's statement was "final action" within the APA and that the question presented was a "purely legal" question. Nevertheless, the matter was unripe in part because of plaintiff's failure to meet the second *Abbott Laboratories* test concerning hardship. The Court noted that the published agency statement was not issued pursuant to delegated rulemaking power and thus did not amount to a regulation with the force and effect of law. The statement was merely a policy statement, said the Court, and as such did not create "adverse effects of a strictly legal kind," which are required for a hardship showing. It is not clear why a practical impact on the parties—whatever its legal designation—should not provide enough hardship to warrant review if the issue is otherwise justiciable. Concurring and dissenting justices felt that the hardship showing was adequate.

The *National Parks* opinion seems a little less enthusiastic about preenforcement review than *Abbott Laboratories* was. The Court makes preenforcement review the exception rather than the rule. "[A] regulation is not ordinarily considered the type of agency action 'ripe' for judicial review under the [APA] until [there is] some concrete action applying the regulation to the claimant's situation in a fashion that harms or threatens to harm him." 538 U.S. at 808. The Court concedes an exception for "substantive rules" that require plaintiff to adjust his conduct immediately, but preenforcement in that setting remains the exception. The Court also signaled that further factual development might be required even if the issue is said to be purely legal, since "further factual development would significantly advance our ability to deal with the legal issues presented ..." 538 U.S. at 812. As in the *Toilet Goods Association* case, where the question to be decided was a legal question (did the statute authorize the agency to suspend certification if access were denied), seeing whether, when, and how the agency actually decided to exercise its claimed power might aid a court in divining the intent of the legislature or assessing the consequences of alternative interpretations.

2. Exhaustion of Administrative Remedies

The rule that administrative remedies must be exhausted before judicial relief is sought had its origin in a discretionary rule adopted by courts of equity that could deny a petitioner equitable relief if similar relief could have been obtained from a court of law. The exhaustion doctrine is said to serve at least two functions. First, it protects agency authority, allowing the agency to proceed to a conclusion on a matter on which Congress has given them primary decisional power. McCarthy v. Madigan, 503 U.S. 140, 145 (1992). In addition, exhaustion protects the exercise of agency discretion and the employment of its expertise. As the Court said, "exhaustion concerns apply with particular force when the action under review involves exercise of the agency's discretionary power or when the agency proceedings in question allow the agency to apply its special expertise." Ibid.

Secondly, as with the ripeness doctrine, the exhaustion rule promotes judicial efficiency by allowing an agency to correct its own errors without the need for judicial action, by not wasting judicial resources on disputes that may become mooted at the agency level, and by providing a fuller record for review in those cases that do ultimately come before the courts. See McCarthy v. Madigan, Id. at 145–146 (1992). See Figure 5.7.

Before we begin our general consideration of exhaustion, there is one special statutory provision that needs attention. If judicial review is sought under

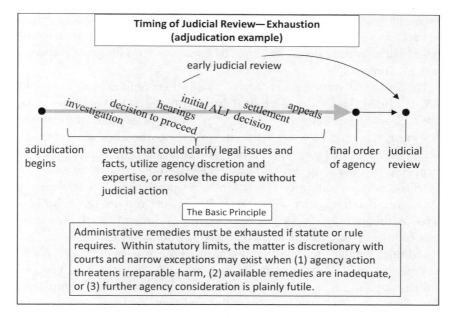

Figure 5.7   Exhaustion of Administrative Remedies

the APA, §704 provides that exhaustion of agency remedies is *not* required unless another statute or agency rule expressly requires it. Darby v. Cisneros, 509 U.S. 137 (1993). Interestingly, this clear provision sat silent and unnoticed by our top litigators, judges, justices and professors for almost 50 years before it was noticed, called to the attention of the Court, and applied. There is hope for us all.

Unless Congress has demanded it, exhaustion is largely within the discretion of the court. McCarthy v. Madigan, 503 U.S. 140 (1992). When a rule of judicial practice is called discretionary, the lawyer needs to know the factors that bear on the judicial exercise of discretion. In the case of exhaustion, the courts have stated a form of balancing test:

> In determining whether exhaustion is required, federal courts must balance the interest of the individual in retaining prompt access to a federal judicial forum against countervailing institutional interests favoring exhaustion. McCarthy v. Madigan, 503 U.S. 140, 146 (1992).

If you reverse the order of these two factors, and if you read "countervailing institutional interests" to include protecting the courts from having to decide undeveloped, hypothetical or abstract questions, you arrive at an analysis very similar to what we found in ripeness. The convention, nevertheless, is that the two doctrines are different. Typically, ripeness is used when there are no remedies a petitioner can exhaust, as would be the case when a final rule is attacked before enforcement.

The classic exhaustion case is Myers v. Bethlehem Shipbuilding Corp., 303 U.S. 41 (1938). The National Labor Relations Board (NLRB) began an unfair labor action against Bethlehem alleging that in one of its plants the company had engaged in unfair labor practices in violation of the labor act. Bethlehem sought to enjoin the Labor Board from proceeding. One of Bethlehem's arguments was that the plant involved was not engaged in interstate commerce — a jurisdictional condition of any action by a federal agency. Bethlehem was not arguing that the agency was wrong in its conclusion about the unfair labor practice (that question had yet to be tried) but that absent an effect on interstate commerce, the federal agency simply had no power over the company. In addition, Bethlehem alleged serious harm in the form of direct costs of the proceeding, loss of time of its officials, and serious impairment of the good will and harmonious relations existing between the company and its employees. Obviously, if an NLRB order against the company was later set aside as beyond the agency's jurisdiction, these costs could not be recouped.

Both the district court and the court of appeals agreed with Bethlehem and granted the injunction, effectively stopping the NLRB from further proceedings against the company. Both lower courts held that on the law as they saw it (the dates were 1936–37) all the courts that had ruled on the matter had concluded that manufacturers were not subject to the NLRB because manufacturing as such was not interstate commerce. Since it seemed clear, therefore, that the NLRB was acting outside its jurisdiction, the courts granted Bethlehem's injunction.

But as you know, timing is everything. Some of the lower court cases the *Bethlehem* lower courts relied on (especially the lower court decision in *Jones & Laughlin Steel*) were themselves on their way to the Supreme Court. By the time *Jones & Laughlin Steel* arrived in the Supreme Court, that Court had undergone a historic shift from its anti-New Deal stance. *Jones & Laughlin* held that manufacturing could be regulated under the Commerce Clause if it had significant impact on interstate commerce. NLRB v. Jones & Laughlin Steel, 301 U.S. 615 (1937). When the *Bethlehem* case arrived in the Supreme Court the next year, therefore, the jurisdiction of the NLRB over manufacturers was established. Under the new doctrine, the NLRB clearly had jurisdiction over a large manufacturer like Bethlehem — whose suppliers and customers were scattered around the United States and, indeed, around the world. With that legal premise settled, it was not difficult for the Supreme Court to reverse the lower courts in *Bethlehem* and allow the NLRB to proceed with its case against the company.

But as you also know, there are decisions and then there are opinions. In the *Bethlehem* opinion by Justice Brandeis there was no mention of the major shift in interstate commerce jurisprudence that had occurred. Instead, he ruled that the district court was without jurisdiction to issue an injunction since the statute gave exclusive decisional power to the NLRB, subject to court of appeals review. Bethlehem argued that it was constitutionally unacceptable to force it to go through a lengthy proceeding that might turn out to be beyond the agency's power. Justice Brandeis cited

> the long-settled rule of judicial administration that no one is entitled to judicial relief for a supposed or threatened injury until the prescribed administrative remedy has been exhausted.... [The exhaustion rule] has been repeatedly acted on in cases where, as here, the contention is made that the administrative body lacked power over the subject matter.... Obviously, the rules requiring exhaustion of the administrative remedy cannot be circumvented by asserting that the charge on which the complaint rests is groundless and that the mere holding of the prescribed administrative hearing would result in irreparable damage. Lawsuits also often prove to have been groundless; but no way has been discovered of relieving a defendant from the necessity of a trial to establish the fact. 303 U.S. at 50–52.

Some critics feel the *Bethlehem* case stated too strict an exhaustion rule—that it seemed to require exhaustion even when agency action was facially improper and that little generosity would be shown to claims of hardship to the parties. See Jaffe, JUDICIAL CONTROL OF ADMINISTRATIVE ACTION 424–26 (1965). Perhaps the opinion's stringent exhaustion rule should be limited to cases where fuller factual development at the agency level will inform later judicial resolution of constitutional issues—typically the case where an action is alleged to be unconstitutional "as applied"—with the exhaustion rule not applied so strictly where the constitutional issue can be decided on the pleadings. Similarly, perhaps one can understand the need, as a general matter, to reject litigation expenses as "irreparable injury." A contrary holding might eliminate the exhaustion rule entirely. But applying the Brandeis principle strictly would unwisely require exhaustion even where early review might be feasible and might save a petitioner from costs of unusual types or magnitudes.

Even if the rule at the federal level is stated with much severity, there remain three recognized exceptions to the exhaustion rule, all of which grow from the implicit premise of the doctrine: that a remedy is in fact available, that it can be timely invoked, and that it will substantially respond to petitioner's claim.

The first exception has to do with "undue prejudice" or "irreparable injury" to the petitioner resulting from delay in review—either agency relief will be unreasonably delayed or the injury needs immediate relief if any relief is to be had at all. An example of the former is agency action subject to very lengthy delay. *Walker v. Southern R. Co.*, 385 U.S. 196 (1966) (possible delay of 10 years in administrative proceedings makes exhaustion unnecessary). An example of the latter would be a case of delay in providing disability benefits or preclusion of a defense in a criminal case. See *Bowen v. City of New York*, 476 U.S. at 483 (disability claimants); *Moore v. East Cleveland*, 431 U.S. 494, 497, n. 5 (1977) (criminal defense) (plurality opinion).

A second cluster of exceptions to the exhaustion rule involve the agency's own lack of authority to provide the type of relief the petitioner seeks. The absence of agency authority may be general (as in the usual statement that agency's lack authority to rule on the constitutionality of their own statutes), *Moore v. East Cleveland*, 431 U.S. 494, 497, n. 5 (1977) (plurality opinion), or it may be that the agency lacks the specific type of remedy the plaintiff seeks. McCarthy v. Madigan, 503 U.S. 140 (1992) (concurring opinion; exhaustion not required when petitioner sought monetary damages that agency had no authority to grant).

Third, and finally, there is the exception sometimes mentioned under the general rubric of "futility." If the agency is truly biased or has otherwise made up its mind on the issue, exhaustion may sometimes be excused. *Houghton v. Shafer*, 392 U.S. 639, 640 (1968) (in view of Attorney General's submission that the challenged rules of the prison were "validly and correctly applied to petitioner," requiring administrative review through a process culminating with the Attorney General "would be to demand a futile act"). Of course, it will take more than a petitioner's concern about an agency's generally negative predisposition toward petitioner. In *Bethlehem*, e.g., the NLRB began its unfair labor practice proceeding only after receipt of employee complaints and after its own investigation. Clearly, the agency did not begin with a wholly neutral state of mind. To excuse exhaustion in such a case would decimate the administrative process. So the futility exception to exhaustion will require a relatively dramatic and focused hostility sufficient to overcome the usual presumption of impartiality. *Association of National Advertisers, Inc. v. FTC*, 627 F.2d 1151, 1156–1157 (D.C. Cir. 1979).

Closely related to the exhaustion doctrine, is a general rule that *issues* not raised before the agency cannot be raised in the reviewing court. The relation to the exhaustion rule is clear: we need a rule that will induce parties to fully reveal their cases early in the process and, in addition, will ensure that reviewing courts will know the agency's view on an argument before they review it. There may be exceptions if miscarriage of justice would result, Paul v. Shalala, 9 F.3d 208 (5th Cir. 1994) (agency misled petitioner), or if the issue could not reasonably have been foreseen. Eagle Eye Fishing Corp. v. U.S., 20 F. 3rd 503 (1st Cir. 1994) (narrow exception; even pro se litigant must raise issue below if a "reasonably well prepared litigant" would have raised it). Some state administrative procedure acts have included the issue exhaustion doctrine in statutory form. See, e.g., Wash. Rev. Statute, § 34.05.445 (2007). While issue exhaustion is mostly applied in adjudications, an occasional court will apply it in the rulemaking context, holding that one cannot challenge a rule on an issue that was not explicitly raised in the public comment on rule. Southwestern Pa. Growth Alliance v. Browner, 121 F.3d 106 (3rd Cir. 1997) (opinion by then-Circuit Judge Samuel Alito).

E. How Is Judicial Review Obtained?

This is a topic for full development in your courses in Federal Courts and Civil Procedure, but there are some special terms in this field that you should know. There are essentially three avenues to judicial relief. First, the agency's own statute may provide for judicial review and may spell out details about where and how review is to be accomplished. In conventional usage among administrative law lawyers, this is called *special statutory review*. Second, the APA provides for judicial review in §§ 701–705. This is called *general statutory review*. Finally, in the rare case where these two avenues are closed, federal courts retain traditional common law and equitable forms of action such as declaratory judgments, mandamus, etc. Although all federal court action must be pursuant to statute, this type of review has acquired the name, *nonstatutory review*. Jurisdiction of federal courts to review federal agency action cases is usually based on the "federal question" jurisdiction granted to the federal courts by 28 U.S.C. § 1331.

F. Primary Jurisdiction

In a legal system as complex as ours, there will be inevitable overlaps of different legal regimes. Where two overlapping regimes are furthering different substantive policies, how do we resolve conflicts that may arise? The most difficult version of the problem arises when one federal regulatory regime would punish behavior that is affirmatively approved by another federal regime. And in a subset of that area, one legal policy may be enforceable through one branch of government (e.g., the judicial branch) and the other through another branch (e.g., the executive branch in the form of an administrative agency). We will examine this subset and the doctrine it has generated called the doctrines of primary jurisdiction. Primary jurisdiction is a cluster of doctrines of unusual subtlety and nuance, a great challenge for the best analyst.

The doctrine of primary jurisdiction arises when an action is begun in court and a claim is made that the matter should be dismissed (or postponed) so that an agency authorized to deal in some manner with the dispute is first given a chance to rule on the matter. So at the outset, it is clear that primary jurisdiction cases are not normally about jurisdiction in any usual sense. Both instrumentalities—court and agency—have jurisdiction, else there would be no conflict. More realistically, the question is which instrumentality should be allowed to exercise its jurisdiction first.

The doctrine had its origin in the transportation field, where on the one hand we had an administrative agency (the Interstate Commerce Commission) with authority over railroad rates and, on the other, federal courts that had developed body of common law principles for judicial resolution of common carrier rate disputes. In 1907, the Supreme Court had such a case. Importantly, the statute authorizing the Commission to act specifically saved any "remedies now existing at common law." 24 Stat. 387 (1887). Nevertheless, the Court ruled that the need for national uniformity in the resolution of railroad rate disputes required a court to dismiss plaintiff's common law action, relegating plaintiff to his remedies before the Commission. Texas and Pac. Ry. v. Abilene Cotton Oil Co., 204 U.S. 426 (1907).

Why does the choice of forum matter to the parties? There may be several kinds of differences between the judicial and the administrative resolutions. It may be simply a matter of geography—a local court may be more friendly to local shipper—than a distant federal agency. It may be a matter of time—relatively prompt judicial decision versus a more drawn out agency proceeding. There may be cost differences in the two processes.

Perhaps the most important impact on the parties arises in cases where the law that will be applied by the court is different from the law that will be applied by the agency. If a workers' compensation commission is created because of dissatisfaction with the generosity of common law juries, the choice of forum could affect the outcome of an injured worker's case. In the antitrust field, competitors sharing price information would find hostility in a court enforcing the Sherman Act but affirmative support in an agency that believes that cooperative action among competitors is important to the health of the industry. And in the bewildering variety of things Congress does, policy con-flicts like this—intended or just the result of less than careful drafting—are not uncommon.

In the 1950s, the government brought an action in a district court to enforce the Sherman Act against an association of shipping companies (carriers) op-erating under the name of the Far Eastern Conference. The complaint alleged that these companies had agreed among themselves to charge lower rates to shippers who used only Conference ships. The Conference would more than likely lose this case because its action would be a per se violation of the Sher-man Act—a classic "conspiracy to restrain trade." The Conference moved to dismiss the judicial action on the ground that the Federal Maritime Board had primary jurisdiction. The Maritime Act created the Federal Maritime Board which had authority to approve some agreements among carriers and, if ap-proved by the Board, the agreements were immune from prosecution under the antitrust laws. Should the court grant the motion to dismiss?

In Far Eastern Conference v. U.S., 432 U.S. 570 (1952), the Supreme Court did dismiss the government's antitrust action, relegating anyone claiming dam-age from Conference practices to their remedy before the Maritime Board. Jus-tices Frankfurter said that

> in cases raising issues of fact not within the conventional experience of judges or cases requiring the exercise of administrative discretion, agencies created by Congress for regulating the subject matter should not be passed over.... Uniformity and consistency in the regulation of business entrusted to a particular agency are secured, and the limited functions of review by the judiciary are more rationally exercised, by preliminary resort for ascertaining and interpreting the circumstances underlying legal issues to agencies that are better equipped than courts. 432 U.S. at 574 (1952).

This is classic primary jurisdiction analysis, and if you retain nothing more from this section than Justice Frankfurter's paragraph, you'll never go far wrong. Note the passage's key elements: a court might dismiss an action on the basis that an agency had primary jurisdiction (1) if there are present in the case technical facts which agency expertise would illuminate, (2) if necessary to honor the con-gressional wish that the decision reflect informed agency discretion, (3) if agency determination would increase uniformity and consistency and (4) if necessary to better ground judicial review should the matter ever come back to the court.

Two dissenting justices argued that the Board did not have power under the Shipping Act to approve an arrangement such as this since the arrangement was aimed at punishing third party carriers. In Justice Frankfurter's view, re-

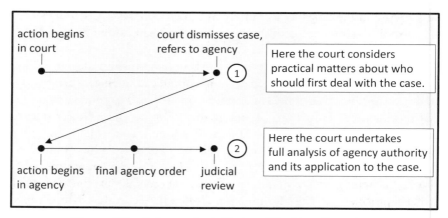

Figure 5.8   Primary Jurisdiction: The Two Questions

sponded that that legal question was premature; courts could better assess the question of the Maritime Board's powers after the Board had reviewed the matter. Thus, prior resort to the Board was necessary "even though the facts after they have been appraised by specialized competence serve as a premise for legal consequences to be judicially defined." Ibid.

In fact, the Board did approve these dual-rate structures but when the matter returned to the Supreme Court, a majority of the Court ruled that the Board had no power to do so—essentially adopting the legal analysis of the dissent in *Far Eastern*. FMB v. Isbrantsen Co., 356 U.S. 481 (1958). Though Justice Frankfurter's opinion in *Far Eastern* clearly contemplated later judicial review, he probably expected the Court to uphold the Board's action. But changes on the Court had apparently altered the Court's view of the powers of the Maritime Board vis a vis the antitrust laws. So Justice Frankfurter—stout champion of primary jurisdiction in *Far Eastern*—becomes a critic of the doctrine in *Isbrantsen*. In dissent, he said that to require plaintiff to consult an agency and then to rule later that the agency had no power to act makes of the doctrine of primary jurisdiction "an empty ritual," a "wasteful futility," a "travesty of law and an abuse of the judicial process." 356 U.S. at 522.

Granting the potential for judicial abuse, the *Isbrantsen* case makes it clear that a court makes two separate and quite different judgments in the two occasions it may have the case before it. Consider Figure 5.8.

When it is considering who has primary jurisdiction, step (1) in the diagram, a court is considering practical matters about where the proceeding should start, the answer turning on questions of expertise, discretion, and the needs for uniformity. Later, when the matter is before the court on judicial review, step (2) in the diagram, the court is considering fully the various factors that bear on the agency's general authority and the particularized elements that permit assessment of how the general authority was applied in this case.

Finally, remember that application of the primary jurisdiction doctrine sometimes results in dismissal of the case, and sometimes merely a postponement to await the agency's initial resolution of a specific question. If the case is dismissed, the dismissal is usually not with prejudice—the plaintiff may later refile the action in court if after the agency is finished with its work a justiciable cause remains.

G. Summary

As we have seen, while judicial review is an important feature of the U.S. administrative law system, much administrative agency action is not subject to review by the courts. The doctrines we have been considering should be understood in light of their functions—to assure judicial review where needed to keep agencies within their legislative charters and legislatures within their constitutional powers, and to do so without imposing inappropriate tasks on courts or permitting courts to intrude inappropriately into matters better resolved elsewhere. Figure 5.9 summarizes the doctrine of availability.

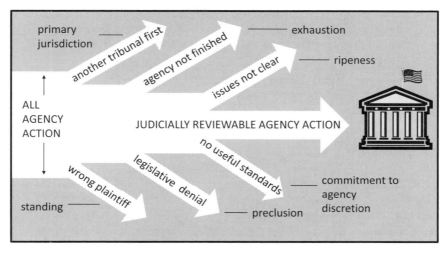

Figure 5.9   Availability of Judicial Review

Checkpoints

- Judicial review of agency action is a critical part of the system that ultimately legitimates the administrative process.

- Despite this, judicial review is not always available, due to certain judge- made doctrines.

- The background premise: in most cases, there is a strong presumption in favor of judicial review. A reverse presumption obtains in some cases (e.g., prosecutorial discretion and like matters are usually unreviewable).

- Statutes can preclude review, explicitly or implicitly. Given the background premise, such statutes are usually construed narrowly.

- Statutes may grant agencies such broad discretion in a matter that courts cannot find any "law to apply." Such courts may conclude that the matter has been committed to agency discretion and unreviewable under § 701 of the APA.

- Not all plaintiffs qualify as petitioners for judicial review.

   - at the constitutional level, the plaintiff must present a "case or controversy" — a specific and likely injury in fact, caused by the agency action challenged.

   - beyond that, the court can further restrict the class of plaintiffs by discretionary qualifiers such as the zone of interest test, the antipathy to reviewing generalized grievances, etc.

- The timing of judicial review is also important. Usually, courts only review final agency actions, actions with respect to which all administrative remedies have been exhausted, and matters that are ripe enough to present issues clear enough for sensible judicial resolution.

- The doctrine of primary jurisdiction is not really part of this set, but functions as to other members of the set to prevent or delay judicial review. The doctrine requires prior resort to an agency if agency action is the more practical road to expert evaluation, uniformity, etc.

Chapter 6

Scope of Judicial Review of Agency Action

Roadmap

- The Importance of Judicial Review
- The Basic Charter: Navigating APA § 706
- Review of Agency Fact Determinations; formal and informal proceedings
- Review of Agency Legal Interpretations — the Historic Cases
- The *Chevron* Revolution
- *Chevron*: Steps One and Two
- Review of Agency Judgment and Exercises of Discretion

A. Introduction

1. The Importance of Scope of Review

The topic to be addressed here can be thought of as the central nerve of administrative law. The Supreme Court has not had occasion to rule on whether judicial review is constitutionally mandated since most agency action is made reviewable by statute, but the importance of that review is clear. As we saw in Chapter 1, a major function of administrative law is the correction of some of the shortfalls in our separated powers form of government — shortfalls that have been caused by the unexpected growth of the regulatory state. One of the greatest infringements that growth has made on strict separation of powers theory is what is perceived to be a substantial transfer of basic policy-making power from accountable elected officials to unelected administrators. To minimize the accountability loss from that delegation, some technique is necessary to keep administrative policy-making faithful to legislative preferences. As we have seen, this can be done in many ways.

While all officials take oaths to support the law, and while most agency legal conclusions made on a day-to-day basis are accepted and carried out without ever having been seen by judges, review by the courts has a special importance. Judges are the most visible and in some senses the most final of the watchmen and potential judicial review casts a shadow over the daily workings of all agencies. Agency efforts to avoid judicial review or to minimize its impact are woven into much agency work. In addition, as former EPA lawyer William Pedersen taught us, judicial review

> reaches beyond those who were concerned with the specific regulations reviewed. They serve as a precedent for future rule-writers and give those who care about well-documented and well-reasoned decision-making a lever with which to move those who do not. William F. Pedersen, Jr., *Formal Records and Informal Rulemaking*, 85 YALE L. J. 38, 60 (1975).

But judicial review doctrine must perform a very delicate operation. It must allow courts to perform their function of policing the legality of agency conduct without interfering with the task the Congress has assigned to the agency. If judicial review is too intensive, policies may be affected by the views of federal judges — persons who would not score high on our index of technical expertise or political accountability. On the other hand, if judicial review is not intensive enough, agency policies may not sufficiently reflect executive or legislative preferences and may not sufficiently reflect rule of law values.

Scope of review doctrines seek to balance these sometimes conflicting values. All understand that the task will require more than doctrine; it will require judges who have a robust sympathy for the democracy project as well as considerable skill and self-discipline. In administrative law, scope of review doctrine is where the rubber hits the road.

2. Some Preliminary Matters

Let us begin with getting some words straight. In describing the scope of review, the literature and the cases are full of adjectives such as strict, generous, permissive, broad, narrow, deep, etc. None of these seems to be wholly free of ambiguity. There is no single word that can calibrate the complex work of judges in this area, but in the discussion that follows we will use the word "intensity" as indicating roughly the depth of judicial review. High-intensity review will be review in which the judge feels reasonably comfortable in substituting his or her own views for that of the agency. At its extreme, we would call this de novo review. At the other end of the spectrum, low-intensity review would be review in which the judge will be highly deferential in reviewing the agency product. In the middle of the spectrum will be the usual gradations. See Figure 6.1. While the qualities of judicial review are far too subtle to be captured on a single linear spectrum, thinking about them in this way gives us a start on comparing different legislative phrases and different judicial attitudes toward review.

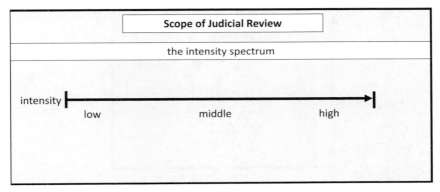

Figure 6.1   Scopes of Review Intensities

It is also useful to keep in mind the relationships of the various players and the exact points in the process to which most discussions of scope of review refer. As indicated in Figure 6.2, in the typical example of judicial review of formal adjudication, e.g., we are likely to find one setting in which a decision by an ALJ has been reviewed by the head of the agency in an internal review process (1), a final order of the agency that has been reviewed by a court of appeals (2), and possibly a court of appeals decision that is reviewed by the Supreme Court (3). In our discussions, we will be mostly concerned with step (2)—where the final administrative order has its first encounter with the courts. As we have seen earlier, at step (1)—where the agency is reviewing its own administrative law judge—§ 557(b) provides that agency review can be highly intensive. At step (3)—where the Supreme Court is reviewing a decision of the court of appeals—review can be relatively unintensive, at least when the high court so chooses. The Court has said (and sometimes remembers it has said):

> Whether on the record as a whole there is substantial evidence to support agency findings is a question which Congress has placed in the

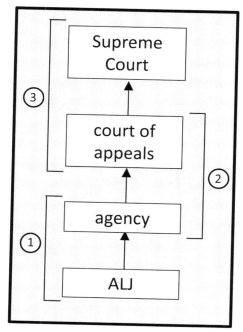

Figure 6.2   The Levels of Review

keeping of the Courts of Appeals. This Court will intervene only in what ought to be the rare instance when the standard appears to have been misapprehended or grossly misapplied. Universal Camera v. NLRB, 340 U.S. 474, 491 (1951).

In any scope of review problem, you must begin with any words of the statute that may signal the legislative preference about the intensity of review. This statutory formula may appear in an agency's own act or in a generally applicable act such as the Administrative Procedure Act. If you read through § 706 of the APA, e.g., you can get a sense of how these formulas are phrased. See Figure 6.3.

Take special note about which formulas apply to which kinds of cases. (You might want to go back and look at Figure 3.5 in Chapter 3 for a comparison of the different review intensities in the judicial and the administrative contexts.) With that statutory formula in hand, we can then go on to see what the formulas mean in operational terms—largely by looking at how judges have used

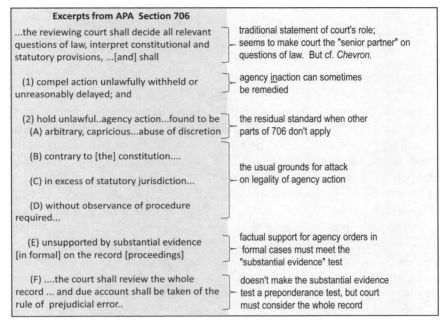

Figure 6.3   The APA Formulas for Judicial Review

them. Figure 6.4 shows our intensity spectrum with some conventional statutory formulas tentatively placed along it.

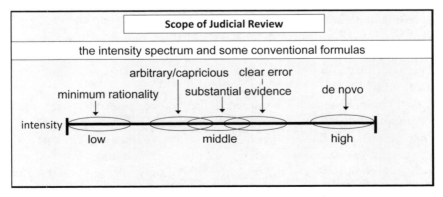

Figure 6.4   Statutory Formulas for Judicial Review

B. Review of Agency Determinations of Ordinary Fact

Let's begin with what is, in doctrinal terms, the easiest kind of judicial review: the task set for the court when the evidential sufficiency of an agency decision is challenged. What is a question of fact? Great doctrinal battles have been fought over the distinction between law and fact, but we needn't get into such deep philosophical waters here. For our purposes, we will use one of the classic statements of the distinction: Professor Jaffe said a finding of fact "is an assertion that a phenomenon has happened or is or will be happening independent of or anterior to any assertion as to its legal effect." Jaffe, JUDICIAL CONTROL OF ADMINISTRATIVE ACTION 548 (1965). The statement of fact can be made by a speaker with no knowledge of the legal implications of the assertion. Under this definition, a statement that the skid marks on the pavement were 46' long would be a statement of fact; the speaker needs no knowledge of speed limits, negligence liability, or any other legal implications of the propositions. By contrast, a proposition of law is a statement of a standard that can be advanced with no knowledge of the facts in a particular case. Thus, the statement that the speed limit on the highway in question was 30 mph is a proposition of law that can be made without knowledge of any particular case that may involve the speed limit.

Of course, such tidy categories will now and then overlap. Where the case turns on an inference drawn from facts (defendant's car must have exceeded the speed limit given the length of the skid marks), or where the decision turns on judgment about factual significance that is colored by policy considerations (speeding in a school zone is especially to be punished) the matter is more complex. For the present, let's stick with what are called "ordinary" facts — facts that answer questions about who did what to whom and with what effects. What is a court's job when assessing the legality of an agency's finding of ordinary fact?

Begin (as always) with the statute. In the judicial world, there are a number of formulas that have been used to assess the quality of evidence in particular contexts, each signaling a somewhat different level of intensity. The list would include familiar phrases such as beyond a reasonable doubt, clear and convincing, preponderance of the evidence, substantial evidence, scintilla of evidence, etc. Under § 706 of the APA there are only two formulas for review of agency fact findings, the substantial evidence test and the arbitrary and capricious test. Section 706 provides that for *formal* proceedings (adjudications or rulemakings required to be conducted on the record and hence under § 556

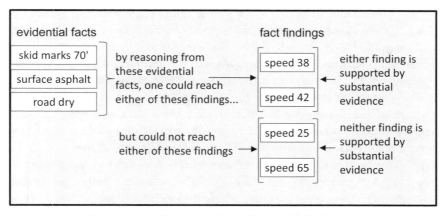

Figure 6.5   Determining Substantial Evidence

and § 557 of the act) the factual adequacy of administrative order is to be determined by the "substantial evidence" test. For findings of fact in *informal* proceedings (notice and comment rulemaking and informal adjudications), § 706 provides for review under the "arbitrary and capricious" test.

1. Substantial Evidence

What degree of review intensity does the substantial evidence test prescribe? It is commonly thought of as a medium-intensity test placed somewhere in the middle of our intensity spectrum. Judicial elaborations of the meaning of substantial evidence have tended to focus on questions of reasonableness — the court defining substantial evidence as "such relevant evidence as a reasonable mind might accept as adequate to support a conclusion." Consolidated Edison *v.* NLRB, 305 U.S. 197, 229 (1938). The sense of the test is perhaps more accurately captured if the word "reasonable" is replaced with the word "reasoning." That is, the question should be whether one could move from the evidence in the record to the findings by the use of a reasoning process. Whether the finding is reasonable in some more general sense should not be important.

With that general guidance in mind, we can say that the task of the reviewing court is to examine each of the agency's fact findings to see if there is evidence in the record from which a reasoning mind could have arrived at the findings. See the example in Figure 6.5.

It has been clear since the leading case of Universal Camera v. NLRB, 340 U.S. 474 (1951) that in making this assessment the reviewing court should take into account not only the evidence supporting the agency's findings but also any evidence that "fairly detracts" from that evidence. Suppose an agency denies a disability claim relying on testimony of its medical expert that the claimant could stand for seven or eight hours in a workday and thus was not disabled. By itself, this testimony would be regarded as substantial and the agency order would stand. But if there were other treating physicians who had testified that the claimant should stand no more than three or four hours per day, the agency's findings would be regarded by the reviewing court as considerably less substantial. This may seem an obvious point, but it took *Universal Camera* and the "whole record" language of § 706 to bring all judges into agreement on the point. This does not mean that the substantial evidence test has been converted into a preponderance test; the judge's job is to decide whether the agency's findings are reasoned, not that they are right—a difficult distinction, but one disciplined judges manage in many places in their work.

In determining whether the evidence in support of the agency action is substantial, what is the significance of a disagreement between the agency and the ALJ on disputed factual questions? We discussed this in Chapter 3 and concluded that while § 557(b) gives the reviewing agency virtually complete power of decision, the reviewing court should not ignore ALJ fact findings that owe something to the demeanor of witnesses. *Universal Camera*, supra, teaches that when such findings are ignored by the agency, the evidence supporting its decision may be regarded by the reviewing court as less substantial. That means that agencies do not have to accept ALJ legal conclusions, policy judgments, exercises of discretion, or even secondary inferences from facts found. And if it explains carefully, the agency on review should be able to use its experience to evaluate the significance of evidence in the record. But *Universal Camera* teaches that it is a wise agency that explains obvious contradictions between its fact findings and those of the ALJ.

2. Arbitrary and Capricious

For reviewing the factual sufficiency of *informal* proceedings such as rulemaking and informal adjudications, § 706(2)(A) of the APA prescribes the arbitrary and capricious test. Since both the substantial evidence and the arbitrary and capricious tests seem in terms to involve some sense of reasonableness, do they reflect different levels of review intensity? Debate has raged over this question for years. Justice Scalia as a circuit court judge expressed the view that the two tests were essentially identical since "it is impossible to conceive of a nonarbitrary factual judgment supported only by evidence that is not substantial in the APA sense." Association of Data Processing Service Organizations v. Board of Governors, 745 F.2d 677, 683 (D.C. Cir. 1984). Others have found a difference in the fact that Congress specifically chose one formula over the other and usually it was in the context of a stated congressional desire to increase the intensity of review. Thus, in agencies such as the OSHA and the FTC, informal proceedings are by the agency's own statutes subjected to the substantial evidence test rather than the APA default arbitrary and capricious test. The legislative history of these acts suggests that Congress intended courts to have a stronger role in supervising the factual adequacy of decisions of these agencies. Strauss, ADMINISTRATIVE JUSTICE IN THE UNITED STATES 347–49 (2d ed. 2002).

A complicating factor is that the arbitrary and capricious test has not been stable in its meaning over time, nor is it used with same intensity for reviewing all kinds of issues or in all kinds of agency proceedings. In the 1930s, the test was very unintensive, but today, as we will shortly see, the test has become considerably more intensive, especially in review of agency discretion (as distinguished from the review of fact findings we are considering here) and most especially when agency discretion is exercised in high-stakes rulemaking. Strauss, *Overseers or "The Deciders"—The Courts in Administrative Law*, 75 U. CHI. L. REV. 815, 821–23 (2008).

Wherever one comes down on the difference between substantial evidence and arbitrary and capricious, note that in Figure 6.4, above, the two tests appear as bands on the continuum, not as points, and that the bands overlap considerably. That seems a reasonably approximate depiction of their relationship.

If the agency action is informal—rulemaking or adjudication—there will not be the sort of record that reviewing courts see in formal proceedings. Where, then, is the judge to look for the evidence that would satisfy the arbitrary and capricious test? We have seen in the rulemaking chapter that modern rulemaking—still stubbornly called "informal" in the administrative law lexicon—can involve mountains of information (in paper and digital form). Where factual sufficiency of agency *rulemaking* is challenged, we will see that the courts will look at anything the agency had before it in making its decision. The best comment remains, Pedersen, *Formal Records and Informal Rulemaking*, 85 YALE L. J. 38 (1975).

On the other hand, informal *adjudications* may leave few traces of the evidence on which the decision is based, making application of the arbitrary and capricious test difficult. If the court is unable to assess the factual adequacy of the order, it may remand for further proceedings. Cf. Citizens to Preserve Overton Park v. Volpe, 401 U.S. 402 (1971). In reviewing either informal rulemaking or informal adjudication for evidential sufficiency, the bottom line is that the test requires that agencies explain and justify their decisions against an ultimate standard of reasonableness. For further discussion, see the informal adjudication section in Chapter 3.

C. Review of Agency Legal Interpretations

1. The Historic Baseline

Agencies interpret statutes as part of their day-to-day implementation and enforcement of legislatively prescribed duties. When an agency's interpretation is presented to a court for review, we confront a very complicated intersection of legislative, executive and judicial powers. Who should be in charge? Who should have the final say? This is probably the most challenging, and certainly the most discussed of all the issues in administrative law.

When an agency's legal interpretation is challenged in court, a lawyer's first instinct might be to say the court should decide the question independently. This instinct has roots as far back as Marbury v. Madison, 5 U.S. 137 (1803), and it seems to be reflected in language of § 706 of the APA which indicates that "the reviewing court shall decide all relevant questions of law, [and] interpret constitutional and statutory provisions...."

Moreover, judicial primacy in law interpretation is supported by several weighty arguments. The first is Justice Marshall's declaration that law interpretation is simply what courts do—a notion premised on his understanding of the nature of the judicial function and the critical role it plays in our constitutional scheme. It has been difficult to dislodge that notion from our settled traditions and understandings; there is something natural—even sacrosanct—about judges deciding what the law means. Now and then, of course, the Court has taken a more practical (and less monopolistic) view of the judicial power, CFTC v. Schor, 478 U.S. 833 (1986), but the centrality of the notion is deeply imbedded in our culture.

It is also said that courts are more appropriate interpreters of the law because they are thought to be more principled, more policy-neutral and more objective than mission-oriented agencies would be. On its face, this is a plausible claim, but there are circumstances in which this could be an argument *against* judicial primacy, at least in settings in which judicial objectivity masks an insensitivity or even hostility to the underlying legislative purpose behind a regulatory scheme. The feeling is also expressed that judges, by training and experience, are more skilled at legal analysis and statutory interpretation than agencies.

On the other hand, some believe agencies are in some circumstances better equipped for interpretation than courts. If the meaning of a statutory term should reflect something of the authoring legislature's purpose or goal, the agency may have been "present at the creation," may have had a hand in promoting and drafting the statute in question and may thus have a sharper or clearer sense of the legislative purpose than a later reviewing court would have.

Further, the agency and its staff may be in a day-to-day working relationship with legislators and their staffs, and with the regulated parties, allowing the agency further insight into the practical implications of alternative interpretations. Further, if the meaning of a statutory term should reflect something of the policy preferences of the elected president, agency staff may be in closer touch with such political considerations; they, after all, are recent presidential appointees or people who work for presidential appointees. And, of course, the agency is much more likely to have technical, scientific, economic or other expertise than a reviewing court is likely to have, and that expertise may in some cases usefully furnish the interpretive process.

Finally, there is the important question of which of the alternative interpreters (courts or agencies) the legislature wished to play the larger role in interpreting a given statute. This will turn out to be a central question in the development of the doctrine today.

There are several ways we might take advantage of agency interpretive strengths. To begin with, a judge might just conclude that an agency interpretation was persuasive and, instead of adopting the interpretation as a judge-made doctrine, speak the language of deference. The *Marbury* dictum, after all, does not prevent a reviewing judge from having either good sense or humility. The most famous example is Justice Jackson's opinion in Skidmore v. Swift, 323 U.S. 134 (1944). In *Skidmore*, the Court gave some interpretive weight to the views of the Administrator of the Wage and Hour Division of the Department of Labor, even though the Administrator had expressed those views informally rather than in notice and comment rulemaking, and even though the Administrator had no power to enforce the act by administrative proceedings, but had to seek injunctions from a court. Justice Jackson's language has become classic:

> We consider that the rulings, interpretations and opinions of the Administrator under this act ... constitute a body of experience and informed judgment to which courts ... may properly resort for guidance. The weight of such a judgment in a particular case will depend upon the thoroughness evident in its consideration, the validity of its reasoning, its consistency with earlier or later pronouncements, and all those factors which give it power to persuade, if lacking power to control. Skidmore v. Swift, 323 U.S. 134, 140 (1944).

The last phrase of this quotation saved the principle of judicial supremacy in legal interpretations, but the whole tenor of the passage is deferential. Indeed, the distinction between what "controls" a judge and what is merely "persuasive" is somewhat elusive. When a judge follows an agency interpretation because it was thoroughly considered and validly reasoned, does it really matter whether we say the judge was persuaded or controlled? I suppose we can imagine a judge who might follow an agency interpretation that was persuasive on those grounds but who, if not required to follow it (was not controlled) might prefer a different interpretation. But in the real world that may be a hard case to find.

Another approach to getting the benefit of agency interpretive strengths is for the court to inquire whether there are parts of the overall interpretive problem that are suitable for judicial resolution and other parts on which deference would seem to be sensible. Something of that sort occurred in NLRB v. Hearst, 322 U.S. 111 (1944). Congress had authorized the NLRB to conduct formal adjudications for the purpose of resolving disputes arising in the labor law field. In such a proceeding, the Board was presented with the question of whether so-called "newsboys" fit within the statutory term "employees" — the category of persons with whom management was required to bargain collectively.

The Court first examined the question of whether Congress had intended to incorporate the common law definition of "employees" in the term as used in the labor act. If Congress had so intended, the employer would probably not be required to bargain with the newsboys; under normal common law analysis, the newsboys would have been independent contractors rather than employees. If, on the other hand, the legislature had intended a meaning of the word employee that was broader than the common law meaning, the newsboys could be within the statutory term and the employer would be required to bargain with them.

The Court concluded, independently, that the legislature had intended the word employee to extend beyond the common law definition. Its discussion included the statutory purpose and the practical problems the common law definition would generate in this setting—i.e., different rules for collective bargaining in different states around the country. The Court concluded that the legislature intended the word employee to cover any person economically related to the newspaper in ways that were relevant to the purposes of the labor act. In this lengthy discussion, there was no suggestion of any deference to the agency's view about the meaning of the statutory term. The Court was simply deciding independently what the legislature meant by the term.

The Court next turned to the question of whether the newsboys in this case had in fact the kind of economic relationship to the newspaper that would make them employees under the broad definition the Court had given the statutory term. On this question, the Court deferred substantially to the agency. Notice that the question at this stage becomes highly fact specific—one needs

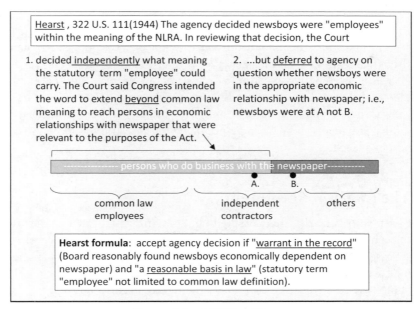

Figure 6.6   NLRB v. Hearst

to know how many newsboys there are, what their economic situation is, what choices they have about the locations from which they sell papers, what hours they work, what prices they charge and who sets the prices, how their compensation is calculated, etc. These are all matters within the knowledge and experience of the agency and present questions about which courts have no special knowledge or experience. Accordingly, the Court accepted the agency's conclusion on this issue, limiting its role to determining whether or not the agency's judgment was reasonable. In the words of the Court, its role in this phase of the case was to determine if the agency decision had a "warrant in the record and a reasonable basis in law." The case is illustrated in Figure 6.6.

Incidentally, any readers who assume determining legislative intent is a relatively simple matter might be interested in knowing that the Court in *Hearst* got the wrong answer. At its next opportunity, Congress amended the act to be sure common law independent contractors were *not* included in the definition of "employee" in the Labor Act. See NLRB v. United Insurance, 390 U.S. 254, 256 (1968). Get used to the idea that determining legislative intent is a very chancy business.

For most of U.S. administrative law's history, these two ways of capturing the benefit of agency interpretive superiority—*Skidmore* and *Hearst*—were sufficient. Courts either gave agency views what persuasive weight they intrinsically warranted on the basis of the thoroughness of their consideration or the validity of their reasoning, or, where Congress had given the agency power to decide the case initially, the courts established by independent analysis the range within which the agency legal interpretations must fall, then allowed the agency relative freedom to decide exactly where within that range it would come down. True, the doctrine was not always predictable as in its nature it was case specific, but the allocation decisions were made on practical and functional judgments about where responsibility for the various interpretive tasks should be placed.

2. The *Chevron* Revolution?

Fasten your seatbelts; this is going to be something of a roller coaster ride. We have here one of the (thankfully) rare events in our jurisprudence where a single case becomes the occasion for an extraordinary outpouring of citations, learned articles, endless discussion, and sharp division among judges at all levels. Since the case was decided (1984), there have been roughly 10,000 citations to it in federal cases alone, and more than 200 major scholarly articles with the case name in the title (which doesn't count discussions without the case name in the title). In addition, the flow shows no signs of stopping; at this writing (summer 2009) more than 1,000 judicial citations were added in the most recent 12-month period and at least 16 major articles. You can be sure the case touched a deep nerve in our legal system and needs to be considered carefully. And given the volume and velocity of the action, we will need a firm grip on the basics to keep our balance.

In 1984, the Court decided Chevron v. NRDC, 467 U.S. 837 (1984) and raised, perhaps unwittingly, a new set of puzzles. The opinion addressed the question of the circumstances under which a court should defer to a legal determination made by an agency, rather than perform a court's more usual role of deciding legal questions independently. That the question should be asked at all expresses what was only implicit in *Skidmore* and *Hearst*—that agencies have a legitimate role in the law-interpretation process. If that is conceded, the question becomes how law-interpreting power should be allocated between court and agency. To give away the final answer, the *Chevron* doctrine—as it has evolved through 25 years of decisions, debate and commentary—is thought by most to call for a somewhat broader role for agency law-interpreting than could be comfortably fitted into the *Skidmore* and *Hearst* approaches.

Here are three principles to get you started in thinking about this allocation decision.

1. Courts and agencies share the process of law creation and application; scope of review doctrines like *Chevron* seek to allocate appropriate roles to each of the players.
2. Congress has the primary authority to make this allocation decision and when it has spoken its allocations (save for constitutional questions) usually will control.
3. When Congress has not spoken, courts have no choice but to make the allocation decision, and they make it independently.

Read that again and let it sink in a bit. We do not view courts and agencies as competitors, rivals, or players differently situated on some hierarchy of authority engaged in a zero sum contest. It is more helpful to think of courts and agencies as partners—partners in a complex system of law creation and application. When primary interpretive authority must be allocated to one or the other, the task is to decide (oversimplifying just a bit) when one of the partners will serve as a senior partner and when as a junior partner. Or, in Peter Strauss's felicitous phrase, whether the court will play a role as a decider or as an overseer. Strauss, *Overseers or "The Deciders"—The Courts in Administrative Law*, 75 U. Chi. L. Rev. 815 (2008).

In the *Chevron* case itself, the Court was reviewing a decision of the court of appeals that had rejected an agency interpretation of a statutory phrase. The court of appeals had disagreed with the agency's interpretation, found it inconsistent with prior judicial rulings and, taking an independent *Marbury*-like view of the matter, rejected the agency's interpretation. In reversing the court of appeals, the Supreme Court, speaking through Justice Stevens, said:

> When a court reviews an agency's construction of the statute that it administers, it is confronted with two questions. First, always, is the question whether Congress has directly spoken to the precise question at issue. If the intent of Congress is clear, that is the end of the matter; for the court, as well as the agency, must give effect to the unambiguously expressed intent of Congress. If, however, the court determines Congress has not directly addressed the precise question at issue, the court does not simply impose its own construction on the statute, as would be necessary in the absence of an administrative interpretation. Rather, if the statute is silent or ambiguous with respect to the specific

issue, the question for the court is whether the agency's answer is based on a permissible construction of the statute. 467 U.S. at 482–83.

Get used to the numbers if you want to be au courant with *Chevron* issues. The Court framed the doctrine in two distinct steps — soon named the "*Chevron* two-step" by the commentariat. Ground your thinking in these two steps, but do not be surprised if academic elaborations produce different enumerations. Stephenson and Vermeule, *Chevron Has Only One Step*, 95 Va. L. Rev. 597 (2009); Merrill and Hickman, *Chevron's Domain*, 89 Geo. L. J. 833, 836 (2001) (suggesting a third step, "Step Zero").

While it is possible to regard *Chevron* as merely restating the *Hearst/Skidmore* doctrine in the field of rulemaking, there are some differences. For example, in defining court/agency roles, the *Hearst/Skidmore* analysis might have owed much to comparative qualifications — the experience of the Administrator of the Wage and Hour Division of the Department of Labor in *Skidmore* and the NLRB's expertise in the field of labor relations issues in *Hearst*. By contrast, *Chevron* and the cases and commentary that followed it seemed to find other reasons for deference. It may be a requirement of separation of powers (courts ought not interfere with executive functions), or of democratic accountability (agencies are more accountable than life-tenured judges are). Sunstein, *Chevron Step Zero*, 92 Va. L. Rev. 187 (2006). In the *Chevron* opinion itself, Justice Stevens seemed to explain deference as a matter of fidelity to legislative intent. There had been a delegation from Congress — either an explicit or implicit delegation — that gave any reasonable agency interpretation "controlling weight."

> If Congress has explicitly left a gap for the agency to fill, there is an express delegation of authority to the agency to elucidate a specific provision of the statute by regulation. Such legislative regulations are given controlling weight unless they are arbitrary, capricious, or manifestly contrary to the statute. Sometimes the legislative delegation to an agency on a particular question is implicit rather than explicit. In such a case, a court may not substitute its own construction of a statutory provision for a reasonable interpretation made by the administrator of an agency. 467 U.S. at 843–44.

As an interesting aside (and some of you might consider the jurisprudential implications of this), it is clear from Justice Stevens's opinion and from his later writings that he did not think he was letting a new genie out of the bottle. He thought he was merely stating a principle that was familiar:

> We have long recognized that considerable weight should be accorded to an executive department's construction of a statutory scheme it is

entrusted to administer, and the principle of deference to administrative interpretations has been consistently followed by this Court
whenever decision as to the meaning or reach of a statute has involved
reconciling conflicting policies, and a full understanding of the force
of the statutory policy in the given situation has depended upon more
than ordinary knowledge respecting the matters subjected to agency
regulations. 467 U.S. at 844.

And more than 25 years later, Justice Stevens still thinks the *Chevron* principle has been read too broadly; he would prefer no deference on "pure" questions of law, and with *Hearst* deference on questions of application and
implementation. Negusie v. Holder, 129 S.Ct. 1159 (2009) (Stevens, concurring and dissenting).

Finally, by way of warning, you will find the *Chevron* principle itself is famously variable. It sometimes appears in a "strong" version (courts with this
view defer frequently and heavily to most agency legal interpretations) and
sometimes in a "weak" version (courts with this view will defer less often and
less deeply). There are rigid versions in which the doctrine is applied mechanically (Justice Scalia?) and there are more subtle versions where the application is on a case-by-case basis (Justice Breyer?). In addition, the doctrine
is simply ignored in many cases. Graham, *Searching For Chevron in Muddy Waters — The Roberts Court and Judicial Review of Agency Regulations*, 60 ADMIN.
L. REV. 229 (2008) (discussing 11 cases in which *Chevron* should have applied
but was not mentioned by the majority). And, as indicated, there is considerable debate about the definition and operation of each of the articulated
steps of *Chevron*. But never forget in all this variation that when a court makes
an allocation decision the ultimate question is always: which allocation of the
senior/junior partner roles makes the most sense from the standpoint of legislative intent and, one hopes, technically sound and accountable decisions.

a. When Does Chevron Apply?

Does *Chevron* require deference to *any* agency legal determination? No, the
Court has not moved that far from *Marbury*. But which kinds of agency interpretations will get *Chevron* deference? Perhaps the safest place to start is with a
test that has been blessed by (most members of) the Supreme Court: the agency
legal interpretations most likely to get *Chevron* deference are those made in the
course of issuing pronouncements that have the "force of law." Christensen v.
Harris County, 529 U.S. 576 (2000). The underlying principle: if Congress has
given the agency the authority to take action of that significance, Congress must
have intended that agency legal interpretations should be respected by the courts.

"Force of law" is not, of course, self defining, but for our purposes regard it as a quality of an agency action that is "not subject to further challenge and which subjects a person who disobeys it to some sanction ..." Merrill and Watts, *Agency Rules with the Force of Law*, 116 HARV. L. REV. 467, 472 (2002). This test would usually mean that courts would give *Chevron* deference to agency legal interpretations made in the course of notice and comment rulemaking and in formal adjudications; in both cases the resulting rule or order must be complied with. *Chevron* deference would not be owing to legal interpretations that do not carry that authoritative weight, i.e., interpretive rules, policy statements, agency manuals or similar agency expressions.

If, as we have argued here, a main purpose of administrative law is to attempt to cure procedural shortfalls that limit neutral and fair decisionmaking, this approach to *Chevron's* applicability makes some sense. If the agency chooses to make a determination informally—where the protections of neutral and fair decisionmaking are limited—more intensive judicial review would seem appropriate. On the other hand, if the agency has followed a more formal procedure which facilitates neutral and fair decisionmaking (such as notice and comment rulemaking or formal adjudication) there is less need for intensive judicial review and *Chevron* deference seems appropriate.

But this blackletter is not satisfying to all. Justice Scalia apparently would grant *Chevron* deference to virtually *any* authoritative agency legal interpretations, irrespective of the formality of the process used in their promulgation.

> *Chevron* sets forth an across-the-board presumption ... Ambiguity means Congress intended agency discretion. Any resolution of the ambiguity by the administering agency that is authoritative—that represents the official position of the agency—must be accepted by the courts if it is reasonable. Mead Corp. v. U.S., 533 U.S. 218, 257 (2001) (Scalia, dissenting).

Like most rule-based approaches, this has the benefit of simplicity, clarity, and predictability. Its disadvantages include its one-size-fits-all nature and its inability to reflect subtle differences in contexts.

The other former administrative law professor on the Court, Justice Breyer, prefers that the question of *Chevron's* applicability be answered on a flexible, case-by-case basis. He would look at a series of factors before concluding whether court or agency was the senior partner in a given interpretative setting. As he explained those factors in his opinion for the Court in *Barnhart*,

> [T]he interstitial nature of the legal question, the related expertise of the Agency, the importance of the question to administration of the statute,

the complexity of that administration, and the careful consideration the Agency has given the question over a long period of time all [should be considered in deciding whether] *Chevron* provides the appropriate legal lens through which to view the legality of the Agency interpretation here at issue. Barnhart v. Walton, 535 U.S. 212, 217 (2002).

Like most standards-based approaches, this has the benefit of accuracy and the ability to tailor a solution to the particular case. Its disadvantages are that it is complex, difficult and largely unpredictable since in most occasions the determination will be case-specific. Some lower courts have followed this approach and have granted deference to relatively informal agency interpretations. See, e.g., Davis v. EPA, 348 F.3d 772 (9th Cir. 2003).

The Court itself varies on the question as various Justices join different majorities. In Mead Corp. v. U.S., 533 U.S. 218 (2001) the Court seemed to follow the black-letter in denying *Chevron* deference to informal letter rulings from Customs offices since the rulings did not have the "force of law." But Justice Souter for the Court said, nevertheless, that deference could be extended to interpretations in agency expressions less formal than rulemaking or formal adjudications if there was "some other indication of a comparable congressional intent." 533 U.S. at 227. And the Court has occasionally agreed with that. Barnhart v. Walton, 535 U.S. 212 (2002).

You can take this home: *Chevron* deference will most likely be shown for agency legal interpretations contained in notice and comment rulemaking and in formal adjudications since such actions have the "force of law." Less formal actions may generate deference if in a particular case the Justice Breyer view captures enough votes, in which event the factors suggested in his statement above will be the salient considerations. If you'd like a quotable epigram, Cass Sunstein has given us this: force of law is a sufficient condition for *Chevron* deference, whether or not it is a necessary condition. Sunstein, *Chevron's Step Zero*, 92 VA. L. REV. 187, 218 (2006).

b. Step One: Is the Statute Ambiguous?

If *Chevron* does apply, how does it work? The original Stevens opinion tells us that the first step is to determine if Congress has "directly addressed the precise question at issue." If it has, of course, there should be no deference to an agency interpretation—the court should simply apply the statute as written. On the other hand, if the statute is "silent or ambiguous with respect to the specific issue" the court may defer. In the first step—determining whether Congress had spoken to the issue—the Court said that determination should be made "employing traditional tools of statutory construction."

This step seems too obvious to bother mentioning, but turns out to be troublesome at several levels. Your first impression on hearing the step described may be to wonder how nine grownups can disagree five to four on a question of whether a statute is clear: whatever else one might think of such a statute, it cannot be "clear." Thus, in Cuomo v. Clearing House, 129 S. Ct. 2710 (2009), five Justices found the statute clear enough to reject an agency rule and four justices found the statute ambiguous and would have deferred to the agency. Further, how do you respond to the litigator who tells you that if Congress really has "directly addressed the precise question at issue" there would have been no litigation in the first place — the statutes that are litigated are those in which Congress has *not* addressed the precise question at issue. On that logic, Step One is meaningless: all statutes that come before the courts are ambiguous.

Some do believe Step One is at least redundant if not wholly meaningless. It is said that the only question is Step Two's question about whether the agency's interpretation is reasonable, and consistency with the statute is part of the reasonableness test. Step One is thus subsumed into Step Two. Justice Scalia has long expressed such a view and it has been debated in recent academic literature. Stephenson and Vermeule, *Chevron Has Only One Step*, 95 VA. L. REV. 597 (2009); Bamberger and Strauss, *Chevron's Two Steps*, 95 VA. L. REV. 611 (2009) (there is independent value in both of *Chevron's* steps). As a practical matter, the real question posed in Step One is not whether the statute is clear in any general sense, but whether it is clear enough to warrant reducing an agency's interpretive role. But even if that more accurately states the question, the Court has given us no very useful metric for calculating an answer.

One's approach to Step One also varies as a function of one's theory of statutory interpretation. Judges who believe the statutory words have to speak for themselves, and those who by contrast think legislative history and perceived legislative purpose have to be factored in, will have greatly different views on the clarity of any particular statute.

And finally, the uncertainty about Step One can make it a strategic step — judges wanting to defer can usually find sufficient ambiguity, and courts with a contrary urge can usually find sufficient clarity. Seidenfeld, *A Syncopated Chevron*, 73 TEX. L. REV. 83, 95 (1994). In such an "eye of the beholder" setting, prediction is difficult. For further discussion and citations to much of the literature on Step One, see Note, *How Clear is Clear*, 118 HARV. L. REV. 1687 (2005).

c. Step Two: Is the Agency's Interpretation Permissible/Reasonable?

If an acceptable case can be made that statutory ambiguity is sufficient to infer legislative delegation of law interpreting power to the agency, the second of *Chevron's* steps is to determine if the interpretive action of the agency was a permissible or reasonable exercise of the power delegated. Here is the way Justice Stevens described the step in the *Chevron* opinion. He said the Court:

> need not conclude that the agency construction was the only one it permissibly could have adopted to uphold the construction, or even the reading the court would have reached if the question initially had arisen in a judicial proceeding. If [the agency's interpretive] choice represents a reasonable accommodation of conflicting policies that were committed to the agency's care by the statute, we should not disturb it unless it appears from the statute or its legislative history that the accommodation is not one that Congress would have sanctioned." 467 U.S. at 845, n.11.

There are the usual differences over whether the standard is generous to the agency ("could any reasonable person have come up with the agency's interpretation?") or whether it has more bite ("is the interpretation a fair accommodation of conflicting statutory policies presented by this case?"). Both versions are covered by the Stevens language and the courts (including the Supreme Court) have not advanced analysis much beyond that.

Some commentators have expressed the view that this step of *Chevron* is indistinguishable from the arbitrary capricious test we have seen in other settings. This seems a plausible contention and has the additional advantage of making relevant some of the elaborations of that test that we have seen in other contexts. More generally, Step Two might be regarded as an occasion to insure that all the standards of review in APA § 706(2) are fully met (i.e., that it meets that section's tests for legal, procedural, factual, and reasoning sufficiency). Bamberger and Strauss, *Chevron's Two Steps*, 95 VA. L. REV. 611(2009). As we will see, of course, the arbitrary and capricious test is highly variable in meaning and intensity depending on the kind of proceeding being reviewed and the kind of issues that are involved. One would hope that sensitivity to context would remain when the test is employed as part of a *Chevron* Step Two analysis.

Figure 6.7 suggests a rationale for the understanding and use of the *Chevron* analysis. This way of perceiving *Chevron* makes clear its connection to the *Hearst* analysis we have considered above.

d. Do Courts Defer to Agency Interpretations of Agency Rules?

One would suppose that when an agency is interpreting not a statute but its own rule, its interpretation should be given substantial deference by reviewing courts. That basic principle was laid down in 1945 when the Court upheld an agency's interpretation of its own regulation with the statement that

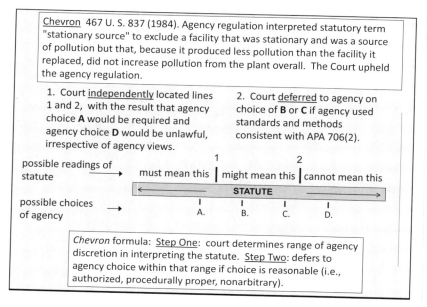

Figure 6.7   Applying the "*Chevron* Two-Step"

the ultimate criterion is the administrative interpretation [of the regulation], which becomes of controlling weight unless it is plainly erroneous or inconsistent with the regulation." Bowles v. Seminole Rock, 325 U.S. 410, 414 (1945).

Notwithstanding that the wartime setting of this regulation almost compelled deference, the principle remains settled today. Auer v. Robbins, 519 U.S. 452 (1997) (agency interpretation controlling unless plainly erroneous, citing *Seminole Rock*). Giving the interpretation "controlling weight" suggests that deference on rule interpretation is even greater than deference on statutory interpretation under *Chevron*, and it is often so held. Cf. Communications Corp. v. FCC, 128 F.3d 735 (D.C. Cir. 1997).

The usual justification for this level of deference is that the agency—as the drafter of the rule—surely knows more than a court what was intended by the rule. Moreover, it is said that such interpretations owe much to agency expertise and experience and that the agency's continuing enforcement responsibilities give it special, practical insight into the interpretive problem. Martin v. OSHRC, 499 U.S. 144 (1991).

There has been strong criticism in the literature of this deference, largely on separation of powers grounds. That is, separation of powers seeks to prevent the writer of the law from being the person who determines its final meaning. Hence, Congress cannot determine the final meaning of a statute; that task has been given to the courts. Granting generous deference to agency interpretation of its own rules involves something of the same problem—agencies function both as law writers and law expositors. The concerns are not frivolous. Some commentators have worried that agencies could write very vague legislative rules, masking their true policy objectives, then announcing those objectives in interpretations of the rule that, given generous *Seminole Rock* deference, are effectively beyond judicial supervision. Manning, *Constitutional Structure and Judicial Deference to Agency Interpretation of Agency Rules*, 96 Colum. L. Rev. 612 (1996). Beyond separation of powers considerations, undue deference to agency rule interpretation also has the practical effect of limiting public participation in new policy development since, as we've seen, most agency interpretations are free from the notice and comment requirements of the APA.

The courts seem not to have responded to this criticism. Substantial deference to legal interpretations of agency rules is common, though occasionally deference will be denied. Gonzalez v. Oregon, 546 U.S. 243 (2006) (no deference to agency interpretation of a rule that merely paraphrases the statute).

e. Some Final Thoughts on the Chevron Doctrine

If you'd like to get a sense of the magnitude of the confusions surrounding *Chevron* today, you can't do better than to look at the annual supplement to Pierce, Treatise on Administrative Law (2000). The 2009 supplement contains about 70 pages discussing *Chevron* litigation between 2002 and 2007. Here are some of the phrases he uses to describe the Court's work with *Chevron*: the Court is "badly divided"; its opinions are filled with "confusing dicta" that "raise more issues than they resolve"; the Court "continues to blur the distinction among types of deference," to "avoid applying *Chevron* even though it should have been clear to all Justices that *Chevron* applied" and to make "a muddle of the law governing application of *Chevron*."

Professor Pierce then turns to a review of almost 50 court of appeals *Chevron*-related decisions in the 2002–09 period. Not surprisingly he finds that "Circuit courts are struggling in their efforts to apply the Supreme Court's increasingly muddled decisions on the scope of *Chevron*."

What is to guide us (and what is to guide the courts) in such a situation? Notice first that as stated the doctrine bristles with opportunities for judicial discretion. All of the factors through which the applicability of *Chevron* is determined have much room for judicial discretion. And once it is decided that the doctrine applies, the Step One questions about whether and to what extent the

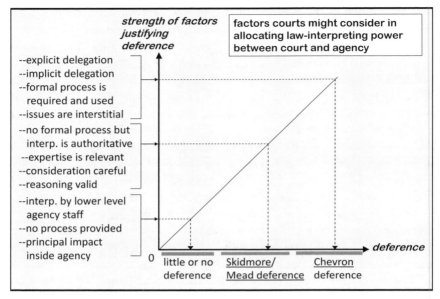

Figure 6.8 *Chevron's* World

statute is ambiguous also leave room for significant judicial discretion. Finally, the Step Two questions about whether the agency interpretation is reasonable are obviously highly discretionary. Whatever rhetorical flourishes a court may have to generate, a court wanting to make an independent judicial interpretation in a particular case may not be significantly cabined by *Chevron*.

If judges have significant discretion about much deference to show an agency's legal interpretations, what should guide the exercise of that discretion? It is to be hoped that courts would provide deference when and to the extent that functional justifications for deference appear in the case—i.e., where the agency's interpretation is authoritative, where its implications do not have effects beyond the agency's assigned responsibilities, where appropriate participation by those affected has been made available and where the question involved, even if legal in form, turns importantly on facts and analysis within the agency's area of expertise. Some of these factors are summarized in Figure 6.8.

The factors touch a variety of concerns. Some of them are related to the legislature (what it has delegated, what process it has required, etc.). Others have to do with the kinds of issues that are involved (interstitial, technical, etc.). Some factors bear on the quality of the agency action (careful, valid reasoning), or its fairness (adequate public participation) and some factors are concerned with the level in the agency where the decision is made (authoritative agency heads versus expressions by lower level staff, etc.). Surely these are factors that should be relevant to a court's allocation of law-interpreting power as between court and agency. Of course, multifactored tests of this kind make prediction difficult. But calls for a simplified, labeling approach to avoid these complexities are persuasive only until one sees how vague the labels are and how easily manipulable.

Finally, before you conclude that there is less to *Chevron* than meets the eye, remember two important facets of the doctrine. First, it reminds us of the basic principle of legislative supremacy—that legislatures can and sometimes do express themselves clearly allocating interpretive power (the statute that says an act applies to "employees as defined by the Administrator" is an explicit allocation of that sort) and courts must respect such allocations when they appear.

Second, *Chevron* sends an important message to the legislature about the consequences of legislative ambiguity. Statutes are ambiguous for many reasons. Sometimes the only way for a legislator to put together a coalition large enough to secure passage is to blur or soften critical language. Sometimes ambiguity is used to avoid publicity or to mask issues that could galvanize opponents. Sometimes ambiguity is sheer inadvertence—an issue arises that no one foresaw. While the reasons for ambiguity are sufficiently numerous and understood as to make it highly unlikely that any given ambiguity can be interpreted as a delegation of law interpreting power to agencies, *Chevron* does provides a background drafting signal to the legislature. It puts the legislature on notice that reasonable agency interpretations of ambiguous statutes will most likely be accepted by the courts. A legislature uncomfortable with that needs to draft with some specificity.

D. Review of Agency Judgment and Exercises of Discretion

Finally, what if the administrative action being reviewed is not comfortably labeled a question of fact or law, or even a "mixed" question of fact and law? For example, suppose the agency must decide on the route for the new highway. Or suppose that in the face of considerable scientific controversy, the agency must decide how many parts per million of a certain chemical will be injurious to human health, what kinds of safety appliances should be required in passenger cars or what level of protection should be afforded workers in factories? However these kinds of issues may be labeled, the plain fact is they are at base policy decisions—decisions requiring value choices that are not fully settled by existing legal standards or by statutory language. Usually, they also involve complex and controverted scientific and technical issues. What level of intensity will a court use in reviewing agency action of this kind?

We can begin with the obvious: courts will have to tread carefully here. The legislature that authorized the exercise of such discretion surely intended agencies to play a primary role in resolving the issues presented. All the reasons sketched above leading to substantial judicial deference apply with most force when a court is reviewing these kinds of decisions. Not only will such decisions often turn on agency skills and experience; they are also more likely to understand and be sympathetic to current legislative policies than courts. And on the accountability index, they'll get a better score than courts.

The statutory formula for review of these kinds of agency determinations is found in § 706(2)(A) of the APA and it turns out to be our old friend, the arbitrary and capricious test. We have two questions to puzzle over: (1) is arbitrariness defined differently in this setting from the way it is defined in reviewing agency fact findings in informal proceedings, and (2) what do courts look at when making decisions based on arbitrariness?

1. Defining Arbitrary

The term is beyond precise definition, may be more in the "I know it when I see it" category. The word has some sense of an outcome that lacks a reasonable or rational explanation. A good Supreme Court discussion is in Motor Vehicle Manuf. Ass'n v. State Farm, 463 U.S. 29 (1983). *State Farm*, incidentally, is a virtual case study of what happens when persuasive science (seat belts and air bags unquestionably save lives) runs into (a) public perceptions about the sanctity of the private automobile, (b) political attitudes about regulation, (c) stiff industry opposition, (d) insurance company interests, (e) the normal complications of the legislative process. There are limits to what science can do. Even though we had belt and air bag technology in the 1960s, these complicating factors resulted in about 20 years of delay in regulations requiring their use, at a cost of 12,000 lives annually.

In *State Farm*, the Court held that the National Highway Traffic Safety Administration acted arbitrarily and capriciously in revoking a rule requiring seat belts or air bags in passenger cars. The Court said the agency failed to present an adequate basis and explanation for rescinding the rule. The failure was in large part the agency's inability to persuade the Court that it had considered all relevant factors and had not omitted consideration of some relevant factors. It was a failure of logic or the inability to explain the logic that was used.

Here are some of the standard quotations from State *Farm* relied on by later courts:

- The test is more intensive than the minimum rationality test used for statutes. "We do not view [the test] as equivalent to the presumption of constitutionality afforded legislation drafted by Congress and the presumption of regularity afforded an agency in fulfilling its statutory mandate connection to reasonableness."
- A "court may not set aside an agency rule that is ... based on consideration of relevant factors [and by implication which avoids reliance on nonpermitted factors]."
- [The] "standard is narrow [unintensive] and a court is not to substitute its judgment for that of the agency."
- The "agency must examine the relevant data and articulate a satisfactory explanation ... including a rational connection between facts found and the choice made."
- The agency must avoid "a clear error of judgment."
- A "[rule will not be upheld if the agency] entirely failed to consider an important aspect of the problem."
- A "[rule will not be upheld if it] is so implausible that it could not be ascribed to ... agency expertise."
- "[Overall, the rule must be] the product of reasoned decisionmaking."

These are the phrases that must occur in your briefs (and exam answers) if you want to deal in the accepted currency. But you can readily see that this list of criteria is internally inconsistent—some elements signal a deferential attitude on the part of the court and some signal an opposite stance. Pretty clearly, the question of whether the arbitrary/capricious test is intensive or the unintensive depends on which of the Court's phrases one emphasizes. What we need are some clues as to what moves a court up or down on the intensity scale. There are a couple of clues.

a. The Historical Movement Toward Intensity

First, there is a clear historical drift of the test from lower to higher intensities. No longer is the Court going to give administrative action the same deference it gives statutes, the formula stated by Justice Brandeis in 1935:

> But where the regulation is within the scope of authority legally delegated, the presumption of the existence of facts justifying its specific exercise attaches alike to statutes, to municipal ordinances, and to orders of administrative bodies. Pacific States Box & Basket v. White, 296 U.S. 176, 186 (1935).

By the late 1960s the courts, especially in reviewing rulemaking, were applying a much more intensive version of the test. Perhaps it was in part a response to the new agencies being brought on line in the 1960s and 1970s. Perhaps it was a growing concern about agency "capture." Perhaps it was the work of a few strong-minded judges in the D.C. Circuit. Whatever its cause, the feeling grew that a firmer judicial hand was warranted. Just as the Court in 1951 saw in the APA and the new Taft-Hartley Act a congressional "mood" calling for somewhat more intensive judicial review, Universal Camera v. NLRB, 340 U.S. 474, 487 (1951), so the courts of appeal in the 1960s and 1970s sensed a new mood. The result was that the arbitrary and capricious test was pushed up the intensity scale a considerable distance from its 1930s position.

The label lower courts put on this new intensive form of arbitrary and capricious review was "hard look" review. In one of its original formulations, Judge Leventhal said a court would overturn agency decisions

> if the court becomes aware … that the agency has not really taken a 'hard look' at the salient problems and has not genuinely engaged in reasoned decisionmaking. Greater Boston Television v. FCC, 444 F.2d 841, 851 (D. C. Cir. 1970).

In some courts, the phrase is now viewed as a requirement not just that the court should be sure the *agency* took a hard look at the problem, but that the *court* should take a hard look at the agency's decision. There is in this shift a further suggestion that review should be notched up the intensity scale a bit.

b. The Obligation to Disclose

One special element in this more intensive review is the obligation of the agency to disclose the material on which its discretionary decision is based, especially to disclose it at the time the proposed rule is initially published. As we have seen, rulemaking agencies will have compiled fairly elaborate studies and analyses to meet the requirements of executive orders, NEPA, the Regulatory Flexibility Act, the Unfunded Mandates Reform Act, etc. One current strand of the arbitrary and capricious test is a requirement that agencies disclose the studies and data on which their analysis is based. U.S. v. Nova Scotia Food Products, 568 F.2d 240 (2d Cir. 1977). Not only are such studies of value to the courts in later review of the rationale of the rule, their disclosure at the time a rule is proposed facilitates commentary by the public, permits commenters to submit rebuttal studies or to discuss the applicability or interpretation of the studies as they pertain to the rule under discussion.

c. The Obligation to Explain

Another factor in arbitrary and capricious review is the requirement that agencies explain the reasoning behind their rule. If a court is to determine rationality, it must find a chain of reasoning through which the factual foundations of the rule can be connected with the final decision. Without an adequate agency explanation, this chain cannot be identified and it is ancient wisdom in this field that courts do not supply these rationales themselves. SEC v. Chenery Corp., 318 U.S. 80 (1943). Something of this element was involved in the *State Farm* case, where the Court could not understand why the agency had failed to consider a major alternative; absent some explanation, the agency action failed.

In FCC v. Fox, 129 S. Ct. 1800 (2009), the Court treated us to an extended debate over the obligation to explain. The case involved broadcasts allegedly violating the FCC's standards about indecent language. Acting in the strong shadow of the First Amendment, the Commission had for many years prohibited such language only if the offending words were used multiple times in a broadcast. In *Fox*, the Commission prohibited a single use of an offending word, though it did not impose fines on the broadcasters as it recognized it was applying a new policy. The Second Circuit reversed on the grounds that the Commission's change of policy was inadequately explained and was, hence, arbitrary under § 706(2)(A).

There were six opinions in the case. Justice Scalia, writing for the majority, found the Commission's explanation for the change adequate to pass muster under the APA. He first reviewed the verbal formulas from *State Farm* (as we have seen, they look in several directions at once, are seldom in themselves dispositive, but they remain mandatory quotes at the beginning of any exam answer or Supreme Court opinion on the arbitrary and capricious test).

Applying the standards, Justice Scalia said an agency can change policy but must explain what it is doing. It must admit that it is changing policy (no *sub silento* overruling), and it must itself believe that the new policy is better than the old. But the agency is under no duty to prove to a court that the new policy is better than the old—all it needs to do is establish that the new policy is rational and within its authority. If the new policy results from changes in facts, laws or policies on which the old policy rested, those changes should be identified and discussed. But there is no need for a treatise on every point. The court should "uphold a decision of less than ideal clarity if the agency's path may reasonably be discerned." 129 Sp.Ct. at 1810.

Justice Breyer in dissent had a tougher version of the duty to explain:

> [T]he agency must explain *why* it has come to the conclusion that it should now change direction. Why does it now reject the considerations

that led it to adopt that initial policy? What has changed in the world that offers justification for the change? What other good reasons are there for departing from the earlier policy? 129 S. Ct. at 1831.

Suppose the real explanation for the change is political, i.e., the new policy reflects the views of the current administration, rejecting the views of the administration in place when the original policy was announced? Justice Rehnquist in *State Farm* thought this could be an acceptable explanation. For a useful analysis, see Watts, Proposing a Place For Politics in Arbitrary and Capricious Review, 119 Yale L.J. 2 (2009).

d. The Obligation to Respond

Finally, the courts have required agencies to respond to important or significant comments received from the public about a proposed rule, the theory being that "the opportunity to comment is meaningless unless the agency responds to significant points raised by the public." ACLU v. FCC, 823 F.2d 1554, 1581 (D.C. Cir. 1987).

In general, the meaning of the arbitrary and capricious test in judicial review of agency policymaking is that there must be an adequate factual foundation to support the agency's policy (with courts no doubt deferring to agency judgments on highly technical factual disputes) and the agency must meet the three obligations mentioned above, to disclose, to explain, and to respond.

More intensive review of rulemaking has had a major impact on the process, as we have suggested in Chapter 2. A good description of the impact on agency work is McGarity, *Some Thoughts on "Deossifying" the Rulemaking Process*, 41 DUKE L. J. 1385 (1992) and Jordan, *Ossification Revisited*, 94 Nw. L. REV. 393 (2000). From an agency's perspective, the problem is the test's open-endedness. Especially after the Supreme Court accepted preenforcement review of rules, Abbott Labs v. Gardner, 387 U.S. 136 (1967) — which deprived rulemaking review of the focus of a specific set of enforcement facts — it became difficult for an agency to tell which of the hundreds of issues raised in a major rulemaking had to be discussed, which of the comments received were "significant" and thus required response, or which of its explanations were not satisfactory and thus had to be elaborated. The only safe course for the agency was to address virtually all the issues raised and all comments received in elaborate detail. The result is that a staggering amount of staff time and other agency resources are needed to complete a major rule today. Recall our case study in Chapter 2. For a major rule today, the "concise, general statement" required by § 553(c) can run into hundreds and hundreds of pages, and can reference thousands of additional pages of studies, reports and other documents.

Hard look review may have great value in health, safety and environmental rulemaking, where substantial burdens can be imposed on private citizens. It is less obvious that this kind of review is of similar value in cases that involve agency "priority- setting, that have relatively little impact on individuals, or are unusually dependent on judgments of a political character. Strauss, ADMINISTRATIVE JUSTICE IN THE U.S. 384 (2d ed. 2002).

On the plus side, hard look review forces agencies to consider and explain the basis of their action in terms outsiders (which includes judges) can understand. This is a victory for transparency and accountability, and no doubt assists in making public comment on proposed rules more meaningful. Beyond that, there is an undoubted self discipline required when one must explain the basis of discretionary action. And the fuller explanation will make judicial review more effective, including making it a little easier for courts to discern when agencies are responding more as "captives" than as promoters of the broader public interest.

On the minus side, there is no doubt that criticisms of the "ossification" of the rulemaking process have weight. Rulemaking, thought by the drafters of the APA to be a quick, simple and inexpensive way to develop and promulgate policy, has become one of the most cumbersome and elaborate processes in government. And to avoid these problems of cost and delay, there is evidence that agencies are shying away from rulemaking in the effort to develop policy by less complicated (and, alas, less comprehensive) means, such as through the adjudication of individual cases or less participatory avenues such as interpretive rules and policy statements.

2. Is There a "Record" for Arbitrary and Capricious Review?

To what documents will a judge resort when asked to review an agency exercise of discretion under the arbitrary and capricious test? For notice and comment rulemaking (as was involved in *Chevron* and *State Farm*) there will be no formal, exclusive record, but there will be the huge accumulation of documents — including public comment on the proposed rule — to which the judge will have access. In informal adjudication (as was involved in Citizens to Preserve Overton Park v.Volpe, 401 U.S. 402 (1971), the court will have to use whatever the agency has preserved in the way of explanatory and supporting materials. And, if that is not enough to accomplish its task — and the Court in *Overton Park* didn't think it was — a court can remand for further agency development.

E. An Overview

Figure 6.9 shows the general situation facing the reviewing court and the classifications and characterizations that bear on the correct formula to describe the reviewing judge's task.

In trying to guess about the actual intensity of judicial review in a given case, there seem to be some important factors—not often articulated—that affect review intensities and that may be briefly listed in aid of understanding some of the deeper currents in this difficult doctrine. Consider such questions as:

- Are there any legislative signals that agency views were to carry special weight? We have seen this in our *Chevron* discussions, but the principle applies more broadly than just in review of agency legal interpretations. Look for a grant of especially broad powers, requirements of relatively formal procedures, or a setting in which the agency is given the first full crack at the decision as indicators of probably less intensive review.
- What kind of question is presented? Review is likely to be more intensive if the question "feels" more like a question of law, i.e., is a general principle, with broad effects, rather than impacting only this case.

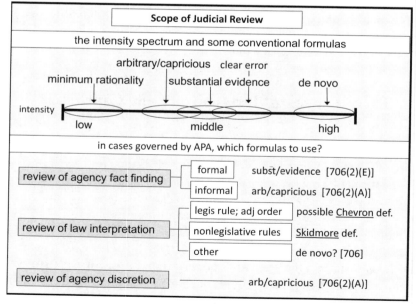

Figure 6.9   Overview of Judicial Review Tests and Formulas

- Is the question best answered by a government body with experience, expertise and long contact with the regulatory setting? If so, less intensive review may be expected.
- How confident is the judge in his or her own abilities to second-guess the agency's technical judgment? Judges differ on this and it matters.
- How satisfied is the judge with the quality of the agency's work? Some agencies develop reputations with judges concerning the commitment of agency leadership to what a judge might regard as objective policymaking and neutral factfinding.
- What is the judge's view of the appropriate judicial role? Expect more intensive review (less *Chevron* deference) from judges who doubt the efficacy of political controls on agencies and who regard courts as effective and legitimate instruments for imposing such controls.
- Does the agency have access to special information or insight on the problem? Was the agency active in proposing, drafting or lobbying for the statute involved? If convincingly shown, less intensive review may result.
- What is the overall quality of the agency decision? Expect less intensive review of agency work product that bears persuasive evidence of thoroughness, fairness and adequate participation by those affected.

Checkpoints

- The intensity of judicial review is a key element in managing our separated powers form of government.

- Different levels of intensity are required by different statutory formulas.

- In reviewing agency fact findings, substantial evidence and arbitrary and capricious are similar, mid-intensity tests looking for reasoned findings.

- Reviewing agency legal determinations is a matter of discerning how the legislature wanted to allocate interpretive functions as between court and agency; controlled today by the famous and massively cited and discussed *Chevron* case.

- *Chevron* applies to most agency legal determinations growing from relatively formal proceedings that have the "force of law."

- *Chevron's* first step: is the agency statute being interpreted capable of bearing several meanings, including the meaning the agency gave it?

- *Chevron's* second step: is the agency's interpretation reasonable and consistent with the standards and methods required by APA § 706(2)?

- Reviewing agency judgment and exercises of discretion is controlled by the arbitrary and capricious test; in rulemaking, a fairly intensive test requiring agencies to disclose, explain and respond.

Chapter 7

The Flow of Information

Roadmap

- Information flows to the agencies
  - Physical inspections
  - Legal authority to inspect
  - Warrants required; exceptions
  - The exclusionary rule in administrative law
  - Records and reports
  - Subpoenas and the Fourth Amendment
  - Subpoenas and the Fifth Amendment
- Information flows to the public
  - Coverage of the Freedom of Information Act and duty to disclose
  - The nine exemptions
  - Enforcement

This chapter sketches some of the legal problems arising in the critical flow of information from the public to the regulatory bodies and the equally critical flow of information from those bodies to members of the public. There are both statutory and constitutional doctrines implicated in this flow, so expect the usual doctrinal vagaries at the edges, with a reasonably clear and predictable center.

A. Information Flows to the Agencies

The basic thing to keep in mind here is that the administrative process runs on information. It cannot perform without this food, and it has a voracious appetite. Millions of reports, documents, forms and other pieces of paper (or clusters of electrons these days) flow from the public to the government yearly.

In addition, an agency's own research, inspections and investigations generate significant amounts of information, as does information from other agencies and research organizations. Physical inspections by government officials
are another source of information. National, state and local governments
promulgate a variety of codes setting forth standards for such things as health,
safety, fire protection, sanitation, light, cleanliness and maintenance. Enforcement of these codes requires records and compliance documents as well
as hundreds of thousands of inspections of businesses and even residences
every year.

This information is essential if the agencies are to perform the tasks the legislature has assigned them. Courts are aware of this, so you can begin with
this: in the vast majority of cases, when push comes to shove an agency is going
to get the information it needs. Yes, the courts are there to help police the
statutory and constitutional limits imposed on government. But knowing how
critical information is to the agency's public mission, courts are not likely to
limit the agencies' fact-gathering powers without a clear and convincing showing of unwarranted intrusions on protected privileges and interests.

Agencies get information from private citizens and businesses essentially in
two ways. First, the agency may require that citizens produce information in
documentary or testimonial form, either "voluntarily" through reports (such
as your annual income tax return) or by compulsion in the form of an agency
subpoena or investigative demand. Secondly, the agency may conduct physical inspection of a citizen's residence or place of business to gather information relevant to some regulatory or enforcement goal.

1. Physical Inspections

Suppose you receive a phone call from a client who tells you there is an
agency inspector at the door seeking entrance to his residence or place of business. In response to your question, you are told the inspector has correct identification but does not have a warrant. The client wants to know if the inspector
should be admitted.

One's first instinct might be to tell the client to resist. After all, the government should not be able to intrude on a private residence or a private place of
business without the judgment of some neutral arbiter to insure that the intrusion is authorized and appropriate. (You might think of the judge issuing
a warrant as that neutral arbiter.) Shouldn't an agency inspector be required
to have a warrant?

There may be tactical reasons for resistance as well. In some circumstances,
resistance might

- buy your client some valuable time (though, as we'll see, not very much)
- eliminate (or at least defer) any costs occasioned by the inspection
- dissuade the agency from proceeding at all
- make the agency clarify its search objectives
- strengthen one's position in bargaining with the agency over the scope of the search
- preserve a legal objection to the search that might be waived if consent is given.

But such benefits should be set against the costs of noncompliance, which might include negative publicity — "Joe's Restaurant Refuses Access to Health Department Inspector" may not be a headline your client would welcome. Resistance might also generate a less "friendly" inspection when it does occur. More generally, never forget that where a client is in a long term regulatory relationship with an agency, good relations with agency staff can be of considerable significance. For reasons of these kinds, an overwhelming majority of owners consent to warrantless searches by official inspectors.

If resistance seems a useful strategy, you will have to consider whether there are legal grounds for resistance. The first question, always, is agency authority. As we've said, agencies have no inherent powers, so the power to investigate must be authorized by its governing statutes and regulations, and the investigation must be consistent with any procedural requirements set out. Those provisions may answer detailed questions as to whether there is authority to conduct the inspection in this way, at this time, by this person, for this purpose, to this degree, and in this manner.

Even clear statutory authority, of course, cannot trump relevant constitutional constraints. Here, we will take a very brief look at protections flowing from the Fourth and Fifth Amendments. In your courses in constitutional law and criminal procedure you will discuss these issues in greater detail. For our purposes, we will sketch in some of the ways those Amendments play out in the field of administrative law.

a. Legal Basis for Resistance

In classic and elegant 18th Century language, the Fourth Amendment states both its proscriptions and their justification. Here is the Amendment in its entirety:

> The right of the people to be secure in their persons, houses, papers, and effects, against unreasonable searches and seizures, shall not be violated, and no Warrants shall issue, but upon probable cause, supported by Oath or affirmation, and particularly describing the place

to be searched, and the persons or things to be seized. U.S. Const. Amendment 4.

Note three things about this language. First, it does not prohibit all searches, it only prohibits *unreasonable* searches. Secondly, it does not in terms require issuance of a warrant in all cases. But the existence of a warrant is an important element in assessing the reasonableness of a search — it is often said that a search pursuant to a warrant is presumed to be reasonable. Finally, the Amendment specifies the conditions for issuance of a warrant, namely, that there be probable cause and that the warrant be relatively specific in its scope.

In 1959, the Supreme Court ruled that administrative inspections could be reasonable within the meaning of the Fourth Amendment even if they were not supported by a warrant. Frank v. Maryland, 359 U.S. 360 (1959). The underlying theory of *Frank* was that Fourth Amendment protections were principally concerned with protecting citizens in a criminal rather than an administrative context. As a result, the Amendment's strictures could be relaxed somewhat in the administrative sphere.

But it became clear that even absent criminal sanctions serious disadvantage to an individual could result from administrative inspection. In 1967, the Court reversed its ground and concluded that a search warrant *was* required before an administrative inspection of a residence or place of business. See v. City of Seattle, 387 U.S. 541 (1967); Camara v. Municipal Court, 387 U.S. 523 (1967). At the same time, the court softened the "probable cause" requirement by permitting these warrants to issue without specific knowledge of potential violations. It is sufficient if the warrant is requested by the agency on the basis of a reasonable agency plan of periodic or area inspections. If the agency has a program that inspects businesses in your client's industry annually, a warrant to inspect your client's business would be issued if a year had passed since the last inspection; it is not necessary that the agency believe there were violations occurring in your client's plant. The underlying requirement of reasonableness remains, however; administration of the agency's search program must be neutral, and inspectors should have due regard for your client's convenience, privacy and dignity.

b. General Exceptions

There are several recognized exceptions to the warrant requirement in administrative law. The first is consent of the owner, the exception raising all the usual questions about when consent is "informed." Another exception is for emergency situations that require prompt inspection, an exception which has produced considerable litigation over the kinds of danger to life and property that will permit a warrantless search. And warrants are not usually needed for searches in parts of a business premises that are open to the public or in "plain view"; government inspections of such places are not considered searches within the meaning of the Fourth Amendment.

Expect the warrant requirement to play out somewhat differently when there are broader issues involved (border inspections) or where the officials have special relationships with those being searched (prisons, hospitals, schools). The recent decision of the Court in Safford Unified School District v. Redding, 129 S.Ct. 1800 (2009) is an example. The case involved the strip search of a 13-year-old girl by public school officials in search of drugs. The Court held that in the public school setting, suspicion well short of probable cause would permit school officials to search the backpack and outer clothing of a student, but a substantially stronger suspicion was needed to permit the search to go further.

c. Special Exceptions for Certain Businesses

With respect to the inspection of business premises, there is another cluster of exceptions to the warrant requirement. The Court has held that a business subject to pervasive and long term government regulation may under some circumstances be subjected to warrantless searches. Colonnade Catering Corp. v. United States, 397 U. S. 72 (1970) (liquor licensee); United States v. Biswell, 406 U.S. 311 (1972) (gun dealer).

The concepts of "pervasive regulation" and "long term government regulation" are not very helpful criteria. For example, warrants are still required in some industries despite extensive and detailed (pervasive?) regulations—think of a manufacturing plant subject to quite detailed OSHA regulation. Marshall v. Barlow's Inc., 436 U.S. 307 (1978). And some businesses are subject to warrantless searches even though they may not be thought of as having been part of a long tradition of close government supervision. Donovan v. Dewey, 452 U.S. 594 (1981) (stone quarries); New York v. Burger, 482 U. S. 691 (1987) ("vehicle dismantling establishments" in Supreme Court talk; "automobile junkyards" or "chop shops" to the rest of us).

Your written briefs will still use the usual phrases about long term and pervasive regulation, but you will probably be better able to predict the outcome of these cases if you see the more general principles behind the phrases. These cases seem to be efforts by the Court to limit Congress's ability to authorize warrantless searches to settings where (a) legitimate expectations of privacy are outweighed by (b) the government's need for prompt—even unannounced—searches. Consider Figure 7.1.

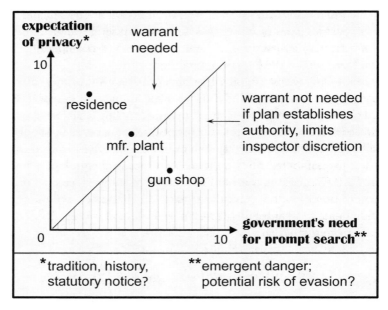

Figure 7.1   Warrant Needed If Expectation of Privacy Outweighs
Government Need

Expectations of privacy may be inferred from tradition, convention, history, and the absence of public notice that unannounced inspections are possible. Thus, one would normally have an expectation of privacy in the case of one's personal residence. Such an expectation would ordinarily not be present with respect to that part of business premises already open to the public. And the need for prompt inspection may appear where danger is special or where frustration of the regulatory goals seems possible. Thus, a stone quarry might present risks of special physical danger where prompt inspection may be important. And an automobile junkyard may be a market for stolen vehicles and parts, where an unsuspected search may be necessary to prevent removal of incriminating evidence.

Warrantless searches are, of course, subject to abuse. Without a neutral arbiter to issue the warrant—a judge who, among other things, will require that the warrant particularly "specify the place to be searched, and the persons or things to be seized"—there is little to restrain abuse by an inspector. For that reason, the Court has limited warrantless searches to situations where the authorizing law provides protection to the property owner that is somewhat equivalent to a warrant. The Court has said that the inspection program must perform the two functions of the warrant: it must make it evident to the owner that the search is according to law, and it must limit the discretion of the inspecting officers with respect to the time, place and scope of the inspection. New York v. Burger, 482 U.S. 691 (1987).

d. Does the Exclusionary Rule Apply?

If an unlawful administrative search takes place, can the agency use information it received in the search in later administrative hearings? The Supreme Court has not decided the issue and there are some differences in the lower courts. But most assume the exclusionary rule does apply, especially where the administrative action to be taken is punitive (fines, bond forfeiture, license revocation, dismissal from employment, expulsion from school, etc.) and where the application of the rule will deter unlawful conduct by agency investigators. For general discussion, see Fave, SEARCH AND SEIZURE 201 (3d ed. 1996).

2. Records, Reports, Subpoenas

The second way agencies collect information is by collecting the information in documentary or testimonial form directly from regulated parties. This may be in the form of reports that regulated parties are required to provide or by compulsion in the form of subpoenas. So voracious is the regulatory state's appetite for reports and forms, Congress has sought to subject it to at least minimal standards of necessity, efficiency, non-duplication and interagency coordination, largely through the Office of Management and Budget in the Executive Branch. See the Paperwork Reduction Act, 44 U.S.C. § 3501 and the Information Quality Act . 44 U.S.C. § 3516 Note. For discussion, see Hecht, *An Information Age*, 31 J. LEGIS. 233 (2005).

Government relies on voluntary disclosures of information for the most part. Every day, citizens provide information to the government in the form of tax returns, periodic reports, answers to telephone inquiries, license and permit applications that require information, etc. When the government seeks information that the citizen is unwilling to disclose, the tools of government compulsion are broken out. The typical tool requiring the production of documents is the subpoena.

As with the inspection, the recipient of an agency subpoena may choose to comply after weighing the costs and benefits discussed above. Note that the federal agency will not have subpoena enforcement power, but must apply to a court for an order of compliance; it is for violating *that* order that one risks a contempt citation with its attendant penalties. So there is a sense in which noncompliance with an agency subpoena is free — no contempt citation will threaten the client for initial resistance, and in the judicial proceeding that the agency must bring to enforce the subpoena, the client will have an opportunity to raise any legal objections. A few statutes provide for fine or even imprisonment for failure to comply with an agency subpoena, but courts typically refuse to enforce them until the respondent fails to comply with a judicial order to comply. Of course, as we have indicated, the agency may have other ways of making the client uncomfortable or the client's business less profitable. Refusing a permit or revoking a license — even temporarily — can be very costly to some clients. In such a setting, negotiation with the agency in an effort to narrow the scope of the demand, or to provide increased time for compliance may be the more practical solution.

If one doesn't comply with a subpoena, on what grounds would a court — to use the historic, colorful verb — "quash" the subpoena? There is, as always, the question of an agency's statutory authority. Subpoena issuance will require statutory authorization and issuance must comply with any limitations or procedures imposed by the statute or the agency's own rules. This is not usually a problem; statutory grants are usually quite broad, typically authorizing an agency to subpoena any documents or require any testimony relevant to any agency proceeding. And while a court might not enforce a subpoena it believed was sought to harass a respondent, generally the courts interpret agency authority broadly. As Judge Selya of the First Circuit said, "as long as the agency's assertion of authority is not obviously apocryphal, a procedurally sound subpoena must be enforced." Indeed, the good judge found the attack on the subpoena in that case so lacking in merit that he dug deep into his lexicon to reject it. "This tergiversation would stand the administrative enforcement process on its head ... We will not encourage so resupinate an exercise." U.S. v. Sturm, Ruger, 84 F.3d 1, 5–6 (1st Cir. 1996).

a. Subpoenas and the Fourth Amendment

If statutory authority is present, and is complied with, any attacks on the subpoena must be made under the constitution. For most of our history, the Fourth Amendment was an important tool in defending citizens from government inquiries. That was a time when Justice Holmes famously prohibited agency "fishing expeditions." FTC v. American Tobacco Co., 264 U.S. 298, 305–06 (1924). But in the 1940s, the Court shifted its tone. Perhaps becoming more comfortable with the regulatory process as its novelty wore off, or its inevitability became clear, the Court developed a very permissive position on the Fourth Amendment in the administrative context. Beyond the requirement that the subpoena be authorized, the Court ruled that subpoenas were consistent with the Fourth Amendment if they sought information *relevant* to the exercise of some agency power, and if they were *not too broad or indefinite*. Oklahoma Press v. Walling, 327 U.S. 186 (1946).

Relevance itself is very broadly viewed; a subpoena will be upheld if the evidence sought is "not plainly incompetent or irrelevant to any lawful purpose of the agency." Endicott Johnson Corp. v. Perkins, 317 U.S. 501, 509 (1943). The agency need not show that it has probable cause to believe that the respondent is guilty of an infraction of the agency's statute or rules. Indeed, the Court has even said that a subpoena enforcement action is not the place to raise questions about *coverage* of the agency's statute. Oklahoma Press v. Walling, 327 U.S. 186 (1946); Endicott Johnson Corp. v. Perkins, 317 U.S. 501 (1943). It is not quite so clear whether a law-based claim that the agency lacks *jurisdiction* could defeat enforcement of an agency subpoena. See EEOC v. Karuk Tribal Housing Authority, 260 F.3d 1071 (9th Cir. 2001) where the Ninth Circuit distinguished between coverage and jurisdiction, and held that since as a pure matter of law EEOC has no jurisdiction over a dispute between the Tribe and its members, the subpoena would not be enforced.

This leaves one resisting enforcement of a subpoena on Fourth Amendment grounds only the argument that it is too broad or indefinite, and this has been a disappointing line of defense for most respondents. On the one hand, if the agency knows the nature of the problem it seeks information about, it will draft its subpoena carefully and it will no doubt pass judicial muster. And if the agency does not yet fully know the extent of the problem, the court will permit general descriptions so as not to limit the agency's ability to find what it needs to know. "Fishing expeditions" are thus not prohibited. The fact is, massive amounts of information may be needed in complex cases and unless the respondent is a small business that would be bankrupted by the costs of compliance, the courts are not likely to impede the agency's work. Usually, the best the respondent can hope for is to make a careful and factual showing that the agency's needs can be met with a less inclusive demand, in which case the court may be able to narrow the scope of the subpoena.

b. Subpoenas and the Fifth Amendment

The Fifth Amendment's strictures on self incrimination has its historic roots in the field of criminal law, as is clear from its language:

> No person shall ... be compelled in any criminal case to be a witness against himself...." U.S. CONSTITUTION, AMEND. V.

While administrative agencies are not normally engaged in criminal law enforcement—the Amendment nevertheless has relevance since some administrative action might lead to later criminal prosecution. The regulatory agency's questions to your client may have only civil regulatory objectives, but testimony developed might later ground criminal proceedings.

Fifth Amendment doctrine is very complex and very much in motion. Due probably to the variety of justifications for its protections and the variety of situations in which those justifications may become relevant, it has been hard for the courts to lay down a clean, consistent body of doctrine. In your courses in constitutional law and criminal procedure you will explore some of these mysteries in greater detail. We touch briefly here a few places where this doctrine intersects administrative law.

Two important broad strokes to help you keep your bearings: First, the Fifth Amendment, like the Fourth, has had to give way to some degree to the regulatory state's appetite for information. As with the Fourth Amendment, the trend of the cases has been unmistakably in the direction of reducing the protection the Amendment once provided. Second, the Amendment's historic roots go back to concerns about torture and coerced confessions. The result is that its language as quoted above seems principally concerned with limiting the state's power to compel *oral testimony* from witnesses. For that reason, there will be less protection for those compelled to produce *documents*, no matter how incriminating those documents may be.

Being historically concerned with protecting individuals from forced confessions, the self-incrimination privilege can only be claimed by natural persons. Although corporations have long been held to be "persons" for due process purposes, they are not "persons" within the meaning of the privilege against self incrimination. The same is true of other so-called "artificial entities" such as partnerships and unincorporated associations. And since the corporation is not entitled to the privilege, neither is the person who is the custodian of the records, even—save in a narrow class of cases—when the documents will incriminate the custodian.

If corporate records are not protected, what about the records of sole proprietorships? And does it make any difference if the records sought from a sole proprietor are business records or personal or private records? Surprisingly, these questions are unsettled, with varying views of courts of appeal and uncertain guidance from the Supreme Court. Beginning with the language of the Amendment, we can say that the only records within the privilege are records (1) whose original production was *compelled*, (2) that are like what a witness would produce—i.e., the documents have some *testimonial* aspect and (3) that are reasonably thought to be *incriminating*.

The first two of these requirements have been difficult for the courts. When we speak of a record as having been *compelled*, we are not talking about the obvious compulsion that results from a subpoena or other form of investigative demand. For Fifth Amendment purposes, the word compelled usually refers instead to the original creation of the document. This is a reason most of the records—personal or business—of the sole proprietor are not protected by the Amendment: their production was not compelled by the government. They were voluntarily created and lack the compulsion element at the heart of Fifth Amendment concerns. The Supreme Court has held that documents in the hands of a sole proprietor were not protected by the Fifth Amendment if they were prepared and maintained voluntarily, since that condition is not within the Amendment's protection of "compelled" testimony. U.S. v. Doe, 465 U. S. 605 (1984). Justice O'Connor, concurring, would have gone further, feeling that "the Fifth Amendment provides absolutely no protection for the contents of private papers of any kind." 465 U.S. at 618.

When we speak of a record having some *testimonial* aspect, we usually mean that production of the document will be in some ways similar to the testimony of witnesses—it will communicate something that is in the mind of the producer of the record. Thus, compulsory blood samples are not testimonial—they communicate physical evidence about the witness's body, but not what is in his or her mind. They are not therefore protected by the Amendment. U.S. v. Patane, 542 U.S. 630 (2004).

If these limits on the Amendment's protection were not enough, the courts have also devised the so-called "required records" doctrine, denying protection to any documents that the government has required to be kept. Since 1911, the Court has held that "public records" are not protected by the Amendment and has defined public records to include "not only to public documents in public offices, but also to [private business] records required by law to be kept."; Wilson v. U.S., 221 U.S. 361, 380. See also, Shapiro v. U.S., 335 U.S. 1(1948). In an era where government record-keeping requirements seem endless, this doctrine could dilute the Amendment's protections to the vanishing point. The Court has not gone quite that far. The required records exception does not apply unless three conditions are met:

- the purpose of the information gathering is essentially regulatory rather than in aid of criminal law enforcement
- the records required are of the sort the individual customarily keeps, and
- the records have acquired some qualities which makes them effectively "public records." See, e.g., Marchetti v. United States, 390 U.S. 39 (1968); Grosso v. United States, 390 U.S. 62 (1968).

These criteria may have eliminated the bogey man raised in the *Shapiro* dissent—that the required records doctrine would make it possible for the government to require all citizens to keep unprotected diaries. But the criteria have not proved useful in predicting outcomes in real cases. After all, (1) the line between regulatory and criminal enforcement may in some cases be difficult to find, (2) even gamblers and criminals "customarily" keep records and (3) there is no principle for determining why a record in which the government has a plausible interest is not a "public record." But that's what we have to work with.

The required records doctrine has another peculiarity that will have been noticed by the careful reader. If *voluntarily* created records are unprotected and *required* records are unprotected, isn't it arguable that *no* personal documents are protected by the Fifth Amendment? That is, doesn't a record have to be either voluntary or compelled? The law has apparently not developed in that neat Aristotelian fashion. There *are* records that fall in neither category that may still be protected by the Amendment. Although the matter is not settled, the required records concept only removes Fifth Amendment protection from the kinds of detailed and prescribed records that highly regulated businesses (think public utilities) have customarily been required to keep. The Amendment's protection could still exist for business records kept under more general regulatory requirements. As Judge Posner has put it, "A statute that merely requires a taxpayer to maintain records necessary to determine his liability for personal income tax is not within the scope of the required records doctrine." Smith v. Richert, 35 F.3d 300, 303 (7th Cir. 1994).

Even for records that fail to pass these various tests, there may be some limited protection available. The Court has long perceived that while the *contents* of a record may not be privileged on one of the foregoing grounds, the very *act of producing* the document may be privileged. U.S. v. Hubbell, 530 U.S. 27 (2000); Brasswell v. United States, 487 U. S. 99 (1988). If a witness is required to produce a document, that very production is an admission that the document exists, that it is authentic and that it is in the possession of the witness. Where those facts are part of a prosecutor's case, production may be privileged. The Court has observed that the questions whether these implied admissions are sufficiently testimonial and incriminating to trigger the Fifth Amendment "perhaps do not lend themselves to categorical answers" but instead depend on the facts and circumstances of particular cases or classes thereof." Fisher v. U.S., 425 U.S. 391, 410 (1976), quoted in Mosteller, *Simplifying Subpoena Law: Taking the Fifth Amendment Seriously*, 73 Va. L. Rev. 1 (1987). As a practical matter, prosecutors will usually obtain the document under an agreement that its custodian will not be identified during the trial.

Finally, the Fifth Amendment's protection may not be available if the government grants immunity to the custodian of the document. The original 1893 statute granting such immunity protected a defendant from prosecution con-

Figure 7.2   Subpoenas and the Fifth Amendment

cerning the *transaction* about which the evidence related. The modern statute is much narrower, protecting the defendant only from the *use* (directly or indirectly) of the evidence obtained. If the prosecutor has other independent evidence of the allegedly criminal transaction, the defendant is still subject to prosecution. See Kastigar v. U.S., 406 U.S. 441 (1972).

Figure 7.2 summarizes some of this learning.

B. Information Flow to the Public — The Freedom of Information Act

The regulatory state's appetite for information has resulted in the accumulation of massive amounts of material. It has been said that annually some 70 billion citizen responses to requests for information are collected by the federal government. The national archives have three million cubic feet of records and five billion electronic data records. Gidiere, FEDERAL INFORMATION MANUAL 1–2 (2006).

Making appropriate information available to citizens is a complex process in which Congress, the president and the regulatory agencies — as well as special sectors such as the media and special interest groups — are players. The system is managed by a complex of statutes such as the Freedom of Information Act (5 U.S.C. § 552), the Privacy Act (5 U.S.C. § 552a), the Paperwork Reduction Act (44 U.S.C. § 3501), the Classified Information Act (18 U.S.C. App.3 §§ 1–16), the Information Quality Act (44 U.S.C. § 3516 Note), the Presidential Records Act (44 U.S.C. § 2111 Note) and other acts with special disclosure provisions, such as the National Environmental Policy Act (42 U.S.C. § 4321) and the Clean Air Act (42 U.S.C. § 7401).

The broadest of these acts is the Freedom of Information Act. The Act is usually referred to in writing by its initials, FOIA, and in speech it goes by the unlovely name, "Foy-uh." This act will be our principal focus here, but do remember that many other statutes, regulations and executive orders may be relevant in fully resolving any information disclosure issue.

FOIA began as a brief sentence in the original Administrative Procedure Act, § 3 of which provided that except for records "requiring secrecy ... or ... relating to the internal management of the agency" "matters of official record shall ... be made available to persons properly and directly concerned, except information held confidential for good cause found." The careful reader will see the vast amount of discretion such language conferred on the agency. Moreover, in the early days courts were not anxious to interfere with the agency discretion. But concerns about agency (and executive branch) secrecy began to emerge in the 1950s and 1960s, and a number of disclosure statute drafts were introduced. The basic FOIA was adopted in 1966. It has been amended several times since then, almost always to broaden disclosure requirements. In the continuing story of disclosure requirements, there has been a structural tension between the legislative wish for more executive branch disclosure and the executive branch's resistance to unlimited disclosure. At one telling historic point, Congress amended the act in 1974; the amendments were vetoed by President Ford, and then passed over his veto by an insistent Congress.

The act remains part of the Administrative Procedure Act (where it appears as 5 U.S.C. § 552). The act begins by insuring that much basic information is publicly available without request. Section 552(a) requires that agencies publish descriptions of their organizations including addresses for contacting the agency, rules of procedure including forms available for all reports and examinations, and all agency substantive rules. Similarly, the section requires that agencies make available for inspection and copying all final opinions and orders in adjudicated cases. Full indexing is required for ease of access, and the act provides that matters not properly published or indexed are not binding on the public unless the persons have actual notice of them. It is routine practice today for federal agencies to have elaborate web sites containing massive amounts of material that can be quickly and cheaply found without the need for formal requests under the FOIA.

The basic principle of the act is unmistakable — maximum disclosure is required: secrecy is bad, openness and transparency are good. All recognize, of course, that such a principle must have limits. Some information cannot be made public without jeopardizing national security, causing competitive injury to citizens supplying the information, or invading personal privacy. To respond to these concerns, the drafters chose a drafting strategy that maximized disclosure. Rather than listing those things that could safely be disclosed, the act requires that *everything* be disclosed subject to certain exclusions and exemptions. Those exclusions and exemptions are narrowly drafted to identify material whose disclosure would be dangerous or harmful. The operative language of the act simply states:

> each agency, upon request for records which ... reasonably describe such records ... shall make such records promptly available to any person. 5 USC § 552(3)(A).

Notice a couple of critical things about this simple declaration. First, the person requesting the information need not identify the record precisely — i.e., with its exact title, date, etc. It is enough if the description is reasonable. This means, too, that the agency must make a good faith search of its files for the requested record, and courts have not been especially generous to agencies whose search efforts were perceived as inadequate. Weisburg v. Dept. of Justice, 705 F.2d 1344 (D.C. Cir. 1983). Second, the request need not be in any particular form; it may be made by simple letter or email. Third, the act says the agency "shall" make the records available — this mandatory language means that when the act applies, the agency has no discretion to withhold. Finally, the act says the records shall be "promptly" made available, suggesting that Congress did not intend for agencies to drag out the response to delay or discourage requests for records. As will appear below, the act's enforcement provisions empowered courts to police the promptness of agency response and while the promise has not always been kept due to workload considerations and resource limits, the intent of Congress is clear.

The act requires all "agencies" to make "records" available to "any person." Each of the terms is defined in the act. "Agencies" refers to most executive branch and independent agencies and to many other federal authorities. It does not cover Congress or the courts. Nor does it cover the many private organizations operating under federal contracts or supported by federal funds.

The term "records" is broadly defined by the act. The courts have said the term includes any document in any format (including electronic format) that has been made or acquired by the agency and is within its control. Tax Analysts v. Dept. of Justice, 845 F.2d 1060 (D.C. Cir. 1988). Thus, private documents submitted to and within the control of the agency are requestable records. On the other hand, personal records of agency officials (calendars, phone logs) are not records unless created for official use. Kissinger v. Reporters Com., 445 U.S. 136 (1980).

The phrase "any person" is much broader than the APA's original "persons properly and directly concerned." The word is broadly defined by the act to include any "individual, partnership, corporation, association, or public or private organization other than an agency." 5 USC § 551(2). It includes foreign governments and aliens, although since 9/11, Congress has adopted some limits on the ability of foreign governments to obtain some kinds of records. 5 USC § 552(a)(3)(A)(E). Notice that there is no requirement that a person requesting records be motivated by a "proper" purpose, as was the case with the original Section 3. Subject to only a couple of narrow exceptions, the purpose of the requester is not relevant to the obligation to disclose. Persons can compel disclosure though they are merely curious, are seeking information for competitive advantage, or who want to embarrass or injure others. As the D.C. Circuit has said, "Congress granted the scholar and the scoundrel equal rights of access to federal records under the FOIA." Durns v. Bureau of Prisons, 804 F.2d 701, 706 (D.C. Cir. 1986).

1. The Exemptions

From that broad pattern of disclosure requirements, one must subtract matters excluded or exempted from the act. Excluded entirely from the act is a narrow category of documents concerning sensitive law enforcement information (e.g., the identity of informers) or that may compromise foreign intelligence or counter intelligence operations.

The principal limits on disclosure are in the nine exemptions. Here, Congress attempted the difficult job of identifying specific types of documents that should not automatically be disclosed. Consistent with its purpose to maximize disclosure, the act puts the burden on the agency to justify application of an exemption. The exemptions are referred to in the cases and in the literature by their statutory number, and that practice will be followed here. The text of the exemptions is included in the APA provisions set out in the Appendix.

Exemption 1 covers much classified material where disclosure could raise important national security issues. The exemption is worded in such a way as to make the decision whether to classify a document itself subject to judicial review. The only documents exempted are those properly classified under criteria established in advance by executive order. The judicial inquiry about the propriety of the classification extends to the question of whether the need for classification of a particular document still exists. Courts are specifically permitted to examine the disputed documents *in camera* both to review the propriety of the classification and to determine whether some parts of the document might be released. Despite this brave effort by Congress to enlist the courts as partners in the disclosure mission, courts have been reluctant—especially in recent times—to require disclosure of any material that plausibly could have a negative impact on national security.

Exemption 2 provides that agencies need not disclose information "related solely to internal personnel rules and practices" of the agency. This exemption is not controversial when one is talking about purely internal matters—parking rules, lunch schedules, sick leave policies. But many matters of internal management can have dramatic effect on the public, such as operating rules, guidelines, manuals of procedure. The Supreme Court has required disclosure where there is a significant public need for it and in the absence of a showing that disclosure would significantly risk circumvention of agency regulations (e.g., by disclosing agency investigative techniques). Dept. of Air Force v. Rose, 425 U.S. 352 (1976). Lower courts continue to struggle with the question, tending not to require disclosure of law enforcement guides and manuals. Crooker v. Bureau, 670 F.2d 1051 (D.C. Cir. 1981).

Exemption 3 allows an agency to withhold information when another statute explicitly so authorizes. How explicit must the withholding statute be? By recent amendment this exemption only allows withholding if the statute on which the agency relies leaves the agency with no discretion in the matter ("thou shall not release") or identifies specific criteria for withholding that the agency has followed. A number of statutes have been held to contain the necessary specificity, including statutes governing the CIA, the Census Bureau and the Internal Revenue Service. For discussion, see Pierce, Shapiro and Verkuil, ADMINISTRATIVE LAW AND PROCESS 460 (5th ed. 2009).

Exemption 4 deals with certain types of information obtained by the agency from a "submitter" who does not want the agency to disclose to others (e.g., to a "requester" who is a competitor of the submitter). The exemption was drafted in a way that left many questions unanswered, and it has been the subject of much litigation. The fourth exemption says the agency need not disclose "trade secrets and commercial or financial information obtained from a person and privileged or confidential. "5 USC § 552(b)(4). If you plot out all the "ors" and "ands" you come up with something shown in Figure 7.3.

The courts have struggled with determining when commercial and financial information is confidential. Should it be enough that the person submit-

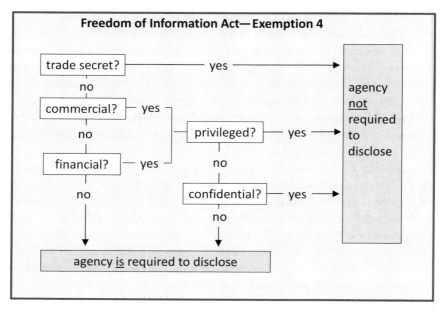

Figure 7.3   The Fourth Exemption in the Freedom of Information Act

ting the information regarded the material as confidential? That would, of course, mean very little disclosure, since most submitters would make that claim. Or should a more objective test be used? In one leading case, the D. C. Circuit opted for an objective test. A matter is regarded as confidential within the meaning of Exemption 4 if (1) disclosing it would impair the government's ability to obtain information in the future (e.g., by making later submitters less likely to volunteer information), or (2) if disclosure of the information would cause substantial competitive harm to the submitter. National Parks v. Morton, 498 F.2d 765 (D.C. Cir. 1974). In later cases, some courts have drawn a distinction between information submitted voluntarily and information obtained by compulsion. If the information was compelled, the court follows the objective test of *National Parks* as described above. But if the information was submitted voluntarily, a subjective standard of confidentiality has been used by some courts—the agency has no obligation to disclose information the submitter itself regards (and customarily treated) as confidential. Critical Mass v. NRC, 830 F.2d 278 (D.C. Cir. 1987).

Exemption 4 has also raised the problem of the so-called "reverse FOIA" action—a suit by a submitter to stop the agency from disclosing exempted material. There may be reasons why an agency would wish to disclose material even if it is within an exemption. May an agency do so? Stated otherwise, does an exemption in the FOIA authorize a court to stop an agency from disclosing information within the exemption? The answer is, "no." The Court has held that the act only mandates disclosure and cannot be used to prohibit disclosure. Chrysler v. Brown, 441 U.S. 281 (1979). So if a submitter provides trade secret information to the agency and someone else requests the information—say, a competitor of the submitter—the agency need not disclose it under Exemption 4 but may decide to disclose it anyway and there is no relief for the submitter under the FOIA.

Protection of submitters lies elsewhere. *Chrysler v. Brown*, supra, held that if disclosure is prohibited by an act other than FOIA, (e.g., the Trade Secrets Act 18 U.S.C. § 1905 prohibits disclosure of trade secrets) disclosure by the agency would violate those acts, and *that* violation could be challenged under the terms of those acts or under the generic provisions of the Administrative Procedure Act. Most agencies have rules today that require submitters to identify any material submitted as confidential, that require the agency to notify submitters if any material so identified has been requested, and that allow the submitter to participate in some fashion in the decision whether to disclose.

Exemption 5 exempts inter- or intra-agency memoranda that reflect the agency's internal decisionmaking process. It is premised on the belief that too much disclosure of the internal agency decisionmaking process would reduce the candor and effectiveness of agency deliberation. Instead of trying to define this category of information itself, Congress has essentially adopted existing rules about disclosure used by courts in protecting candid discussion. Accordingly, Exemption 5 exempts information that would "fall within the ambit of a privilege against [disclosure] under judicial standards that would govern litigation against the agency that holds it." Department of Interior v. Klamath Water Users Protective Ass'n, 532 U.S. 1, 8(2001). Thus, the agency may not need to disclose information that would ordinarily be protected in litigation—such as government deliberations within the "executive privilege," certain attorney/client discussions, or some attorney work product, etc.

A key feature of the developed doctrine of Exemption 5 is the distinction between "pre-decisional" records—records made before the decision is taken and which are protected from disclosure in aid of candid deliberations—and "post-decisional" records—records made after the decision, describing the rationale or interpretation of the decision which, being part of the working law of the agency, should be available to the public. NLRB v. Sears, 421 U.S. 132 (1975).

Exemption 6 is an attempt to protect the personal privacy of those who submit information to the government. It allows the agency to withhold "personnel or medical files and similar files the disclosure of which would constitute a clearly unwarranted invasion of personal privacy." To decide whether a given disclosure would be "clearly unwarranted" the court will have to balance the injury that disclosure will inflict on the individual concerned against the public interest in disclosure. In striking this balance, the only relevant public interest in disclosure is that disclosure would contribute to public understanding of the operations of government. Thus, if the requested disclosure shows nothing relevant to government action, there is nothing on the public interest side of the scale; disclosure will not be required. Hertzberg v. Veneman, 273 F. Supp. 2d 67, 86 (D.C. Cir. 2003) (disclosure of names of fire victims would shed no light on how government responded, hence the names are within Exemption 6). Note that the balancing test of Exemption 6 is one of the few places in the act where the identity and the motives of the requester may be relevant to the disclosure decision.

Exemption 7 is a much-amended section which seeks to protect legitimate law enforcement activities from unnecessary disclosure. As with Exemption 6, it is one of the few places where the identity and motives of the requester become relevant. The Exemption covers "records or information compiled for law enforcement purposes" and permits an agency to withhold information if one of six specific conditions are present. Withholding is authorized if disclosure:

A. could interfere with law enforcement proceedings that are currently pending
B. would deprive a person of a fair trial
C. could cause an unwarranted invasion of personal privacy (cf. Exemption 6)
D. could disclose identity of informants
E. would disclose law enforcement techniques if disclosure would risk circumvention of the law, *or*
F. could be expected to endanger the life or physical safety of individuals (law enforcement personnel, witnesses, etc.)

As one might expect in a provision emerging from sharp controversies — as this exemption has — the language bristles that drafting subtleties. Notice that the "clearly unwarranted" invasion of privacy exempted in Exemption 6 becomes merely "unwarranted" in this exemption. In 1989, the words "or information" were added to the word "record" in identifying what material might be exempt. And notice the shift in meaning which occurs when the drafter chooses between the word "could" and the word "would" in identifying when the consequences of disclosure warrant the exemption. The cases here bear close reading.

Exemption 8 concerns information relating to the regulation of financial institutions, historically an area where public disclosure of information has been greatly limited. It remains to be seen whether current calls for more intensive regulation of these institutions will undercut that historic bias against disclosure.

Exemption 9 protects geological and geophysical information, maps and data concerning oil wells. It is not often invoked and has not been the subject of judicial interpretation.

2. Enforcement

The true efficacy of an information act lies not only in its coverage but in its enforcement. The Freedom of Information Act began in 1967 with fond hopes for agency compliance, but experience quickly showed the need for more "teeth" in its enforcement provisions. As it stands today, it is regarded as a reasonably effective act, though in one particular it still falls short of the congressional intent. Congress's clear desire for "prompt" agency response has been frustrated by agency workload problems—no one came even close to guessing the volume of requests the act would generate. To take only one example, the Social Security Administration received 19 million FOIA requests in fiscal year 2007. FOIA ANNUAL REPORT FOR THE SOCIAL SECURITY ADMINISTRATION FOR FISCAL YEAR 2007. While agency staff dedicated to handling record requests has grown greatly, few agencies are staffed to handle large and complex FOIA searches and analyses. Courts have been understandably sympathetic to the plight of the agencies and the result is that truly "prompt" agency response is limited to relatively simple requests.

The act is designed so that enforcement relies heavily on the courts. When a request for documents is made to an agency, the act requires an agency response in 20 days and, if the response is negative, an explanation and information about internal agency appeals. 5 USC § 552(a)(6). Internal agency appeals are subject to a similarly short time frame, and when the agency has finally decided not to comply with a request, the requester is entitled to immediate judicial review in a federal district court. 5 USC § 552(a)(4)(B). The statute provides that the judge is to decide such an issue "de novo"—i.e., with no special deference to any prior agency determination, and the burden of proof is on the agency to justify its failure to disclose. 5 USC § 552(a)(B). The agency is required to file a complete index listing all documents within the scope of the request and an identification of which exemption the agency is relying on to withhold the records. Further, the statute provides that a requester who "substantially prevails" in his judicial action may be awarded attorney fees and costs by the court. 5 USC § 552(a)(E) .

Beyond the courts, executive branch attitudes, practices and regulations have had an important effect on FOIA enforcement. Different presidential administrations have had different levels of enthusiasm for disclosure and those differences have been of consequence in the practical meaning of the act. Take one example: suppose an agency is considering a request for records under the FOIA. If the agency denies the request and litigation ensues, will the agency be defended by the official government law office (the Department of Justice)? Shortly after 9/11 — and in part because of national security concerns — then Attorney General John Ashcroft issued a memorandum indicating that the Department of Justice *would* defend any agency decision to withhold information requested under the FOIA so long as the decision had a sound legal basis. Office of the Attorney General, *Memorandum on the Freedom of Information Act* (October 12, 2001). General Ashcroft was saying to agencies disposed to deny requests on technical, legal grounds, "I've got your back." Studies seemed to show that the memo resulted in fewer FOIA disclosures.

The Obama administration rescinded the Ashcroft memo and in its place promulgated a new policy. On the question of litigation support for agencies denying FOIA requests, the memo says the Department will *not* defend every denial of a FOIA request. The Department will defend the agency "only if ... the agency reasonably foresees that disclosure would harm an interest protected by one of the statutory exemptions." Office of the Attorney General, *Memorandum for Heads of Executive Departments and Agencies, (The Freedom of Information Act)* March 19, 2009. To assure litigation support, the agency must go beyond establishing a legal basis for withholding, must also make a reasonable finding that disclosure would cause harm to relevant interests.

The new AG's memo also confirms the presumption of openness embodied in the FOIA, instructs agencies to think of FOIA requests as raising questions about what can be released rather than what can be withheld, encourages discretionary disclosure of exempt material where that is lawful, and makes other recommendations to improve speedy and coordinated implementation of the act. On such practical details, much turns.

Checkpoints

Information to agencies

- Information is critical to agency work; courts respect that.

- All agency information-securing power must come from statute.

- Warrants are needed for physical inspections; probable cause usually not needed.

- There is an exception to the warrant requirement for pervasively regulated businesses; courts will balance government need against citizen's expectation of privacy.

- Records and the Fourth Amendment: the agency can subpoena records if it has authority, the records are relevant and the request is not oppressively broad.

- Records and the Fifth Amendment: the agency can subpoena corporate records and some (but not all) private records; incriminating testimony usually protected.

Information to public

- Freedom of Information Act applies very broadly; strong bias in favor of disclosure.

- The nine exemptions limit disclosure of records about matters such as classified material, internal agency matters, confidential material, records affecting personal privacy, and law enforcement records.

- Enforcement in courts; statute requires prompt agency action but complex requests may take years.

Mastering Administrative Law Master Checklist

Chapter 1 • The Role of Administrative Law
- ❏ Administrative Law is a set of doctrines designed to correct separation of powers shortfalls caused by the unexpected growth of the regulatory process. Specifically, administrative law considers:
  - o how agencies get authority
  - o how agency procedures can be kept fair
  - o how agency policies can be kept accountable
- ❏ The three central functions of administrative law doctrines are:
  - o to facilitate legislative control of agency procedure
  - o to insure that tasks given courts in judicial review are appropriate
  - o to incorporate basic "rule of law" factors into the process

Chapter 2 • Rulemaking
- ❏ Making general rules for the future is a most important part of the regulatory process.
- ❏ So-called "legislative rules" are promulgated under § 553's basic notice and comment procedure, have legal effects similar to statutes.
- ❏ Notice and comment process today requires agencies to disclose studies and research on which their proposed rule is based.
- ❏ So-called "nonlegislative rules" can be promulgated without § 553 process, but many must be published; they do not have the legal effect of statutes.
- ❏ Beyond § 553 procedures, §§ 556-57 process may be required for formal rulemaking, and additional procedures may be required by Congress (hybrid rulemaking), by agency rule or by executive order.
- ❏ Agency officials engaged in rulemaking are treated as legislators not judges, have considerable freedom from courtroom-like strictures.

Chapter 3 • Adjudication
- ❏ Formal adjudication under §§ 556-57 is required only if another statute calls for a hearing "on the record."

o Formal adjudications usually presided over by an Administrative Law Judge whose independence is sought by removing agency control over selection, tenure and salary
o Formal adjudication procedures are court-like with some flexibility, cover burdens of proof, evidence, discovery, witnesses, bias, etc.
o Decisions in formal adjudications must be based exclusively on the hearing record
o Initial decisions of ALJ can be appealed to agency, then to court if needed
❏ Informal adjudication is used in other cases. Very few APA procedures here, though other statutes and agency rules may have requirements.

Chapter 4 • Constitutional Requirements for Fair Process
❏ Due process applies if the issues and the claimant's interests warrant protection of hearing.
o Disputed issues of adjudicative fact usually suffice
o Interests qualify for due process protection if they are property interests (claimant has a legitimate claim of entitlement to something the agency is affecting) or liberty interests (serious deprivations without property connections, such as restrictions on movement, damage to reputation, etc. Law is very unclear.)
❏ When due process applies, it requires hearing procedures the formality of which varies as a function of
o the extent of loss to the claimant
o the degree to which the procedure asked for will improve accuracy of decision
o the cost of providing the procedure and other related costs

Chapter 5 • Availability of Judicial Review
❏ Judicial review is critical to process, is usually presumed to be available, though contrary presumption may appear in cases of prosecutorial discretion or the like.
❏ Statutes sometimes preclude review, or grant agencies such broad discretion that review is not feasible.
❏ Not all persons have standing to seek review, only those who can show present or threatened concrete injury from the agency act complained of.
❏ Timing of review is important:
o Courts historically have not reviewed agency action if there were unexhausted administrative remedies; today, APA says exhaustion not required unless statute so requires
o Courts do not review issues that are not yet ripe (not clear enough for sensible judicial resolution)

Chapter 6 • Scope of Judicial Review

❏ Intensity of judicial review is a critical marker in managing our separation of powers system—high intensity review puts power in courts; low intensity review puts power in legislative and executive branches.

❏ Intensity is initially signaled by statutory formulas such as de novo, clear error, arbitrary and capricious, substantial evidence, etc.

❏ Formal agency determinations of ordinary fact are reviewed under the substantial evidence test, essentially to see if one could reach agency findings from evidence in the record by the process of reasoning.

❏ Review of agency legal determinations is today governed by the famous *Chevron* doctrine which suggests substantial deference to agency views where the statute is unclear and the agency's interpretation is reasonable. Many, many questions remain.

❏ Exercises of agency discretion are reviewed under the arbitrary and capricious test, a much more intensive test than it was in the 1930s; especially in high-stakes rulemaking where it requires that agencies disclose material considered, explain the theory of their action and respond to public comment.

Chapter 7 • The Flow of Information

❏ Information flow to agencies

    o The Fourth Amendment applies to agency inspections but warrants are not usually hard to get (probable cause not needed) and there are some exceptions for emergencies and pervasively regulated businesses.

    o The Fourth Amendment applies to agency subpoenas, but courts are generous today, permit extensive inquiries if authorized, relevant and not too broad.

    o The Fifth Amendment applies to agency requests for testimony that might be incriminating.

    o The Fifth amendment offers less protection for records, does not protect corporate records, voluntarily kept private records, or records required to be kept.

❏ Information flow to public

    o Freedom of Information Act provides broad public disclosure of information in hands of government.

    o The nine exemptions limit disclosure of records about such things as classified material, internal agency matters, confidential records, personal privacy, and law enforcement.

    o Enforcement in courts; statute requires prompt agency action but staff and resource problems mean that complex requests can take years.

Appendix

Federal Administrative Procedure Act
United States Code. Title 5

§ 551. Definitions

For the purpose of this subchapter—

(1) "agency" means each authority of the Government of the United States, whether or not it is within or subject to review by another agency, but does not include—
    (A) the Congress;
    (B) the courts of the United States;
    (C) the governments of the territories or possessions of the United States;
    (D) the government of the District of Columbia; or except as to the requirements of section 552 of this title—
    (E) agencies composed of representatives of the parties or of representatives of organizations of the parties to the disputes determined by them;
    (F) courts martial and military commissions;
    (G) military authority exercised in the field in time of war or in occupied territory; or
    (H) functions conferred by sections 1738, 1739, 1743, and 1744 of title 12; chapter 2 of title 41; subchapter II of chapter 471 of title 49; or sections 1884, 1891-1902, and former section 1641(b)(2), of title 50, appendix;

(2) "person" includes an individual, partnership, corporation, association, or public or private organization other than an agency;

(3) "party" includes a person or agency named or admitted as a party, or properly seeking and entitled as of right to be admitted as a party, in an agency proceeding, and a person or agency admitted by an agency as a party for limited purposes;

(4) "rule" means the whole or a part of an agency statement of general or particular applicability and future effect designed to implement, interpret, or prescribe law or policy or describing the organization, procedure, or practice requirements of an agency and includes the approval or prescription for the fu-

ture of rates, wages, corporate or financial structures or reorganizations thereof, prices, facilities, appliances, services or allowances therefor or of valuations, costs, or accounting, or practices bearing on any of the foregoing;

(5) "rule making" means agency process for formulating, amending, or repealing a rule;

(6) "order" means the whole or a part of a final disposition, whether affirmative, negative, injunctive, or declaratory in form, of an agency in a matter other than rule making but including licensing;

(7) "adjudication" means agency process for the formulation of an order;

(8) "license" includes the whole or a part of an agency permit, certificate, approval, registration, charter, membership, statutory exemption or other form of permission;

(9) "licensing" includes agency process respecting the grant, renewal, denial, revocation, suspension, annulment, withdrawal, limitation, amendment, modification, or conditioning of a license;

(10) "sanction" includes the whole or a part of an agency—
   (A) prohibition, requirement, limitation, or other condition affecting the freedom of a person;
   (B) withholding of relief;
   (C) imposition of penalty or fine;
   (D) destruction, taking, seizure, or withholding of property;
   (E) assessment of damages, reimbursement, restitution, compensation, costs, charges, or fees;
   (F) requirement, revocation, or suspension of a license; or
   (G) taking other compulsory or restrictive action;

(11) "relief" includes the whole or a part of an agency—
   (A) grant of money, assistance, license, authority, exemption, exception, privilege, or remedy;
   (B) recognition of a claim, right, immunity, privilege, exemption, or exception; or
   (C) taking of other action on the application or petition of, and beneficial to, a person;

(12) "agency proceeding" means an agency process as defined by paragraphs (5), (7), and (9) of this section;

(13) "agency action" includes the whole or a part of an agency rule, order, license, sanction, relief, or the equivalent or denial thereof, or failure to act; and

(14) "ex parte communication" means an oral or written communication not on the public record with respect to which reasonable prior notice to all parties is not given, but it shall not include requests for status reports on any matter or proceeding covered by this subchapter.

§ 552. Public information; agency rules, opinions, orders, records, and proceedings

(a) Each agency shall make available to the public information as follows:

(1) Each agency shall separately state and currently publish in the Federal Register for the guidance of the public—

(A) descriptions of its central and field organization and the established places at which, the employees (and in the case of a uniformed service, the members) from whom, and the methods whereby, the public may obtain information, make submittals or requests, or obtain decisions;

(B) statements of the general course and method by which its functions are channeled and determined, including the nature and requirements of all formal and informal procedures available;

(C) rules of procedure, descriptions of forms available or the places at which forms may be obtained, and instructions as to the scope and contents of all papers, reports, or examinations;

(D) substantive rules of general applicability adopted as authorized by law, and statements of general policy or interpretations of general applicability formulated and adopted by the agency; and

(E) each amendment, revision, or repeal of the foregoing.

Except to the extent that a person has actual and timely notice of the terms thereof, a person may not in any manner be required to resort to, or be adversely affected by, a matter required to be published in the Federal Register and not so published. For the purpose of this paragraph, matter reasonably available to the class of persons affected thereby is deemed published in the Federal Register when incorporated by reference therein with the approval of the Director of the Federal Register.

(2) Each agency, in accordance with published rules, shall make available for public inspection and copying—

(A) final opinions, including concurring and dissenting opinions, as well as orders, made in the adjudication of cases;

(B) those statements of policy and interpretations which have been adopted by the agency and are not published in the Federal Register; (C) administrative staff manuals and instructions to staff that affect a member of the public; (D) copies of all records, regardless of form or format, which have been released to any person under paragraph (3) and which, because of the nature of their subject matter, the agency determines have become or are likely to become the subject of subsequent requests for substantially the same records; and (E) a general index of the records referred to under subparagraph (D); unless the materials are promptly published and copies offered for sale. For records created on or after November 1, 1996, within one year after such date, each agency shall make such records available, including by computer telecommunications or, if computer telecommunications means have not been established by the agency, by other electronic means. To the extent required to prevent a clearly unwarranted invasion of personal privacy, an agency may delete identifying details when it makes available or publishes an opinion, statement of policy, interpretation, staff manual, instruction, or copies of records referred to in subparagraph (D). However, in each case the justification for the deletion shall be explained fully in writing, and the extent of such deletion shall be indicated on the portion of the record which is made available or published, unless including that indication would harm an interest protected by the exemption in subsection (b) under which the deletion is made. If technically feasible, the extent of the deletion shall be indicated at the place in the record where the deletion was made. Each agency shall also maintain and make available for public inspection and copying current indexes providing identifying information for the public as to any matter issued, adopted, or promulgated after July 4, 1967, and required by this paragraph to be made available or published. Each agency shall promptly publish, quarterly or more frequently, and distribute (by sale or otherwise) copies of each index or supplements thereto unless it determines by order published in the Federal Register that the publication would be unnecessary and impracticable, in which case the agency shall nonetheless provide copies of such index on request at a cost not to exceed the direct cost of duplication. Each agency shall make the index referred to in subparagraph (E) available by computer telecommunications by December 31, 1999. A final order, opinion, statement of policy, interpretation, or staff manual or instruction that affects a member of the public may be relied on, used, or cited as precedent by an agency against a party other than an agency only if—

(i) it has been indexed and either made available or published as provided by this paragraph; or

(ii) the party has actual and timely notice of the terms thereof.

(3)(A) Except with respect to the records made available under paragraphs (1) and (2) of this subsection, and except as provided in subparagraph (E), each agency, upon any request for records which (i) reasonably describes such records and (ii) is made in accordance with published rules stating the time, place, fees (if any), and procedures to be followed, shall make the records promptly available to any person.

(B) In making any record available to a person under this paragraph, an agency shall provide the record in any form or format requested by the person if the record is readily reproducible by the agency in that form or format. Each agency shall make reasonable efforts to maintain its records in forms or formats that are reproducible for purposes of this section.

(C) In responding under this paragraph to a request for records, an agency shall make reasonable efforts to search for the records in electronic form or format, except when such efforts would significantly interfere with the operation of the agency's automated information system.

(D) For purposes of this paragraph, the term "search" means to review, manually or by automated means, agency records for the purpose of locating those records which are responsive to a request.

(E) An agency, or part of an agency, that is an element of the intelligence community (as that term is defined in section 3(4) of the National Security Act of 1947 (50 U.S.C. 401a(4))) shall not make any record available under this paragraph to—

(i) any government entity, other than a State, territory, commonwealth, or district of the United States, or any subdivision thereof; or

(ii) a representative of a government entity described in clause (i).

(4)(A)(i) In order to carry out the provisions of this section, each agency shall promulgate regulations, pursuant to notice and receipt of public comment, specifying the schedule of fees applicable to the processing of requests under this section and establishing procedures and guidelines for determining when such fees should be waived or reduced. Such schedule shall conform to the guidelines which shall be promulgated, pursuant to notice and receipt of public comment, by the Director of the Office of Management and Budget and which shall provide for a uniform schedule of fees for all agencies.

(ii) Such agency regulations shall provide that—

(I) fees shall be limited to reasonable standard charges for document search, duplication, and review, when records are requested for commercial use;

(II) fees shall be limited to reasonable standard charges for document duplication when records are not sought for commercial use and the request is made by an educational or noncommercial scientific institution, whose purpose is scholarly or scientific research; or a representative of the news media; and

(III) for any request not described in (I) or (II), fees shall be limited to reasonable standard charges for document search and duplication.

In this clause, the term "a representative of the news media" means any person or entity that gathers information of potential interest to a segment of the public, uses its editorial skills to turn the raw materials into a distinct work, and distributes that work to an audience. In this clause, the term "news" means information that is about current events or that would be of current interest to the public. Examples of news-media entities are television or radio stations broadcasting to the public at large and publishers of periodicals (but only if such entities qualify as disseminators of "news") who make their products available for purchase by or subscription by or free distribution to the general public. These examples are not all-inclusive. Moreover, as methods of news delivery evolve (for example, the adoption of the electronic dissemination of newspapers through telecommunications services), such alternative media shall be considered to be news-media entities. A freelance journalist shall be regarded as working for a news-media entity if the journalist can demonstrate a solid basis for expecting publication through that entity, whether or not the journalist is actually employed by the entity. A publication contract would present a solid basis for such an expectation; the Government may also consider the past publication record of the requester in making such a determination.

(iii) Documents shall be furnished without any charge or at a charge reduced below the fees established under clause (ii) if disclosure of the information is in the public interest because it is likely to contribute significantly to public understanding of the operations or activities of the government and is not primarily in the commercial interest of the requester.

(iv) Fee schedules shall provide for the recovery of only the direct costs of search, duplication, or review. Review costs shall include only the direct costs incurred during the initial examination of a document for the purposes of determining whether the documents must be disclosed under this section and for the purposes of withholding any portions exempt from disclosure under this section. Review costs may not include any costs incurred in resolving issues of law or policy that may be raised in the course of processing a request under this section. No fee may be charged by any agency under this section—

(I) if the costs of routine collection and processing of the fee are likely to equal or exceed the amount of the fee; or

(II) for any request described in clause (ii)(II) or (III) of this subparagraph for the first two hours of search time or for the first one hundred pages of duplication.

(v) No agency may require advance payment of any fee unless the requester has previously failed to pay fees in a timely fashion, or the agency has determined that the fee will exceed $250.

(vi) Nothing in this subparagraph shall supersede fees chargeable under a statute specifically providing for setting the level of fees for particular types of records.

(vii) In any action by a requester regarding the waiver of fees under this section, the court shall determine the matter de novo: *Provided,* That the court's review of the matter shall be limited to the record before the agency.

(viii) An agency shall not assess search fees (or in the case of a requester described under clause (ii)(II), duplication fees) under this subparagraph if the agency fails to comply with any time limit under paragraph (6), if no unusual or exceptional circumstances (as those terms are defined for purposes of paragraphs (6)(B) and (C), respectively) apply to the processing of the request.

(B) On complaint, the district court of the United States in the district in which the complainant resides, or has his principal place of business, or in which the agency records are situated, or in the District of Columbia, has jurisdiction to enjoin the agency from withholding agency records and to order the production of any agency records improperly withheld from the complainant. In such a case the court shall determine the matter de novo, and may examine the contents of such agency records in camera to determine whether such records or any part thereof shall be withheld under any of the exemptions set forth in subsection (b) of this section, and the burden is on the agency to sustain its action. In addition to any other matters to which a court accords substantial weight, a

court shall accord substantial weight to an affidavit of an agency concerning the agency's determination as to technical feasibility under paragraph (2)(C) and subsection (b) and reproducibility under paragraph
(3)(B).

(C) Notwithstanding any other provision of law, the defendant shall serve
an answer or otherwise plead to any complaint made under this subsection within thirty days after service upon the defendant of the pleading in
which such complaint is made, unless the court otherwise directs for good
cause shown.

[(D) Repealed. Pub.L. 98-620, Title IV, § 402(2), Nov. 8, 1984, 98 Stat. 3357]

(E)(i) The court may assess against the United States reasonable attorney
fees and other litigation costs reasonably incurred in any case under this
section in which the complainant has substantially prevailed.

   (ii) For purposes of this subparagraph, a complainant has substantially prevailed if the complainant has obtained relief through either—
      (I) a judicial order, or an enforceable written agreement or con-
      sent decree; or
      (II) a voluntary or unilateral change in position by the agency, if
      the complainant's claim is not insubstantial.

(F)(i) Whenever the court orders the production of any agency records
improperly withheld from the complainant and assesses against the United
States reasonable attorney fees and other litigation costs, and the court
additionally issues a written finding that the circumstances surrounding the
withholding raise questions whether agency personnel acted arbitrarily or
capriciously with respect to the withholding, the Special Counsel shall
promptly initiate a proceeding to determine whether disciplinary action is
warranted against the officer or employee who was primarily responsible
for the withholding. The Special Counsel, after investigation and consideration of the evidence submitted, shall submit his findings and recommendations to the administrative authority of the agency concerned and
shall send copies of the findings and recommendations to the officer or
employee or his representative. The administrative authority shall take the
corrective action that the Special Counsel recommends.

   (ii) The Attorney General shall—
      (I) notify the Special Counsel of each civil action described under
      the first sentence of clause (i); and
      (II) annually submit a report to Congress on the number of such
      civil actions in the preceding year.
   (iii) The Special Counsel shall annually submit a report to Congress
   on the actions taken by the Special Counsel under clause (i).

(G) In the event of noncompliance with the order of the court, the district court may punish for contempt the responsible employee, and in the case of a uniformed service, the responsible member.

(5) Each agency having more than one member shall maintain and make available for public inspection a record of the final votes of each member in every agency proceeding.

(6)(A) Each agency, upon any request for records made under paragraph (1), (2), or (3) of this subsection, shall—

    (i) determine within 20 days (excepting Saturdays, Sundays, and legal public holidays) after the receipt of any such request whether to comply with such request and shall immediately notify the person making such request of such determination and the reasons therefor, and of the right of such person to appeal to the head of the agency any adverse determination; and

    (ii) make a determination with respect to any appeal within twenty days (excepting Saturdays, Sundays, and legal public holidays) after the receipt of such appeal. If on appeal the denial of the request for records is in whole or in part upheld, the agency shall notify the person making such request of the provisions for judicial review of that determination under paragraph (4) of this subsection.

The 20-day period under clause (i) shall commence on the date on which the request is first received by the appropriate component of the agency, but in any event not later than ten days after the request is first received by any component of the agency that is designated in the agency's regulations under this section to receive requests under this section. The 20-day period shall not be tolled by the agency except—

    (I) that the agency may make one request to the requester for information and toll the 20-day period while it is awaiting such information that it has reasonably requested from the requester under this section; or

    (II) if necessary to clarify with the requester issues regarding fee assessment. In either case, the agency's receipt of the requester's response to the agency's request for information or clarification ends the tolling period.

(B)(i) In unusual circumstances as specified in this subparagraph, the time limits prescribed in either clause (i) or clause (ii) of subparagraph (A) may be extended by written notice to the person making such request setting forth the unusual circumstances for such extension and the date on which a determination is expected to be dispatched. No such notice shall specify a date that would result in an extension for more than ten working days, except as provided in clause (ii) of this subparagraph.

(ii) With respect to a request for which a written notice under clause (i) extends the time limits prescribed under clause (i) of subparagraph (A), the agency shall notify the person making the request if the request cannot be processed within the time limit specified in that clause and shall provide the person an opportunity to limit the scope of the request so that it may be processed within that time limit or an opportunity to arrange with the agency an alternative time frame for processing the request or a modified request. To aid the requester, each agency shall make available its FOIA Public Liaison, who shall assist in the resolution of any disputes between the requester and the agency. Refusal by the person to reasonably modify the request or arrange such an alternative time frame shall be considered as a factor in determining whether exceptional circumstances exist for purposes of subparagraph (C).

(iii) As used in this subparagraph, "unusual circumstances" means, but only to the extent reasonably necessary to the proper processing of the particular requests —

(I) the need to search for and collect the requested records from field facilities or other establishments that are separate from the office processing the request;

(II) the need to search for, collect, and appropriately examine a voluminous amount of separate and distinct records which are demanded in a single request; or

(III) the need for consultation, which shall be conducted with all practicable speed, with another agency having a substantial interest in the determination of the request or among two or more components of the agency having substantial subject-matter interest therein.

(iv) Each agency may promulgate regulations, pursuant to notice and receipt of public comment, providing for the aggregation of certain requests by the same requestor, or by a group of requestors acting in concert, if the agency reasonably believes that such requests actually constitute a single request, which would otherwise satisfy the unusual circumstances specified in this subparagraph, and the requests involve clearly related matters. Multiple requests involving unrelated matters shall not be aggregated.

(C)(i) Any person making a request to any agency for records under paragraph (1), (2), or (3) of this subsection shall be deemed to have exhausted his administrative remedies with respect to such request if the agency fails to comply with the applicable time limit provisions of this paragraph. If the Government can show exceptional circumstances exist and that the agency is exercising due diligence in responding to the request, the court may retain jurisdiction and allow the agency additional time to complete its review of the records. Upon any determination by an agency to comply with a request for records, the records shall be made promptly available to such person making such request. Any notification of denial of any request for records under this subsection shall set forth the names and titles or positions of each person responsible for the denial of such request. (ii) For purposes of this subparagraph, the term "exceptional circumstances" does not include a delay that results from a predictable agency workload of requests under this section, unless the agency demonstrates reasonable progress in reducing its backlog of pending requests.

(iii) Refusal by a person to reasonably modify the scope of a request or arrange an alternative time frame for processing a request (or a modified request) under clause (ii) after being given an opportunity to do so by the agency to whom the person made the request shall be considered as a factor in determining whether exceptional circumstances exist for purposes of this subparagraph.

(D)(i) Each agency may promulgate regulations, pursuant to notice and receipt of public comment, providing for multitrack processing of requests for records based on the amount of work or time (or both) involved in processing requests.

(ii) Regulations under this subparagraph may provide a person making a request that does not qualify for the fastest multitrack processing an opportunity to limit the scope of the request in order to qualify for faster processing.

(iii) This subparagraph shall not be considered to affect the requirement under subparagraph (C) to exercise due diligence.

(E)(i) Each agency shall promulgate regulations, pursuant to notice and receipt of public comment, providing for expedited processing of requests for records—

> (I) in cases in which the person requesting the records demonstrates a compelling need; and
>
> (II) in other cases determined by the agency.

(ii) Notwithstanding clause (i), regulations under this subparagraph must ensure—

> (I) that a determination of whether to provide expedited processing shall be made, and notice of the determination shall be provided to the person making the request, within 10 days after the date of the request; and

(II) expeditious consideration of administrative appeals of such determinations of whether to provide expedited processing.

(iii) An agency shall process as soon as practicable any request for records to which the agency has granted expedited processing under this subparagraph. Agency action to deny or affirm denial of a request for expedited processing pursuant to this subparagraph, and failure by an agency to respond in a timely manner to such a request shall be subject to judicial review under paragraph (4), except that the judicial review shall be based on the record before the agency at the time of the determination.

(iv) A district court of the United States shall not have jurisdiction to review an agency denial of expedited processing of a request for records after the agency has provided a complete response to the request.

(v) For purposes of this subparagraph, the term "compelling need" means—

(I) that a failure to obtain requested records on an expedited basis under this paragraph could reasonably be expected to pose an imminent threat to the life or physical safety of an individual; or

(II) with respect to a request made by a person primarily engaged in disseminating information, urgency to inform the public concerning actual or alleged Federal Government activity.

(vi) A demonstration of a compelling need by a person making a request for expedited processing shall be made by a statement certified by such person to be true and correct to the best of such person's knowledge and belief.

(F) In denying a request for records, in whole or in part, an agency shall make a reasonable effort to estimate the volume of any requested matter the provision of which is denied, and shall provide any such estimate to the person making the request, unless providing such estimate would harm an interest protected by the exemption in subsection (b) pursuant to which the denial is made.

(7) Each agency shall—

(A) establish a system to assign an individualized tracking number for each request received that will take longer than ten days to process and provide to each person making a request the tracking number assigned to the request; and

(B) establish a telephone line or internet service that provides information about the status of a request to the person making the request using the assigned tracking number, including—

(i) the date on which the agency originally received the request; and

(ii) an estimated date on which the agency will complete action on the request.

(b) This section does not apply to matters that are—

(1) (A) specifically authorized under criteria established by an Executive order to be kept secret in the interest of national defense or foreign policy and (B) are in fact properly classified pursuant to such Executive order;

(2) related solely to the internal personnel rules and practices of an agency;

(3) specifically exempted from disclosure by statute (other than section 552b of this title), provided that such statute (A) requires that the matters be withheld from the public in such a manner as to leave no discretion on the issue, or (B) establishes particular criteria for withholding or refers to particular types of matters to be withheld;

(4) trade secrets and commercial or financial information obtained from a person and privileged or confidential;

(5) inter-agency or intra-agency memorandums or letters which would not be available by law to a party other than an agency in litigation with the agency;

(6) personnel and medical files and similar files the disclosure of which would constitute a clearly unwarranted invasion of personal privacy;

(7) records or information compiled for law enforcement purposes, but only to the extent that the production of such law enforcement records or information (A) could reasonably be expected to interfere with enforcement proceedings, (B) would deprive a person of a right to a fair trial or an impartial adjudication, (C) could reasonably be expected to constitute an unwarranted invasion of personal privacy, (D) could reasonably be expected to disclose the identity of a confidential source, including a State, local, or foreign agency or authority or any private institution which furnished information on a confidential basis, and, in the case of a record or information compiled by criminal law enforcement authority in the course of a criminal investigation or by an agency conducting a lawful national security intelligence investigation, information furnished by a confidential source, (E) would disclose techniques and procedures for law enforcement investigations or prosecutions, or would disclose guidelines for law enforcement investigations or prosecutions if such disclosure could reasonably be expected to risk circumvention of the law, or (F) could reasonably be expected to endanger the life or physical safety of any individual;

(8) contained in or related to examination, operating, or condition reports prepared by, on behalf of, or for the use of an agency responsible for the regulation or supervision of financial institutions; or

(9) geological and geophysical information and data, including maps, concerning wells.

Any reasonably segregable portion of a record shall be provided to any person requesting such record after deletion of the portions which are exempt under this subsection. The amount of information deleted, and the exemption under which the deletion is made, shall be indicated on the released portion of the record, unless including that indication would harm an interest protected by the exemption in this subsection under which the deletion is made. If technically feasible, the amount of the information deleted, and the exemption under which the deletion is made, shall be indicated at the place in the record where such deletion is made.

(c)(1) Whenever a request is made which involves access to records described in subsection (b)(7)(A) and —

(A) the investigation or proceeding involves a possible violation of criminal law; and

(B) there is reason to believe that (i) the subject of the investigation or proceeding is not aware of its pendency, and (ii) disclosure of the existence of the records could reasonably be expected to interfere with enforcement proceedings,

the agency may, during only such time as that circumstance continues, treat the records as not subject to the requirements of this section.

(2) Whenever informant records maintained by a criminal law enforcement agency under an informant's name or personal identifier are requested by a third party according to the informant's name or personal identifier, the agency may treat the records as not subject to the requirements of this section unless the informant's status as an informant has been officially confirmed.

(3) Whenever a request is made which involves access to records maintained by the Federal Bureau of Investigation pertaining to foreign intelligence or counterintelligence, or international terrorism, and the existence of the records is classified information as provided in subsection (b)(1), the Bureau may, as long as the existence of the records remains classified information, treat the records as not subject to the requirements of this section.

(d) This section does not authorize withholding of information or limit the availability of records to the public, except as specifically stated in this section. This section is not authority to withhold information from Congress.

§ [552a. Privacy Act [omitted]

§ 552b. Open Meetings Act [omitted]

§ 553. Rule making

(a) This section applies, according to the provisions thereof, except to the extent that there is involved—

(1) a military or foreign affairs function of the United States; or

(2) a matter relating to agency management or personnel or to public property, loans, grants, benefits, or contracts.

(b) General notice of proposed rule making shall be published in the Federal Register, unless persons subject thereto are named and either personally served or otherwise have actual notice thereof in accordance with law. The notice shall include—

(1) a statement of the time, place, and nature of public rule making proceedings;

(2) reference to the legal authority under which the rule is proposed; and

(3) either the terms or substance of the proposed rule or a description of the subjects and issues involved.

Except when notice or hearing is required by statute, this subsection does not apply—

(A) to interpretative rules, general statements of policy, or rules of agency organization, procedure, or practice; or

(B) when the agency for good cause finds (and incorporates the finding and a brief statement of reasons therefor in the rules issued) that notice and public procedure thereon are impracticable, unnecessary, or contrary to the public interest.

(c) After notice required by this section, the agency shall give interested persons an opportunity to participate in the rule making through submission of written data, views, or arguments with or without opportunity for oral presentation. After consideration of the relevant matter presented, the agency shall incorporate in the rules adopted a concise general statement of their basis and purpose. When rules are required by statute to be made on the record after opportunity for an agency hearing, sections 556 and 557 of this title apply instead of this subsection.

(d) The required publication or service of a substantive rule shall be made not less than 30 days before its effective date, except—

(1) a substantive rule which grants or recognizes an exemption or relieves a restriction;

(2) interpretative rules and statements of policy; or

(3) as otherwise provided by the agency for good cause found and published with the rule.

(e) Each agency shall give an interested person the right to petition for the issuance, amendment, or repeal of a rule.

§ 554. Adjudications

(a) This section applies, according to the provisions thereof, in every case of adjudication required by statute to be determined on the record after opportunity for an agency hearing, except to the extent that there is involved —

> (1) a matter subject to a subsequent trial of the law and the facts de novo in a court;
>
> (2) the selection or tenure of an employee, except an administrative law judge appointed under section 3105 of this title;
>
> (3) proceedings in which decisions rest solely on inspections, tests, or elections;
>
> (4) the conduct of military or foreign affairs functions;
>
> (5) cases in which an agency is acting as an agent for a court; or
>
> (6) the certification of worker representatives.

(b) Persons entitled to notice of an agency hearing shall be timely informed of —

> (1) the time, place, and nature of the hearing;
>
> (2) the legal authority and jurisdiction under which the hearing is to be held; and
>
> (3) the matters of fact and law asserted.

When private persons are the moving parties, other parties to the proceeding shall give prompt notice of issues controverted in fact or law; and in other instances agencies may by rule require responsive pleading. In fixing the time and place for hearings, due regard shall be had for the convenience and necessity of the parties or their representatives.

(c) The agency shall give all interested parties opportunity for —

> (1) the submission and consideration of facts, arguments, offers of settlement, or proposals of adjustment when time, the nature of the proceeding, and the public interest permit; and
>
> (2) to the extent that the parties are unable so to determine a controversy by consent, hearing and decision on notice and in accordance with sections 556 and 557 of this title.

(d) The employee who presides at the reception of evidence pursuant to section 556 of this title shall make the recommended decision or initial decision required by section 557 of this title, unless he becomes unavailable to the agency. Except to the extent required for the disposition of ex parte matters as authorized by law, such an employee may not —

> (1) consult a person or party on a fact in issue, unless on notice and opportunity for all parties to participate; or

(2) be responsible to or subject to the supervision or direction of an employee or agent engaged in the performance of investigative or prosecuting functions for an agency.

An employee or agent engaged in the performance of investigative or prosecuting functions for an agency in a case may not, in that or a factually related case, participate or advise in the decision, recommended decision, or agency review pursuant to section 557 of this title, except as witness or counsel in public proceedings. This subsection does not apply—

(A) in determining applications for initial licenses;

(B) to proceedings involving the validity or application of rates, facilities, or practices of public utilities or carriers; or

(C) to the agency or a member or members of the body comprising the agency.

(e) The agency, with like effect as in the case of other orders, and in its sound discretion, may issue a declaratory order to terminate a controversy or remove uncertainty.

§ 555. Ancillary matters

(a) This section applies, according to the provisions thereof, except as otherwise provided by this subchapter.

(b) A person compelled to appear in person before an agency or representative thereof is entitled to be accompanied, represented, and advised by counsel or, if permitted by the agency, by other qualified representative. A party is entitled to appear in person or by or with counsel or other duly qualified representative in an agency proceeding. So far as the orderly conduct of public business permits, an interested person may appear before an agency or its responsible employees for the presentation, adjustment, or determination of an issue, request, or controversy in a proceeding, whether interlocutory, summary, or otherwise, or in connection with an agency function. With due regard for the convenience and necessity of the parties or their representatives and within a reasonable time, each agency shall proceed to conclude a matter presented to it. This subsection does not grant or deny a person who is not a lawyer the right to appear for or represent others before an agency or in an agency proceeding.

(c) Process, requirement of a report, inspection, or other investigative act or demand may not be issued, made, or enforced except as authorized by law. A person compelled to submit data or evidence is entitled to retain or, on payment of lawfully prescribed costs, procure a copy or transcript thereof, except that in a nonpublic investigatory proceeding the witness may for good cause be limited to inspection of the official transcript of his testimony.

(d) Agency subpenas authorized by law shall be issued to a party on request and, when required by rules of procedure, on a statement or showing of general relevance and reasonable scope of the evidence sought. On contest, the court shall sustain the subpena or similar process or demand to the extent that it is found to be in accordance with law. In a proceeding for enforcement, the court shall issue an order requiring the appearance of the witness or the production of the evidence or data within a reasonable time under penalty of punishment for contempt in case of contumacious failure to comply.

(e) Prompt notice shall be given of the denial in whole or in part of a written application, petition, or other request of an interested person made in connection with any agency proceeding. Except in affirming a prior denial or when the denial is self-explanatory, the notice shall be accompanied by a brief statement of the grounds for denial.

§ 556. Hearings; presiding employees; powers and duties; burden of proof; evidence; record as basis of decision

(a) This section applies, according to the provisions thereof, to hearings required by section 553 or 554 of this title to be conducted in accordance with this section.

(b) There shall preside at the taking of evidence —
    (1) the agency;
    (2) one or more members of the body which comprises the agency; or
    (3) one or more administrative law judges appointed under section 3105 of this title.
This subchapter does not supersede the conduct of specified classes of proceedings, in whole or in part, by or before boards or other employees specially provided for by or designated under statute. The functions of presiding employees and of employees participating in decisions in accordance with section 557 of this title shall be conducted in an impartial manner. A presiding or participating employee may at any time disqualify himself. On the filing in good faith of a timely and sufficient affidavit of personal bias or other disqualification of a presiding or participating employee, the agency shall determine the matter as a part of the record and decision in the case.

(c) Subject to published rules of the agency and within its powers, employees presiding at hearings may —
    (1) administer oaths and affirmations;
    (2) issue subpenas authorized by law;

(3) rule on offers of proof and receive relevant evidence;

(4) take depositions or have depositions taken when the ends of justice would be served;

(5) regulate the course of the hearing;

(6) hold conferences for the settlement or simplification of the issues by consent of the parties or by the use of alternative means of dispute resolution as provided in subchapter IV of this chapter;

(7) inform the parties as to the availability of one or more alternative means of dispute resolution, and encourage use of such methods;

(8) require the attendance at any conference held pursuant to paragraph (6) of at least one representative of each party who has authority to negotiate concerning resolution of issues in controversy;

(9) dispose of procedural requests or similar matters;

(10) make or recommend decisions in accordance with section 557 of this title; and

(11) take other action authorized by agency rule consistent with this subchapter.

(d) Except as otherwise provided by statute, the proponent of a rule or order has the burden of proof. Any oral or documentary evidence may be received, but the agency as a matter of policy shall provide for the exclusion of irrelevant, immaterial, or unduly repetitious evidence. A sanction may not be imposed or rule or order issued except on consideration of the whole record or those parts thereof cited by a party and supported by and in accordance with the reliable, probative, and substantial evidence. The agency may, to the extent consistent with the interests of justice and the policy of the underlying statutes administered by the agency, consider a violation of section 557(d) of this title sufficient grounds for a decision adverse to a party who has knowingly committed such violation or knowingly caused such violation to occur. A party is entitled to present his case or defense by oral or documentary evidence, to submit rebuttal evidence, and to conduct such cross-examination as may be required for a full and true disclosure of the facts. In rule making or determining claims for money or benefits or applications for initial licenses an agency may, when a party will not be prejudiced thereby, adopt procedures for the submission of all or part of the evidence in written form.

(e) The transcript of testimony and exhibits, together with all papers and requests filed in the proceeding, constitutes the exclusive record for decision in accordance with section 557 of this title and, on payment of lawfully prescribed costs, shall be made available to the parties. When an agency decision rests on official notice of a material fact not appearing in the evidence in the record, a party is entitled, on timely request, to an opportunity to show the contrary.

§ 557. Initial decisions; conclusiveness; review by agency; submissions by parties; contents of decisions; record

(a) This section applies, according to the provisions thereof, when a hearing is required to be conducted in accordance with section 556 of this title.

(b) When the agency did not preside at the reception of the evidence, the presiding employee or, in cases not subject to section 554(d) of this title, an employee qualified to preside at hearings pursuant to section 556 of this title, shall initially decide the case unless the agency requires, either in specific cases or by general rule, the entire record to be certified to it for decision. When the presiding employee makes an initial decision, that decision then becomes the decision of the agency without further proceedings unless there is an appeal to, or review on motion of, the agency within time provided by rule. On appeal from or review of the initial decision, the agency has all the powers which it would have in making the initial decision except as it may limit the issues on notice or by rule. When the agency makes the decision without having presided at the reception of the evidence, the presiding employee or an employee qualified to preside at hearings pursuant to section 556 of this title shall first recommend a decision, except that in rule making or determining applications for initial licenses—

> (1) instead thereof the agency may issue a tentative decision or one of its responsible employees may recommend a decision; or
> (2) this procedure may be omitted in a case in which the agency finds on the record that due and timely execution of its functions imperatively and unavoidably so requires.

(c) Before a recommended, initial, or tentative decision, or a decision on agency review of the decision of subordinate employees, the parties are entitled to a reasonable opportunity to submit for the consideration of the employees participating in the decisions—

> (1) proposed findings and conclusions; or
> (2) exceptions to the decisions or recommended decisions of subordinate employees or to tentative agency decisions; and
> (3) supporting reasons for the exceptions or proposed findings or conclusions.

>> The record shall show the ruling on each finding, conclusion, or exception presented. All decisions, including initial, recommended, and tentative decisions, are a part of the record and shall include a statement of—

(A) findings and conclusions, and the reasons or basis therefor, on all the material issues of fact, law, or discretion presented on the record; and

(B) the appropriate rule, order, sanction, relief, or denial thereof.

(d)(1) In any agency proceeding which is subject to subsection (a) of this section, except to the extent required for the disposition of ex parte matters as authorized by law—

(A) no interested person outside the agency shall make or knowingly cause to be made to any member of the body comprising the agency, administrative law judge, or other employee who is or may reasonably be expected to be involved in the decisional process of the proceeding, an ex parte communication relevant to the merits of the proceeding;

(B) no member of the body comprising the agency, administrative law judge, or other employee who is or may reasonably be expected to be involved in the decisional process of the proceeding, shall make or knowingly cause to be made to any interested person outside the agency an ex parte communication relevant to the merits of the proceeding;

(C) a member of the body comprising the agency, administrative law judge, or other employee who is or may reasonably be expected to be involved in the decisional process of such proceeding who receives, or who makes or knowingly causes to be made, a communication prohibited by this subsection shall place on the public record of the proceeding:

(i) all such written communications;

(ii) memoranda stating the substance of all such oral communications; and

(iii) all written responses, and memoranda stating the substance of all oral responses, to the materials described in clauses (i) and (ii) of this subparagraph;

(D) upon receipt of a communication knowingly made or knowingly caused to be made by a party in violation of this subsection, the agency, administrative law judge, or other employee presiding at the hearing may, to the extent consistent with the interests of justice and the policy of the underlying statutes, require the party to show cause why his claim or interest in the proceeding should not be dismissed, denied, disregarded, or otherwise adversely affected on account of such violation; and

(E) the prohibitions of this subsection shall apply beginning at such time as the agency may designate, but in no case shall they begin to apply later than the time at which a proceeding is noticed for hearing unless the person responsible for the communication has knowledge that it will be noticed, in which case the prohibitions shall apply beginning at the time of his acquisition of such knowledge.

§ 558. Imposition of sanctions; determination of applications for licenses; suspension, revocation, and expiration of licenses

(a) This section applies, according to the provisions thereof, to the exercise of a power or authority.

(b) A sanction may not be imposed or a substantive rule or order issued except within jurisdiction delegated to the agency and as authorized by law.

(c) When application is made for a license required by law, the agency, with due regard for the rights and privileges of all the interested parties or adversely affected persons and within a reasonable time, shall set and complete proceedings required to be conducted in accordance with sections 556 and 557 of this title or other proceedings required by law and shall make its decision. Except in cases of willfulness or those in which public health, interest, or safety requires otherwise, the withdrawal, suspension, revocation, or annulment of a license is lawful only if, before the institution of agency proceedings therefor, the licensee has been given—
> (1) notice by the agency in writing of the facts or conduct which may warrant the action; and
> (2) opportunity to demonstrate or achieve compliance with all lawful requirements.

When the licensee has made timely and sufficient application for a renewal or a new license in accordance with agency rules, a license with reference to an activity of a continuing nature does not expire until the application has been finally determined by the agency.

§ 559. Effect on other laws; effect of subsequent statute

This subchapter, chapter 7, and sections 1305, 3105, 3344, 4301(2)(E), 5372, and 7521 of this title, and the provisions of section 5335(a)(B) of this title that relate to administrative law judges, do not limit or repeal additional requirements imposed by statute or otherwise recognized by law. Except as otherwise required by law, requirements or privileges relating to evidence or procedure apply equally to agencies and persons. Each agency is granted the authority necessary to comply with the requirements of this subchapter through the issuance of rules or otherwise. Subsequent statute may not be held to supersede or modify this subchapter, chapter 7, sections 1305, 3105, 3344, 4301(2)(E), 5372, or 7521 of this title, or the provisions of section 5335(a)(B) of this title that relate to administrative law judges, except to the extent that it does so expressly.

[Judicial Review]

§ 701. Application; definitions

(a) This chapter applies, according to the provisions thereof, except to the extent that—

(1) statutes preclude judicial review; or

(2) agency action is committed to agency discretion by law.

(b) For the purpose of this chapter—

(1) "agency" means each authority of the Government of the United States, whether or not it is within or subject to review by another agency, but does not include—

(A) the Congress;

(B) the courts of the United States;

(C) the governments of the territories or possessions of the United States;

(D) the government of the District of Columbia;

(E) agencies composed of representatives of the parties or of representatives of organizations of the parties to the disputes determined by them;

(F) courts martial and military commissions;

(G) military authority exercised in the field in time of war or in occupied territory; or

(H) functions conferred by sections 1738, 1739, 1743, and 1744 of title 12; chapter 2 of title 41; subchapter II of chapter 471 of title 49; or sections 1884, 1891–1902, and former section 1641(b)(2), of title 50, appendix; and

(2) "person", "rule", "order", "license", "sanction", "relief", and "agency action" have the meanings given them by section 551 of this title.

§ 702. Right of review

A person suffering legal wrong because of agency action, or adversely affected or aggrieved by agency action within the meaning of a relevant statute, is entitled to judicial review thereof. An action in a court of the United States seeking relief other than money damages and stating a claim that an agency or an officer or employee thereof acted or failed to act in an official capacity or under color of legal authority shall not be dismissed nor relief therein be denied on the ground that it is against the United States or that the United States is an indispensable party. The United States may be named as a defendant in any such action, and a judgment or decree may be entered against the United States: *Provided*, That any mandatory or injunctive decree shall specify the Federal officer or officers (by name or by title), and their successors in office, personally responsible for compliance. Nothing herein (1) affects other limitations on judicial review or the power or duty of the court to dismiss any action or deny relief on any other appropriate legal or equitable ground; or (2) confers authority to grant relief if any other statute that grants consent to suit expressly or impliedly forbids the relief which is sought.

§ 703. Form and venue of proceeding

The form of proceeding for judicial review is the special statutory review proceeding relevant to the subject matter in a court specified by statute or, in the absence or inadequacy thereof, any applicable form of legal action, including actions for declaratory judgments or writs of prohibitory or mandatory injunction or habeas corpus, in a court of competent jurisdiction. If no special statutory review proceeding is applicable, the action for judicial review may be brought against the United States, the agency by its official title, or the appropriate officer. Except to the extent that prior, adequate, and exclusive opportunity for judicial review is provided by law, agency action is subject to judicial review in civil or criminal proceedings for judicial enforcement.

§ 704. Actions reviewable

Agency action made reviewable by statute and final agency action for which there is no other adequate remedy in a court are subject to judicial review. A preliminary, procedural, or intermediate agency action or ruling not directly reviewable is subject to review on the review of the final agency action. Except as otherwise expressly required by statute, agency action otherwise final is final for the purposes of this section whether or not there has been presented or determined an application for a declaratory order, for any form of reconsideration, or, unless the agency otherwise requires by rule and provides that the action meanwhile is inoperative, for an appeal to superior agency authority.

§ 705. Relief pending review

When an agency finds that justice so requires, it may postpone the effective date of action taken by it, pending judicial review. On such conditions as may be required and to the extent necessary to prevent irreparable injury, the reviewing court, including the court to which a case may be taken on appeal from or on application for certiorari or other writ to a reviewing court, may issue all necessary and appropriate process to postpone the effective date of an agency action or to preserve status or rights pending conclusion of the review proceedings.

§ 706. Scope of review

To the extent necessary to decision and when presented, the reviewing court shall decide all relevant questions of law, interpret constitutional and statutory provisions, and determine the meaning or applicability of the terms of an agency action. The reviewing court shall—

(1) compel agency action unlawfully withheld or unreasonably delayed; and

(2) hold unlawful and set aside agency action, findings, and conclusions found to be—

(A) arbitrary, capricious, an abuse of discretion, or otherwise not in accordance with law;

(B) contrary to constitutional right, power, privilege, or immunity;

(C) in excess of statutory jurisdiction, authority, or limitations, or short of statutory right;

(D) without observance of procedure required by law;

(E) unsupported by substantial evidence in a case subject to sections 556 and 557 of this title or otherwise reviewed on the record of an agency hearing provided by statute; or

(F) unwarranted by the facts to the extent that the facts are subject to trial de novo by the reviewing court.

In making the foregoing determinations, the court shall review the whole record or those parts of it cited by a party, and due account shall be taken of the rule of prejudicial error.

[Administrative Law Judges]

§ 3105. Appointment of administrative law judges

Each agency shall appoint as many administrative law judges as are necessary for proceedings required to be conducted in accordance with sections 556 and 557 of this title. Administrative law judges shall be assigned to cases in rotation so far as practicable, and may not perform duties inconsistent with their duties and responsibilities as administrative law judges.

§ 7521. Actions against administrative law judges

(a) An action may be taken against an administrative law judge appointed under section 3105 of this title by the agency in which the administrative law judge is employed only for good cause established and determined by the Merit Systems Protection Board on the record after opportunity for hearing before the Board.

(b) The actions covered by this section are—

    (1) a removal;

    (2) a suspension;

    (3) a reduction in grade;

    (4) a reduction in pay; and

    (5) a furlough of 30 days or less;

but do not include—

    (A) a suspension or removal under section 7532 of this title [national security];

    (B) a reduction-in-force action under section 3502 of this title [RIF]; or

    (C) any action initiated under section 1215 of this title [special counsel proceedings].

Index